Law and Sexuality in
Tennessee Williams's America

The Fairleigh Dickinson University Press Series in Law, Culture, and the Humanities

General Editor: Caroline Joan "Kay" S. Picart, M.Phil. (Cantab), PhD, JD, Esquire
Attorney at Law/Of Counsel, Tim Bower Rodriguez, PA

The Fairleigh Dickinson University Press Series in Law, Culture, and the Humanities publishes scholarly works in which the field of Law intersects with, among others, Film, Criminology, Sociology, Communication, Critical/Cultural Studies, Literature, History, Philosophy, and the Humanities.

Publications

Jacqueline O'Connor, *Law and Sexuality in Tennessee Williams's America* (2016).
Caroline Joan "Kay" S. Picart, Michael Hviid Jacobsen, and Cecil E. Greek, *Framing Law and Crime: An Interdisciplinary Anthology* (2016).
Caroline Joan "Kay" S. Picart, *Law In and As Culture: Intellectual Property, Minority Rights, and the Rights of Indigenous Peoples* (2016).

On the Web at http://www.fdu.edu/fdupress

Law and Sexuality in Tennessee Williams's America

Jacqueline O'Connor

FAIRLEIGH DICKINSON UNIVERSITY PRESS
Madison • Teaneck

Published by Fairleigh Dickinson University Press
Copublished by The Rowman & Littlefield Publishing Group, Inc.
4501 Forbes Boulevard, Suite 200, Lanham, Maryland 20706
www.rowman.com

Unit A, Whitacre Mews, 26-34 Stannary Street, London SE11 4AB

Copyright © 2016 by Jacqueline O'Connor

All rights reserved. No part of this book may be reproduced in any form or by any electronic or mechanical means, including information storage and retrieval systems, without written permission from the publisher, except by a reviewer who may quote passages in a review.

British Library Cataloguing in Publication Information Available

Library of Congress Cataloguing-in-Publication Data Available
The hardback edition of this book was previously catalogued by the Library of Congress as follows:

O'Connor, Jacqueline, author.
Law and sexuality in Tennessee Williams's America / by Jacqueline O'Connor.
Madison [New Jersey] : Fairleigh Dickinson University Press, 2016. | Series: The Fairleigh Dickinson University Press Series in Law, Culture, and the Humanities | Includes bibliographical references and index.
LCCN 2016021138 (print) | LCCN 2016036475 (ebook)
LCSH: Williams, Tennessee, 1911-1983--Criticism and interpretation. | Sexual orientation in literature. | Male homosexuality in literature. | Sex and law.
LCC PS3545.I5365 Z7954 2016 (print) | LCC PS3545.I5365 (ebook) | DDC 812/.54--dc23
LC record available at https://lccn.loc.gov/2016021138

ISBN 978-1-61147-893-8 (cloth : alk. paper)
ISBN 978-1-61147-895-2 (pbk.: alk. paper)
ISBN 978-1-61147-894-5 (electronic)

∞™ The paper used in this publication meets the minimum requirements of American National Standard for Information Sciences Permanence of Paper for Printed Library Materials, ANSI/NISO Z39.48-1992.

Printed in the United States of America

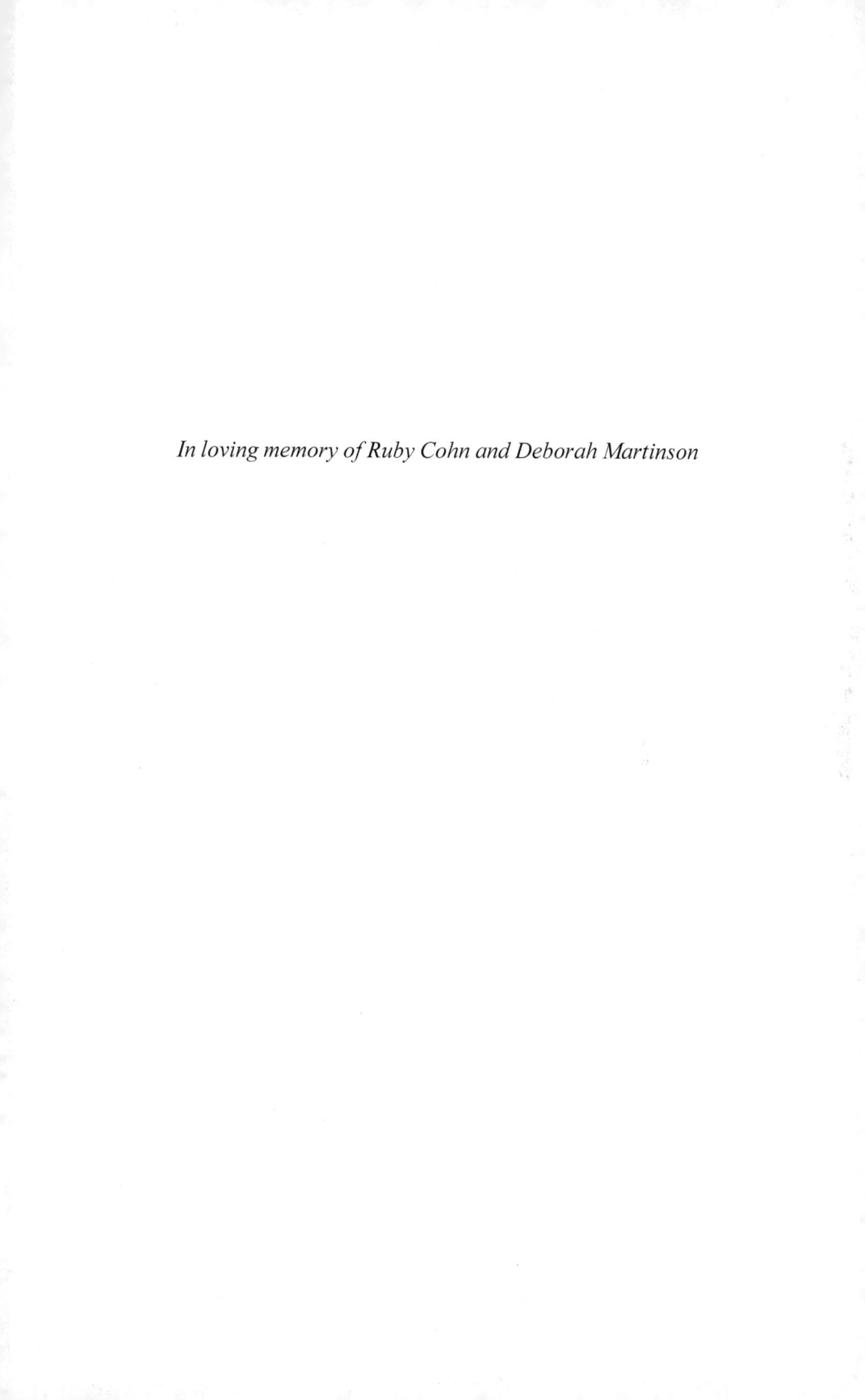

In loving memory of Ruby Cohn and Deborah Martinson

Contents

Acknowledgments		ix
Introduction: Illegal Bodies		1
1	Privacy and Identity	25
2	The Power of Disgust	57
3	The Fugitive Kind	101
4	The Politics of Recognition	149
Conclusion: With Dignity for All		191
Bibliography		199
Index		207

Acknowledgments

The idea for this book emerged from my participation in a National Endowment for the Humanities Summer Institute in 2009. The institute topic, "The Rule of Law: Legal Studies and the Liberal Arts," and the five weeks of intensive work in the field of law and humanities provided me the opportunity to reimagine my scholarly work in literary studies and American drama. One evening our group of participants screened the film version of *A Streetcar Named Desire*, and I agreed to make some opening remarks. It was the first time that I considered the questions, "What did Tennessee Williams know about the law? Where does it appear in his work?" So did this project begin, in a dormitory common room at the University of New England, and the book would not exist if not for those five rainy summer weeks in Biddeford, Maine. I am grateful to institute directors Matthew D. Anderson and Cathrine O. Frank, to the distinguished visiting faculty, and to my fellow institute participants.

Among my records from that summer is a chain of e-mail exchanges with Leslie Durham, who has been my most treasured friend and colleague since we both joined the faculty at Boise State University in 2001. Every project I have undertaken since we met has benefitted from her sharp intellect, her sound advice, and her unwavering support. This book is no exception. It is impossible to measure my debt to her or imagine my life without her.

An exceptional and diverse group of scholars and teachers have dedicated their careers to Tennessee Williams studies and to the publication and performance of his texts. Their names fill my bibliography, demonstrating my indebtedness to their work. Thanks in particular to Robert Bray, founding editor of the *Tennessee Williams Annual Review* and Conference Director of the Tennessee Williams Scholars' Conference held in New Orleans each spring.

Support for research travel and writing time at every stage of this book project has been crucial to its completion. The Harry Ransom Humanities Research Center at the University of Texas at Austin awarded me a research fellowship in 2011. Closer to home, an Idaho Humanities Council Research Fellowship provided time for writing, and a Boise State University Arts and Humanities Institute Research Fellowship in 2012 funded a semester away from teaching, travel to Columbia University Rare Books and Manuscript Library, and office space at Boise State's Yanke Research Park. Boise State University granted me a sabbatical leave in 2014 to revise my completed draft. The College of Arts and Sciences at Boise State provided travel funds for a presentation at the Tennessee Williams Scholars' Conference in 2013. The Department of English funded travel to annual meetings of the Association for the Study of Law, Culture and the Humanities in 2011 and 2012, where I presented my research on this topic. English department chair Michelle Payne approved my requests for research leave, and associate chair Roger Munger facilitated the necessary course schedule changes.

Thanks to the students in my 2013 graduate seminar on Tennessee Williams, and to the undergraduate and graduate students in an interdisciplinary course I taught in 2014 on "Mapping the Writer's Life: Tennessee Williams" for their interest in and enthusiasm for the author and his work. Gender studies student Janne Knight read parts of the manuscript and provided useful feedback.

I am grateful to all of my department colleagues for their friendship and support, especially Tom Hillard, Russell Willerton, Whitney Douglas, Bruce Ballenger, Matt Hansen, Jeff Westover, Cheryl Hindrichs, Steven Olsen-Smith, and Linda Marie Zaerr. Special thanks go to my colleague Tara Penry, who buoyed my confidence at every stage and came to my rescue during final revisions. Her expertise in writing and editing scholarly arguments guided me as I made some challenging but necessary changes. My colleague and friend Christy Vance read, commented on, and made many corrections to the manuscript, and it is better for her careful and thoughtful attention. Suzanne Sherman Aboulfadl did excellent work completing the index.

Special thanks to Harry Keyishian, director of Fairleigh Dickinson University Press, for his prompt attention to my proposal submission, his enthusiastic support of the book, and for his advice and guidance throughout the editorial process. Thanks also to Brooke Bures and Zachary Nycum at Rowman & Littlefield.

My husband and partner in all things, Derek Jeffery, contributed to the success of this project at every stage. He is my "cleft in the rock of the world," and our life together inspires me daily.

Permission to quote the following from published and unpublished materials by Tennessee Williams was made possible by the kind assistance of Rachel Brooke, permissions manager of Georges Borchardt, Inc., Christopher Wait, permissions editor of New Directions Press, and Rick Watson, head of Reference Services at the Harry Ransom Center at the University of Texas at Austin.

Excerpts from *Memoirs* by Tennessee Williams, ©1975 by The University of the South. Reprinted by permission of New Directions Publishing Corp. and Georges Borchardt, Inc. for the Estate of Tennessee Williams.

Excerpts from *New Selected Essays: Where I Live* by Tennessee Williams, ©1945 by The University of the South. Reprinted by permission of New

Directions Publishing Corp. and Georges Borchardt, Inc. for the Estate of Tennessee Williams.

Excerpts from *Selected Letters: Volume I, 1920–1945* by Tennessee Williams, ©2000 by The University of the South. Reprinted by permission of New Directions Publishing Corp. and Georges Borchardt, Inc. for the Estate of Tennessee Williams.

Excerpts from *Selected Letters: Volume II, 1945–1957* by Tennessee Williams, ©2002 by The University of the South. Reprinted by permission of New Directions Publishing Corp and Georges Borchardt, Inc. for the Estate of Tennessee Williams.

Excerpts from *Stairs to the Roof* by Tennessee Williams, ©2000 by The University of the South. Reprinted by permission of New Directions Publishing Corp. and Georges Borchardt, Inc. for the Estate of Tennessee Williams.

Excerpts from *Stopped Rocking and Other Screenplays* by Tennessee Williams, ©1984 by The University of the South. Reprinted by permission of New Directions Publishing Corp. and Georges Borchardt, Inc. for the Estate of Tennessee Williams.

Excerpts from *The Collected Stories of Tennessee Williams* by Tennessee Williams, ©1985 by The University of the South. Reprinted by permission of New Directions Publishing Corp. and Georges Borchardt, Inc. for the Estate of Tennessee Williams.

Excerpts from *The Theatre of Tennessee Williams, Vol. I* by Tennessee Williams, ©1971 by The University of the South. Reprinted by permission of New Directions Publishing Corp. and Georges Borchardt, Inc. for the Estate of Tennessee Williams.

Excerpts from *The Theatre of Tennessee Williams, Vol. III* by Tennessee Williams, © 1971 by The University of the South. Reprinted by permission of New Directions Publishing Corp. and Georges Borchardt, Inc. for the Estate of Tennessee Williams.

Excerpts from *The Theatre of Tennessee Williams, Vol. IV* by Tennessee Williams, ©1972 by The University of the South. Reprinted by permission of New Directions Publishing Corp. and Georges Borchardt, Inc. for the Estate of Tennessee Williams.

Excerpts from *The Theatre of Tennessee Williams, Vol. V* by Tennessee Williams, ©1976. Reprinted by permission of New Directions Publishing Corp. and Georges Borchardt, Inc. for the Estate of Tennessee Williams.

Excerpts from *The Theatre of Tennessee Williams, Vol. VII* by Tennessee Williams, ©1981 by The University of the South. Reprinted by permission of New Directions Publishing Corp. and Georges Borchardt, Inc. for the Estate of Tennessee Williams.

Excerpts from Tennessee Williams's *Notebooks*, © 2006 by The University of the South Reprinted by permission of Georges Borchardt, Inc. for the Estate of Tennessee Williams.

Excerpt from screenplay draft of "One Arm," from Tennessee Williams Papers. Copyright ©2015 The University of the South. Reprinted by permission of Georges Borchardt, Inc. for the Estate of Tennessee Williams.

Excerpt from unpublished letter from Harold Hart from Tennessee Williams Papers, April 1970. Copyright ©2015 The University of the South. Reprinted by permission of Georges Borchardt, Inc. for the Estate of Tennessee Williams.

Excerpt from unpublished letter from Stephen M. Lachs from Tennessee Williams Papers, August 1981. Copyright ©2015 The University of the South. Reprinted by permission of Georges Borchardt, Inc. for the Estate of Tennessee Williams.

Excerpt from Honorary Doctorate of Literature Award from the University of Hartford from Tennessee Williams Papers, December 1972. Copyright ©2015 The University of the South. Reprinted by permission of Georges Borchardt, Inc. for the Estate of Tennessee Williams.

Excerpt from letter from Sacred Heart College, Tennessee Williams Papers. Copyright © 2015 The University of the South. Reprinted by permission of Georges Borchardt, Inc. for the Estate of Tennessee Williams.

I am indebted to the Harry Ransom Center at the University of Texas at Austin for permission to quote from several letters and manuscripts in the Tennessee Williams Collection.

An essay excerpted from chapter 2 of this book appeared in the 2014 volume of the *Tennessee Williams Annual Review*. A revised version of it is reprinted with the permission of editor Robert Bray.

Introduction

Illegal Bodies

In November 1949 author Tennessee Williams, his lover Frank Merlo, and his grandfather Walter Dakin arrived in Key West, Florida, by automobile, taking up residence at a rented cottage on Duncan St. that Williams purchased the following year. In a letter to agent Audrey Wood, Williams described life as "one of those sentimental ballads of Irving Berlin, blue skies, cottage small, sunshine and so forth." The city was the winter White House for then President Harry S. Truman and his family, and Williams told Wood that his grandfather and Frank watched the presidential motorcade pass along Duval Street.[1] By April of the following year, however, the trio was preparing to leave the city sooner than expected, and Williams wrote to friend Oliver Evans that the early departure had been planned in order to avoid attack or arrest: "Last month a forty-three-year-old queen was clubbed to death by an ash-tray and a sailor, and as a reprisal for this terrible offense on the part of the queen, all the Bohemians in town are being picked up on the street and booked for vagrancy, given heavy fines and twelve hours to get off the Key. There are sixteen different kinds of vagrancy in Florida law and I'm sure Frank and I, and perhaps even grandfather, would come under at least one of them!"[2] As a gay man who had spent much of the last decade cruising various U.S. cities for sexual companions, Williams had personal experience with both the legal and the physical dangers of the casual pickup. In a journal entry from July 3, 1942, Williams wrote that he and his friend Paul Bigelow had an encounter with the police in Macon, Georgia; the two were questioned at the local precinct after being reported as "'suspicious characters;'" Williams did not have his draft card on his person, which was grounds for detainment.[3] In a letter to Donald Windham about the incident, he added that he and Bigelow were picked up on Cherry Street, part of a Macon neighborhood known for its gay bars, because of his "dark glasses and cigarette holder."[4] Williams's descriptions of the detainment indicated that he recognized the likelihood that he and his companion were "suspicious" because of their appearance and their location rather than any specific behavior.

In January 1943, while staying in the Hotel St. George in Brooklyn, he invited a sailor to his room and was beaten up by him. In his journal he wrote that he was "relatively the innocent party," and that "it was a case of guilt and shame" on the part of the sailor; Williams posed the question, "Why do they strike us?" and answered it as follows: "We offer them a truth which they cannot bear to confess except in privacy and the dark—a truth which is inherently as bright as the morning sun."[5] The following year, back in New York City, Williams was detained by the police crossing the park after midnight and once again he did not have his draft registration card with him (his status was 4F because of poor eyesight). This time, he wrote James Laughlin, he was "turned over to the FBI and incarcerated for the night," an experience he called "fearful." He went on to describe the city's atmosphere as "sweltering with suspicion and prurience and petty malice. It is sad to see one's friends caught here and becoming infected with it, especially when they came here as such fresh and sensitive individuals."[6] These encounters occurred during World War II, when servicemen, in training or in transit, descended upon U.S. cities in large numbers, and men who were not in uniform were often subject to heightened scrutiny because they were assumed to be inadequate for service or indifferent to patriotism.

The descriptions Williams provided in the immediate aftermath of these events make clear his astuteness in reading these situations and recognizing the vulnerability of his own illegal body: a cigarette holder carried the suggestion of effeminacy, and his sexuality sparked both attraction and repulsion for the sailor with homoerotic urges. In the 1950 Key West letter he may have been feigning imminent personal danger for dark comic effect; by then a famous playwright and resident of the community, his concern that he and his companions would be arrested and charged under one or more of the sixteen types of vagrancy laws was no doubt exaggerated. But the details he provided in all of these first-person documents demonstrate his knowledge of the legal ramifications and the specific laws that restricted homosexual activity and that unofficially targeted those who exhibited a certain kind of "bohemian" visibility. Fame and money afforded him considerable protection, but he was aware of the possibility of punishment, by a violent sailor or by the authorities, for sexually transgressive acts or for being identified as an illegal body. His travels, his residences in urban boarding houses and hotels, and his decades of nightlife outings beginning in 1939 had already provided him with first-hand observations about the private and public lives of Americans whose sexual identities and practices situated them outside the law, whether male or female, gay or straight, rich or poor.

Throughout his life, Williams created plays and stories by circling back to events from these years when he first lived within close proximity of violence and with the constant dangers of imprisonment, and witnessed many other people living in analogous circumstances. His early adulthood was spent living along law's edge and taking regular excursions over the lines drawn by a variety of local, state, and federal statutes regulating sexual behavior, and he was aware that a determination of suspiciousness was subject to individual interpretation. Indeed, laws regulating sexuality during the midcentury were purposefully vague, allowing that many and various situations might be considered harmful to society and therefore require police intervention. The ambiguity of language served the government by allowing considerable latitude about new applications of restrictive laws that existed to control behavior, and as the United States entered a space race, waged a cold war of ideologies, and carved out its position as a global powerhouse, authorities in the federal government and in the military, in statehouses and in local precincts took advantage of language elasticity to direct citizens toward seemly lives.

The diary and epistolary histories Williams left behind provide details on the writer's daily life, his travels, his personal and professional relationships, and his writing habits. These documents have supported painstaking scholarly reconstructions of his complex and extensive writing and revision processes, and they have helped to pinpoint the origins of the names and places that Williams transformed into metaphoric and atmospheric richness in his creative texts. They chart the development of his private and public identities, and despite some fallow periods, they provide a record of documentation from age eight until the final years of his life. As texts that reveal much more than the specifics of a time and place, and considering Williams's commitment to their successful production over decades, they establish his extensive work in these genres of personal history. Albert Devlin, a co-editor of two volumes of *Selected Letters*, analyzes the correspondence between Williams and agent Wood, who represented him for thirty-one years, "in order to understand better the role that letters may have played in forming and sustaining Tennessee Williams's far-flung literary life."[7] The goal in this introduction is to take Devlin's lead in a different direction: to consider how his notebooks and letters played a role in "forming and sustaining" his "far-flung" sexual life, its development, and its intersections with the cultural worlds he resided in as well as those he created for his characters.

Edmund White remarked in his review of Williams's *Notebooks* (2006) that the journals provided a view of a gay life lived during the decades leading up to the Stonewall riots in 1969, and White advised young gays today to read, "just to learn about how much the oppression of the past distorted the oppressed. If Williams was always lonely and insecure, if he met so few gay couples, if the other gays he knew all deplored their condition, this was characteristic of the period three decades before the beginning of gay liberation."[8] The extensive record of first-person writing that Williams left behind in journals, letters, and essays, not to mention his published *Memoirs*, make it possible to explore his sexual attitudes and experiences unfiltered by the overlay of fiction, which is not to say that these personal musings lack embellishment and drama. His letters chart the freedom he was able to achieve and maintain in the pursuit of companionship and love even as they reflect the challenges facing anyone who risks self-exposure to find intimacy. He would go on, in his work, to use what he experienced and what he observed about pre- and postwar American life to create narratives that convey as much about certain social and political milieus as they do about the emotional and psychological lives he chronicled. His depictions of transient street life, of the performance of sexuality, of the legislation against diversity, and of the violence that often threatens the most afflicted and vulnerable citizens constitute a complex record of the times in which he lived and wrote, one that encompasses personal fates, family lives, and cultural and historical legacies. These first-person narratives chart the creation of a writer whose materials emerged, at least in part, from a self in conflict with the law and culture of its time. They contain specific evidence of his knowledge of the law and his complicated relationship to its repressive features; they remind us that someone whose life includes criminal activity may craft an identity informed by the circumscription of living outside of law and therefore in danger of legal prosecution.

In his notebooks, Williams recalled a conversation he had with Oliver Evans in New Orleans in September 1941; Evans had argued that the gay population "'ought to be exterminated for the good of society.'" In response, Williams argued that if homosexuals were exterminated, "society would lose some of its most sensitive, humanitarian members." He continued: "I am a deeper and warmer and kinder man for my deviation. More conscious of need in others, and what power I have to express the human heart must be in large part due to this circumstance. Someday society will take perhaps the suitable action—but I do not believe that it will be or should be extermination."[9] Williams's statement of defense for the deviant has some distinct cultural markings: he was well aware of and may have internalized social attitudes about homosexuality, both the heightened emotion and the deviance of those members. But he argued for the increased compassion that resulted from the mixture of sensitivity and difference. Hinted here and explored elsewhere in his work is the troubling possibility that some "suitable action" might be taken for the "good of society." Evans, at an historical moment when millions of "undesirables," including homosexuals, were being exterminated in Europe, suggested a similar solution for all homosexuals. Whether or not he was serious, his remarks reflected the attitudes that endangered those deemed different or threatening, and suggested the sway such attitudes could have even on the "deviant" themselves.

Williams's life and work indicate, however, that despite his defense of deviance, living a life that others condemned was not easy; the particular place he occupied, on the margins yet desperate to be embraced, artistically at least, by mainstream America, was a precarious one. Late in his career, he expressed in his *Memoirs* the challenge that comes with showing a true self to the world without being rejected because of such exposure: "I often wonder how Anna Magnani managed to live within society and yet to remain so free of its conventions. She was as unconventional a woman as I have known in or out of my professional world, and if you understand me at all, you must know that in this statement I am making my personal estimate of her honesty, which I feel was complete." As for his own status, he continued: "Of course I also existed outside of conventional society while contriving somewhat precariously to remain in contact with it. For me this was not only precarious but a matter of dark unconscious disturbance."[10] The position he described, outside of but within contact of conventional society, may have been precarious, but it enabled him to explore the tensions between the deviant and the orthodox in his work.

Elsewhere in *Memoirs* Williams conveyed what he claimed was "perhaps the most important recognition of all, at least in the quest for balance of mind."[11] He recalled the miracle of coming to understand his place in the world as "being one among many of my kind," an insight that came to him while composing a poem as he walked alone in the streets of Amsterdam. Fifty years later, he reminisced about the moment of the poem's composition, and about the "marching feet" of "endless throngs of strangers" who filled the poem both literally and emotionally. In *Memoirs* he called this idea of connectivity and commonality the "most important recognition for us all to reach now," describing it as "being a member of multiple humanity with its multiple needs, problems and emotions, not a unique creature but one, only one among the multitude of its fellows."[12] If, as his work often suggested, the characters he created were not so different from audience members, for they embodied lives and struggles familiar to the "endless throngs," then playgoers and readers might better understand and accept the unorthodoxy his works celebrated.

Born in 1911, Williams was a member of a generation of men and women whose lives were shaped by modernity, by the Depression and World War II, and by the Cold War that followed. Opportunity and limitation coexisted. Americans lived with the tension between the wide open spaces of the nation's future, our guide the scientists and engineers who emerged from World War II with advanced technologies, and the gnawing fear that the individual's life loomed ahead as a narrow path of regular checkpoints for success, happiness, honor. For those ill-suited to such regulated living, there were possibilities for carving out a fulfilling existence, but contentment and security were only possible with extra layers of effort, attention, and contemplation. For Williams, who was determined to live life as openly as possible given the times, and to do so within the public eye, it meant commitment to a lifetime of diligence about presenting the appropriate identity for each occasion. As a result of this experience, his creative texts often interrogate the gap between what could and could not be exposed, narrating or dramatizing the pain and fear that originates in the disjuncture of selves, no matter the cause.

Social changes that occurred over the course of Williams's life helped to create the possibility for his relatively open gay life. Increased visibility of gay culture on the streets of New York City during the Prohibition years of 1920–1933, according to historian George Chauncey, created a "pansy craze" that swept the city; gay men "became the subject of newspaper headlines, Broadway dramas, films, and novels" and "visible gay life moved from the margins of the city—from the waterfront and the Bowery, Harlem, and Greenwich Village—into Times Square, the city's most prestigious cultural center."[13] In New York and other large cities, Chauncey argues, prohibition had limited hotel profits by depriving these establishments of liquor-related sales, and as a result some of the second-class hotels in midtown Manhattan began to allow prostitutes and speakeasies space on their premises to conduct illegal business. The criminalization of liquor was, to a large extent, "the criminalization of nightlife," which had "far-reaching implications for the culture of the city, but one of its most immediate consequences was to undermine the policing of the city's nightlife in ways that benefited gay meeting places."[14] The presence of gay men in nightclubs and in popular culture media began what has been the long journey toward visibility and public acknowledgment of this segment of America's population.

The repeal of the Eighteenth Amendment, however, was accompanied by a "powerful backlash to the Prohibition-era 'pansy craze,'" and this backlash gathered momentum during the second half of the 1930s as a reaction against the previous decade's cultural freedom and experimentation. What was perceived as an increased presence of homosexuals in midtown Manhattan helped to fuel the reaction, and in New York and other cities concerted efforts were made to exclude gay men and lesbians from the public sphere.[15] In many jurisdictions, existing laws legislating sexual behavior multiplied, whether through the expansion of existing laws or through new laws created to contain or suppress activity deemed deviant. William N. Eskridge Jr. argues that with sex panic surges occurring before and after World War II, "homosexuals became the new enemy of the people" and the "perfect repository for Americans' obsession with and guilt about sexual pleasure, gender-bending, and even racial segregation."[16] With the development of "urban anonymity and a new ethics of gender relations" in the twentieth century, says David A. J. Richards in his book *The Sodomy Cases*, a significant cultural shift occurred in the conception of homosexuality: the development of the definition from men who had sex with boys to men in subcultures who are members of a third or intermediate gender.

The conditions of homosexual life in modern America increasingly involved a surrender of rights and an exposure to public contempt, conditions that exacted a cost not previously levied against "men who had sex with boys." Homosexuals forfeited their rights as dominant males, and they were often treated with contempt as a kind of male whore.[17] The additional cost was political and cultural agency, for with the loss of access to the power of the dominant male came a life-changing condition of identity. The word "gay" originally was applied to prostitutes, but it was transferred to homosexuals as the male homosexual became culturally assimilated to the female prostitute: as Richards argues, male homosexuals, "traditionally even more culturally marginalized than women, were the dissidents to male gender that the female prostitutes were to their gender." The love of homosexual men for each other "not only challenged the male gender norm of aggressive competition with other men but its very object (love between men) unspeakably affirmed what traditional advocates of heterosexual love anxiously did not want even to discuss, let alone debate (real equality in love)."[18] He concludes that patriarchal gender hierarchy rendered the very idea of homosexual love a "conceptual absurdity, an unnatural act, which made such a man loving another man doubly disgraced and stigmatized, not a man, and, as a woman, a fallen woman." Therefore, he maintains, the "greater dehumanization of the homosexual over the prostitute was in this double disgrace, so disgraceful, indeed, that its disgrace could not even be spoken."[19] Williams's knowledge and exploration of the sexual categories that Richards describes is visible in his draft process, for he often changed characters, specifically sexually transgressive ones, from one gender to another, and he compared the lives of male and female prostitutes, situating them in similar public or semi-public milieus: street corners, bars, boarding houses.

Chauncey reminds us of the ongoing danger that homosexuals faced, in both law and self-perception; for example, many men frequented "tearooms" (slang for t-rooms or public toilets) to search for sexual partners, and such encounters affected how "even men little involved in other aspects of the gay world regarded that world." The association between homosexual sex and public restrooms amplified negative perceptions, for they "seemed to offer vivid confirmation of the cultural association of homosexuality with degeneracy by putting homosexuality and homosexuals almost literally in the gutter." Even the men who used tearooms as sexual meeting places absorbed cultural attitudes that viewed such locales and practices as disgusting.[20] Although some aspects of this "sexual underworld" were visible, many of them remained invisible, Chauncey claims, for "gay men had to contend with the threat of vigilante anti-gay violence as well as with the police."[21] The tension between the seen and the unseen cannot be understated, and Williams drew upon this particular environmental reality of the "sexual underworld" in order to explore and expose cultural status and community values.

As World War II brought the infusion of large groups of single people to cities, Allan Bérubé argues, this influx included gay men and women, and off-duty passes for visits to the "bustling war-boom cities promised gay male and lesbian GIs the allures of fun, romance, and sex—a chance to let down their hair, let off steam, and take part in the wartime excitement of civilian life."[22] However, he continues, "military officials set out to bring this wartime boom in gay life under their control," and they used "wartime vice control powers, which had been developed to eliminate heterosexual venereal disease and prostitution, to regulate the gay life as well."[23] The interaction of diverse populations during a period of enhanced military authority meant that urban social settings became sites of sexual anxiety and danger, and Williams drew upon these developments in his stories and plays about contemporary relationships. Indeed, the ways that transgressive sex acts are represented in the law and in Williams's texts during the period demonstrate the construction of homosexuality as the "perfect repository" for these complex social anxieties. As both Eskridge and Chauncey make clear, homosexuals coming of age in the 1930s, as Williams did, found themselves entering a public sphere in which gay culture was already highly developed, on the one hand, but was coming under increased scrutiny, restriction, and attack in the years prior to, during, and following World War II.

It was this complex and contradictory cultural reality that Williams entered when he left his family behind to forge his career as a writer. Although Williams wrote and published stories and had his plays produced by amateur theaters while he was still in college, his personal life had been to a large extent defined and circumscribed by his family life until he was twenty-seven years old. Brief residences at several universities he attended and summer respites spent with his beloved grandparents in Mississippi or Memphis had provided regular but temporary departures from his parents' home in St. Louis. He graduated from the University of Iowa in August 1938 and spent a few months living with his parents in St. Louis while attempting to secure a job through the Works Project Administration in Chicago. At the end of the year, he departed for New Orleans to seek his future, "a journey that would last the rest of his life," for, as biographer Lyle Leverich notes, Williams would "return home again, but briefly, then take off, only to alight somewhere else. He had become a wayfarer."[24] Years later Williams wrote in his *Memoirs* that while finishing up his classes at Iowa in the summer of 1938 he had been lonely and frightened: "I took to wandering aimlessly about the streets at night to escape the stifling heat of my room. I didn't know the next step. I was finally fully persuaded that I was 'queer,' but had no idea what to do about it. I didn't even know how to accept a boy on the rare occasions when one would offer himself to me."[25] As biographer John Lahr suggests, "Williams's own transition from timid virgin to florid gay man was his defining struggle."[26] For a long time, Lahr argues, because Williams had been influenced by his mother's "fear of the flesh," he had "allowed his instinctual life to be ruled by his mother's dicta. By refusing to acknowledge his own sexuality, he elected to remain a child well into his twenties. He had no clear sexual identity and no sexual body."[27] Given the family circumstances, the time period, and Williams's determination to forge a public life and career, it is little wonder that his personal documents during this period of "transition from timid virgin to florid gay man" included the details of his developing sexual identity.

By the end of 1938, innocence was met by experience, his own and that of others; even though employment with the WPA eluded him in New Orleans, just as it had in Chicago, the move proved to be a formative one. For he discovered what he described in his journal as a "completely new scene—New Orleans—the Vieux Carré," about which he was convinced, after only three hours, that it "surely is the place I was made for if any place on this funny old world."[28] Three days later, on New Year's Day 1939, he reported: "What a nite!—I was introduced to the artistic and Bohemian life of the Quarter with a bang! All very interesting, some utterly appalling."[29] This entry marked the beginning of regular, sometimes daily recordings in his notebooks and letters describing the nightlife and street life he participated in for decades and from which he drew details for fictional scenarios about public sexuality in all its many forms. Casual sexual encounters and the "excitement of pickups" proved satisfying to Williams, according to Lahr, because by "being desired, Williams was emptied of need: the stranger became the needy one. In that sense, Williams's cruising held the promise of another kind of emotional relief—each time it succeeded, he had been chosen, he had been taken in, he knew he was real."[30] Indeed, for all his apparent trepidation about finding companionship in strange cities, he took to the vagabond life in many ways, describing the ease with which he was able to identify a community of people to spend time with, no matter where or in what circumstances he landed.

However, it does not appear that Williams took immediate advantage of either what he called the "Bohemian life" or what he referred to as the "utterly appalling" element of the Quarter nightlife, for a few months later in Los Angeles he recorded a "rather horrible night with a picked-up acquaintance Doug whose amorous advance made me sick to my stomach—Purity—Oh God—It is dangerous to have ideals." In her annotations, *Notebooks* editor Margaret Bradham Thornton speculates that with "no prior mention of a homosexual experience it is likely that this is Williams' first homosexual encounter." But her note also includes this information: "Years later in a television interview, Williams would name the New Year's Eve in New Orleans as his 'first time.'"[31] What is, of course, most pertinent is not when he began acting on his homosexual desires, but that he did so in part because of his changed circumstances: free from family, living in communal settings in strange cities, and enjoying nighttime encounters on streets and in bars. Furthermore, he began to record these activities in his personal documents, narrating the various aspects of his sexual self in great detail. John S. Bak notes that if "prior to January 1940, Williams wrote endlessly in his notebooks about his art and his desire for success and for freedom from his father's control, after this date his notebooks become filled with his sexual predilections."[32] The author transplanted and transformed such experiences into his plays and stories, using them to comment on the transient nature of love, the vulnerability of desire expressed and acted upon in public places, the punishment rained down on the participants in such experiences by various authority figures, and the relentless need for connection despite the dangerous circumstances he and others in his circles experienced.

Removing himself geographically from his family and leaving behind the stultifying atmosphere of St. Louis were significant to his development, personally and professionally, but doing so proved complicated. Two months before his departure, he had written in his journal: "Once again I feel dangerously cornered, cut off—wonder how I am going to fight my way through." He continues: "Soon as I gather my forces (and I shall!) I must make a definite break—because this stagnation is debilitating my will. . . . Perhaps I can get hold of about $20, and just bum out for Florida—bum my way South—Sounds too improbable for words—but something desperate should be done to escape this."[33] While he manages to do better than "just bum out for Florida," due in large part to the fact that he continued to depend on his family's financial support after he left home, the ties that bound him to his family are evident. As Leverich explains, "At the center of his existence, there was the pull of his family: his love for his mother, intertwined with the more intense, guilt-ridden attachment for his sister, further bound in by his love-hatred toward his father." [34] He managed to escape physically, but he remained faithful to his family, never fully dismissing the value of their viewpoints or the need for their approval. His letters and journals provide evidence of this pull, even as they reveal another, criminal self that he developed beyond the family sphere. Despite its dangers of private, public, or legal censure, the embrace of his homosexuality, and therefore of a lifestyle and identity considered transgressive, offered Williams the deepening appeal of nonconformist exploration and escape from the imprisonment that a conventional life signaled to him. It also offered him other communities to join, and his personal documents provide a detailed view of the circles he joined or formed as he created that life.

One of his lifelong passions was swimming, and it proved over the years to be a way of meeting men, for friendship and for sex. In his journal entry from New Orleans on January 14, 1939, he reported that he was swimming at the YMCA every day, a detail that is annotated by *Notebooks* editor Thornton: "By World War I, a number of YMCAs had become centers of sex and social life for gay young men."[35] Chauncey similarly notes that the Ys of the 1930s, 1940s, and 1950s served as gay social centers, and these decades corresponded to the time when

Williams lived in a wide range of communal settings, including the New York YMCA. As Chauncey describes the communities that formed at the city's Ys, he explains that they served as places where many gay New Yorkers rented rooms, used the pool, ate meals, and socialized. As important, and more ironic, "given reformers' intentions," was the "crucial role the hotels often played in introducing young men to the gay world. It was at the Y that many newcomers to the city made their first contacts with other gay men."[36] While spending the autumn of 1941 in New Orleans, Williams wrote to Paul Bigelow that a membership at the New Orleans Athletic Club, with its saltwater pool and Turkish bath, had facilitated his friendship with the "prettiest Creole belles in town." He goes on: "I actually pass for 'butch' in comparison and am regarded as an innovation—'The Out-door Type'!—and am consequently enjoying a considerable *succés*."[37] This entry is one of many in which Williams dissected the varieties of gay stereotypes and the recognition of his own sexual fluidity within well-defined or shifting parameters.

In their description of homosexual life during and after World War II, John D'Emilio and Estelle B. Freedman assert that the war "created substantially new erotic opportunities that promoted the articulation of a gay identity and the rapid growth of a gay subculture," especially in cities newly populated by young men and women of Williams's age group. For a "generation of young Americans, the war created a setting in which to experience same-sex love, affection, and sexuality, and to participate in the group life of gay men and women."[38] Donna Penn writes similarly about the period after World War II: "This belief that homosexuals, like prostitutes, now constituted an expanding quasi-organized sexual underworld was not merely a homophobic phantasmagoria but was a reflection of real social and cultural shifts taking place as a consequence of the war," as many gay men and lesbians "took advantage of wartime social dislocation and employment opportunities to leave their families of origin and pursue the ever-increasing possibilities for establishing a gay way of life in many of the nation's urban centers."[39] This group life did not end with war's end, for "having experienced so great a transformation in their sexual and emotional lives, [gay men and lesbians] did not return to prewar patterns," even though the national commitment to contain Communism led to increased attention to and attempts to identify suspected homosexuals and restrict their social and sexual activities.[40] Homosexuals were not the only unmarried people whose lives changed as a result of access to new sexual freedoms in the 1940s: the war accelerated the shift to city living, provided youth with more autonomy and freedom, and presented unprecedented opportunities for premarital experience. Personal documents provide extensive evidence that the young Tennessee Williams was an astute observer of his gay and his straight peers, that he recorded daily examples of and insights into sexual desire and behavior, and that he drew from these records to create his fictional works.

The community that welcomed him at the New Orleans Athletic Club was one of many groups that provided him physical and spiritual acceptance and pleasure. When he wrote Paul Bigelow about the police detaining him during his visit to Macon, it was less than three years since his introduction to what he called the "Bohemian" life of New Orleans; his contacts in the latter city now included, according to him, old-money families as well as members of the public and even flamboyant homosexual community. Bigelow, the recipient of the letter, represented an example of the friends on whom Williams depended: the playwright met Bigelow and his companion Jordan Massee when Williams was in New York following the unsuccessful Theater Guild production of his play *Battle of Angels* in 1940. At that time he was staying at the apartment of his friends Donald Windham and Fred Melton, and Leverich reports that Williams "enjoyed Paul's invigorating companionship and the company of other friends. He would say that, more than anyone, Paul not only appealed to his sense of humor but gave him the kind of support and encouragement of an older and wiser man."[41] Scores of letters to the friends listed above and many other men and women over the years demonstrate Williams's capacity to create enduring bonds; he created a life within a complex family tree of relationships, not ties determined by blood but ones built on various levels of commitment to artistic lives and rejection of restrictive living arrangements.

One striking feature of his communiques about sexual activities is the gender-bending code-switching he employed. With other gay men friends and several women with whom he enjoyed close friendships, he spoke openly about his lovers, about cruising with friends, about picking up and bringing home strangers. Janna Malamud Smith argues that a letter to a close friend can display "playfulness and frank mean ease," addressing the reader while "revealing debates with the self that 'I' use the friend to help me resolve."[42] For Williams, the frankness was often mitigated by what appeared as a coy covertness, for in some of the most revealing depictions he used nicknames and the female pronoun for himself and for some of his paramours. Malamud Smith argues that one's autonomy and well-being are based on the individual's choice about what to reveal, and the "capacity to assert a self rests on not having your definition of events continually impede or drown out mine. But also because the gratification of writing, of self-expression generally, is—psychologically—about nothing so much as control."[43] In Williams's letters, his efforts to control notions of self were manifested in the negotiations he made between revelation and concealment or at least misdirection.

With his confidantes, of course, the moves to shield identity, whether his own or others', had the result of increasing intimacy, for the implication was that the recipients could translate the coded language and thus participate in group privacy. He emphasized his commitment to creating a network of sexual connections wherever he landed, then used the stories that resulted as a way to remain intimate, even from a geographic distance, with those in his closest circles. In other cases, Williams was open about the nature of his sexual encounters, as in this letter to his friend Oliver Evans, from Rome in 1948: "My first night on the Boulevard I met a young Neopolitan who is a professional lightweight boxer. How I thought of you! Thick glossy black hair and a small but imperial torso! The nightingales burst their larynx!" While overtly hesitant to say too much—"I wish I could tell you more about this boxer, details, positions, amiabilities—but this pale blue paper would blush!" and "such confidences are only meant to be whispered in the bed-chamber," he went on to use very descriptive language: "Orally! The tongue has inflections which the typewriter wants!" Such intimate details, especially the letter's suggestion of oral sex, would have been scandalous even if he was not describing two men, for the act was criminal for heterosexuals too. The bold determination to document his activities and his erotic relationships extended to other documents. As he tells Evans: "I can hardly wait for you to come over this Spring: by that time my address book will probably be running into the tricentennial edition in gold and scarlet morocco with illustrations hand-painted."[44] The 1940s personal address book of the single man was, of course, the record and symbol of his romantic and erotic success.

The timing of this revelatory missive was significant, its year coinciding with the appearance of Alfred C. Kinsey's book *Sexual Behavior in the Human Male* (1948). As the first major figure in the field of American sexology peeled back the layers of secrecy about sexual activity, so did the autobiographical texts produced by Williams. In *Understanding Privacy*, Daniel J. Solove considers the possibility that "more disclosures about people's private lives might change attitudes," an argument that he reports is often made for outing gays. But Solove is skeptical about the outcome of such outing, for while it is true "that if every person's private life were exposed, society might change its attitudes and beliefs," in reality, he argues, "the revelation of people's personal secrets often does damage to the individuals without having much effect of changing them."[45] Multiple conflicting tensions intersect, as the necessity of privacy conflicts with the human drive to reveal a true self to the world; the potential benefits of such revelations for opening hearts and minds are at odds with the possibility of social ostracism, legal prosecution, or retaliatory violence.

Williams's letters demonstrated his success in maintaining separate yet coexistent identities, and the following example illustrates the benefits of the division he was able to create. In early 1941, Williams was rewriting *Battle of Angels* while staying in Key West in the slave quarters of Clara Atwood Black, who Williams described in a letter to Lawrence Langner as a "clergyman's widow who gives me lodging at a ridiculously low price because I remind her of her son who was an aviator recently killed in a crash." The letter goes on to make clear he had begun to keep his two selves, puritan and prurient, separate from each other, and to enjoy the tension between them: "I lead an exciting double life here, writing all morning, spending my afternoons in an English widow's cabana on the beach where I associate with people like John Dewey, James Farrell and Elizabeth Bishop and in the evening consorting, in dungarees, with B-girls, transients and sailors at Sloppy Joe's or the Starlight Gambling Casino."[46] Consorting with such latter types provided him colorful material for his plays and stories while educating him on the range of diverse sexual activities of men and women, the "double life" he lived heightening his awareness of the rich tension between "bohemia" and "suburbia." But the double life also made him realize, not long after he left home for good, that he would have to carefully negotiate a space between two very different worlds if he wanted to access both.

As he became more famous, the likelihood increased that all he wrote, even the most intimate narratives of his life recorded in the thousands of letters and journal entries, would at some point be released into the public sphere. This apparent contradiction, indicative of his complex negotiation of the private and the public, is evident in two letters he wrote in the early 1960s. The first letter, dated September 8, 1962, was to Lucy Freeman, who assisted Williams's mother in writing a memoir about her son: *Remember Me to Tom*, published in 1963. In the letter, he expressed concern that book dealer and literary estate consultant Andreas Brown, who had been hired by agent Audrey Wood to catalogue Williams's archives, had accessed certain personal papers from his parents' home. "I find it hard to believe that I would ever have left so intimate an item as a personal journal in her house. He has dug up so many things from such widely varied sources, even love-letters that I wrote twenty-some years ago that if he did not seem a gentleman and a scholar I would be quite alarmed about it."[47] Although he claimed not to have heard of Brown, a letter from the same period from Williams to Brown indicates otherwise, for in it he complained to Brown about Freeman's access to his private papers: "We were all a bit upset when excerpts from the 'Macon Journal' and from some other journal I kept in New York cropped up in the typed MS. of Lucy Freeman's book, but fortunately Miss Freeman was quite discreet in her selections and all that troubles me is that these intimate materials might get into less scrupulous hands someday." He goes on to direct Brown to "keep the Macon Journal or any other material of that degree of intimacy until you turn it over to me personally . . . it was never meant for anyone but myself, as you may readily imagine. That is, during my lifetime. Eventually the journals should be published as a sort of emotional record."[48] He wanted to believe in the significance of all that

Introduction 15

he wrote; he had a sense that documentation of his life and career would be meaningful, and that private details should eventually be made public, no matter how damning they might be. But he recognized the risks, and those risks were both social and familial.

In other earlier documents, he discussed his fears that his immediate family might discover the "secret" of his homosexuality. In a letter to companion Pancho Rodriguez y Gonzalez in late April of 1946, Williams warned his lover not to reveal too much about their relationship or their plans to cohabit in Taos in communiques to him while he was staying with his parents in St. Louis: "We have two phones, one upstairs and one down and Mother usually listens at the other phone. I was terrified that you would say something. She had already opened and read your telegram and [my parents] are full of conjecture and suspicion occasioned by that." He concluded with the plea to "please be extremely careful what you put in any communication addressed here."[49] Malamud Smith notes that the "letters of greatest interest tend to be those written to close friends or relatives to whom the writer feels able to speak freely," but she recognizes that "even private letters are various," for there are letters, she argues, "that the recipient might show casually, letters that can be shared with intimates, and letters that the writer hopes will not be shared at all."[50] Williams's letter to Pancho makes clear that he could not trust his mother to respect his privacy, for her desire to know was so great. Indeed, Malamud Smith argues, the private letter is "vulnerable to intrusion exactly because the freshness it contains is so attractive. The pleasure of reading other people's private letters stems from the wish to see what they have not chosen to show."[51] The secrets of his life that Williams attempted to keep from his parents may seem surprising given all that he revealed via his stories and plays, but it is consistent with the tension between the need for connection, in this case to his past and his familial history, and the need for a certain amount of privacy when it came to the personal life he constructed after leaving home.

There is another element here, one made plain by Kevin M. Crotty's discussion of the confession, which contextualizes Williams's letters as confessions of a sort, for although they are technically private, transmission by mail made them vulnerable to investigation. Crotty argues that the confession "does not appear to be a progressive force: it does not evidently challenge the law to broaden its perspectives or expand its vision." If anything, he continues, "it further entrenches law: confession entails the acceptance—or at least the acknowledgement—of the law's authority. The confessing party accuses not the law, but *himself*, of being out of line [emphasis in the original]."[52] What is most striking about all of these examples from Williams's letters and journals is the very specific documentation they provide us with, not only of his own erotic life, but of the circumstances in which same-sex pairings, and particularly those that were passing or impromptu, required caution on multiple fronts.

Moreover, they provide evidence that he was acutely aware of the legal ramifications of the life he led; that he would regularly include such details in his work is therefore no more surprising than his penchant for using person and place names, Southern phrases, and the many other details that migrated from reality to fiction under his hand.

While much scholarship on Tennessee Williams argues that his work places sexual desire at its center, what has not yet been considered is how his many representations of desire, along with the rights and restrictions placed on its pursuit, might be further informed by critical legal studies and its examinations of sexuality and privacy, morality and freedom. Directed by legal history and informed by multiple strands of Williams studies criticism, textual and cultural, this book explores the interplay of select topics defined and debated in law's texts with those same topics in Williams's personal and imaginative texts. Contextualized by the history of laws that governed sexual behavior, his life and work become striking in their focus on the formation, maintenance, and revision of multiple illegal bodies, his characters' and his own. From this rich site of critical common ground emerges a narrative positioning Williams's work as central to our understanding of twentieth-century American life, particularly in its insights on legal and cultural dialogues about sexuality, identity formation, intimacy, disgust, and difference. Extensive textual evidence, in personal documents and in his creative texts, detail his persistent emphasis on cultural perceptions of and legal restrictions on sexual activities that were considered transgressive; his ongoing interest in private and public identities and rights; his extensive knowledge of laws that incorporated the language of disgust to fabricate moral consensus and garner cultural acceptance. The complex representations in plays and prose lead to ambiguous resolutions that often combine social or legal punishment with individual compassion and transcendence.

The first book-length critical study of Williams and his drama, Nancy Tischler's 1961 *Tennessee Williams: Rebellious Puritan*, set the tone for what would become the critical consensus about him and his work for the next two decades. In the conclusion of her book, Tischler summarized Williams's career to date and his significance. As a dramatist, he had extended frontiers here and abroad, and because of his plays, Tischler argues, the "angry young Britons were better able to vent their rage," and plays such as *Krapp's Last Tape*, *Zoo Story*, and *The Balcony* reflected the same world out of which Williams writes." Because of him, "prostitution, dope addiction, homosexuality are now permissible dramatic subjects" expected at a "'serious' play." The "boundary expansion," she continues, "has been almost entirely in the sexual area," since that was the area "most infected by taboos." Above the belt, however, "Tennessee Williams has had little to offer . . . he is no intellectual; his decisions are usually emotional rather than rational, and he has not developed any clear or consistent philosophy. His most positive tenet is that the world needs romanticism."[53] This assessment of Williams's first two decades as a playwright would be expanded and modified, of course, but its focus on the "emotional rather than the rational" determined to a large extent what would be expected of, and valued in, his performance and published texts. His attempts to engage audiences with political or philosophical issues were seen as inconsistent with his romantic vision and therefore dismissed as artistic missteps. Tischler's book was published just as Williams's success was waning, and the early works she analyzes continued to receive the lion's share of scholarly attention some two decades after her study appeared. But his expansive genius, not to mention the sheer volume of creative work he produced consistently until his death in 1983, ensured that his legacy could not be so narrowly confined.

By the 1990s, the ties that bound his reputation to a string of Broadway hits, and to an apolitical Southern sensibility, had been loosened. The dissemination of texts that the playwright had deposited at various research archives around the country meant that previously unproduced plays received major productions and additional stories, poetry, and one-acts were published. Furthermore, the wealth of new biographical material available in the first volume of a comprehensive biography (1995), two volumes of selected letters (2000, 2004), and a massive edition of his notebooks (2006) inspired multiple new directions in scholarship on Williams. Simultaneously, developments in gender and cultural studies provided new perspectives on Williams's complex representations of sexuality, whether of himself as an openly gay man, or of his characters, many of whom narrate or dramatize sexual attitudes or behavior that overstep heteronormative boundaries of the period. David Savran argues in his 1992 book, *Communists, Cowboys, and Queers: The Politics of Masculinity in the Work of Arthur Miller and Tennessee Williams*, that Williams's exposure of the anxiety of masculinity that marked the Cold War era "offers an urgent challenge to the stubborn antitheses between the political and the sexual," adding that his plays "redefine and reconfigure resistance so that it is less the prerogative of rebellious individuals than a potential always ready at play within both social organization and dramatic structure."[54] Such studies repositioned Williams as a writer actively engaged in grappling with the public tensions in American life over five decades, as equality and freedom of choice slowly displaced the prejudice and repression of the past. To date, however, neither Williams's homosexual identity or lifestyle nor his persistent representation of various kinds of sexual transgression have been examined as legal matters, as acts that, during their time, interrogated and defied the rule of law.

In 1992 Marc Robinson proposed that it is the topic of sex in Williams's work that defines him as radical: "Only someone who never stayed long enough in one place to learn and abide by its standards of what was 'appropriate' and 'decent' would have risked as much as he did." He disputes Susan Sontag, whose assessment was that Williams's radicalism was not one of form and therefore could not be called "radical;" she argued that he limited his experimentation to topics that the theater had long avoided, sex being one of them. Robinson claims that "Sontag underestimated the degree to which such a choice of subject matter would in fact change one's idea of form," and he "made room in his plays for a startling frankness about erotic attraction."[55] In 2011, Amiri Baraka defines Williams's political identity as one of identity politics, beginning by suggesting that the getting and maintaining of power is at the heart of politics: "One of the most open struggles in our society is whether you even have sufficient power to be what you are—or not be to—without suffering at the hands of those with more power." If you are "black, or a woman, or gay, or poor, it should be obvious that you have to struggle to simply be who you are."[56] In his book on homosexuality in Cold War America, Robert J. Corber summarizes prior assessments of Williams's treatment of the politics of gender and sexual identity, noting that some postwar critics were bothered by the focus on female experience, assuming that these characters were no more than gay men in drag whose encounters with men "were a projection of Williams's own desire." The generation of gay male critics that wrote about Williams in the early years of gay liberation saw him as a "casualty of the closeted gay male subculture of the fifties, the stereotypical self-hating gay man who was unable to come to terms with his homosexuality." Corber determines to reconceive Williams as "out" in his plays, "locating the gay elements in his plays in their focus on female experience" but arguing that this "focus reflected an identification with women that was not Oedipal but political." While the plays "eroticize subjugated forms of masculinity (working-class, ethnic, and so on)," they treat these forms of masculinity "as symptomatic of patriarchal structures of oppression and foreground the sexual violence to which they invariably lead."[57] What continues to be in development in the critical commentary is the extent to which sexual politics in his works are as political as they are sexual.

Williams's reputation as a writer concerned primarily with poetic representations has supported the neglect of legal and political investigations of the diverse sexualities featured regularly in his drama and fiction. Such neglect has persisted despite the fact that his depictions of illegal sex are included in texts he wrote throughout his career, a period coinciding with radical and often highly contested revisions to laws and social attitudes regarding sexual activity and sexual identity. Such investigation need not be deferred any longer, for legal history and theory have paved new pathways for considering the laws that govern sexual behavior in a free society, particularly as these laws have been formulated or influenced by moral beliefs, emotional responses, and imaginative texts. Landmark Supreme Court cases provide documentation of the challenges made on both sides, and these cases are useful for charting the gradual expansion of sexual freedoms and demonstrating the multiple legal intersections of sexuality and privacy. Williams's continued preeminence in theaters, in classrooms, in new critical and popular texts written about him—indeed, in multiple realms that regularly influence public opinion and shape cultural values— make this examination a timely and useful one. In many ways, his influence on contemporary life is as significant as it was during his lifetime, and the issues that his creative texts grapple with are pertinent to some of the most pressing legal debates of the twenty-first century. What emerges from my study of law and Williams is that he worked assiduously on crafting diverse perspectives about sexual behavior that were reflective of his times; as lawmakers, medical and social scientists, psychologists, and other professionals grappled with the complexities of diverse sexualities, Williams did this work as well.

Multiple drafts of key plays and stories provide evidence of Williams's knowledge of the law, particularly as it applied to what he accurately called "lewd vagrancy," echoing the statutes that prohibited a variety of transgressive behavior and demonstrating a career-long interest in the legal consequences for the "fugitive kind" that populate his works.[58] His letters and journals documented his awareness of his own illegality and of legislation restricting the liberty of homosexuals, single women, and people of color. Legal statutes that defended the need for sexual prohibitions often defined all sexual activity outside of marriage as "disgusting," "degenerate," "unnatural," words that fill Williams's plays and stories. Scenes in or references to prisons or other spaces of confinement, mob retaliation, and public shaming, that is, to sites or types of punishments inflicted upon the promiscuous in Williams's works, all make evident his commitment to exposing the cultural suspicion and condemnation of sexual desire in the period. What I propose is to use the law as a framework for a new narrative of Williams's work and life. I propose a narrative that connects work and life but not as a one-to-one correspondence, not as a more traditional view of biography would trace life events in the fiction, or trace fictional events in their connection to biography. Rather, like law's narratives, the progression will be in fits and starts; it will feature shadowy confusion alongside traces of clarifying insight; it will reflect the beauty in a turn of phrase. It will demonstrate the constancy of a worldview alongside its conflicts and contradictions.

The road and the roadhouse tend to offer up certain kinds of stories, and the social flexibility of the Depression era influenced Williams in his depictions of transitory lives and spirits, broken by illness, madness, and sadness while being boosted by unusual alliances and unexpected gifts of kindness. His apprentice plays include the portraits of his tuberculin men with blood-stained pillowcases that then echo through his work only to reappear in a late memory play that in performance recalls the intricacies of boarding house intimacy that he experienced in his salad days with a trunk and a typewriter. Even in the early, rather crude, sketches of these men, Williams evokes the risk that intimacy offers in the face of physical illness as well as its persistent need. Certainly the shock value of his subject matter has been much noted: drawn to the grotesque from the beginning of his writing career, he married the shameful with the scintillating and, in doing so, produced compelling conflict. In the case of physical incapacity, disgust carries with it a tension that emphasizes the undesirability of the very person who is most in need of sympathy and, more importantly, contact. But whether the struggle is to care for the physically or psychically maimed, it becomes a measure of human potential and value to overcome the repulsion that providing such care might involve. That the transient, the mentally ill, the chronically ill, and the physically mutilated are still often hidden from society's view make his creation of such protagonists during the mid-century an unparalleled achievement. The transgressors that fill his plays and stories are often criminals, and the crimes they are guilty or accused of are sex crimes: sodomy, adultery, lewd vagrancy among the most common, but also prostitution, rape, and pedophilia; punishments exacted or threatened in response to these transgressive sexual behaviors include castration, murder, suicide, lobotomy, and cannibalism.

As recently as 2002, George W. Crandell describes a "current topic in Williams scholarship, namely Williams's unwillingness or inability (because of social prohibitions) to disclose the truth—at least onstage— about sensitive topics such as homosexuality or race relations."[59] The scholarly neglect of Williams's interest in the law and, most particularly, in the ways that he focuses on legal prohibitions against diverse sexual behaviors, has helped to undermine the extent to which his work not only disclosed but debated the very sensitive and oddly invisible attempts to legally contain those citizens whose bodies and actions were deemed "deviant," and therefore illegal, in many states. Williams's texts brought such issues to page and stage well before they were raised in the courts, and eventually in the high court. His use of the language of disgust was not, as it might first appear, the act of a self-loathing homosexual or of an artist determined to seek and maintain mainstream popularity: it was the expression of a complex and often contradictory construction of a social and sexual framework. It acknowledged both the frequency of and the judgment of all sexual activity that was not sanctioned by marriage and even some that was. On a larger scale, particularly when it comes to the treatment of sexual activity and identity, legal perspectives on privacy have continued to proliferate throughout the twentieth century; such perspectives provide numerous avenues for a detailed examination of Williams's literary and theatrical texts. His construction of sexual diversity is a commonplace of the critical commentary that has established him as a major literary and theatrical figure, but there are myriad ways that the existing scholarship on Williams can be advanced with the addition of issues raised here. Bringing the law to bear on his work yields new insights on his texts and their enduring legacy in the cultural and political landscape of the twentieth century. Law's statutes and judicial decisions about sexual behavior, when read as a history of/series of opinions drafted at various moments in time and at multiple levels of jurisprudence, become analogous to and revelatory for our study of Williams's body of texts (and his body as text), which work similarly, albeit artistically, to interrogate the issue.

Chapter 1, "Privacy and Identity," analyzes *A Streetcar Named Desire* and *The Night of the Iguana* within the context of several key Supreme Court debates and decisions on sexual restriction and freedom. Both plays were composed and produced during the height of the Cold War, a period when issues of privacy, individual freedom, and national security were center stage. *Streetcar* is one of Williams's best known plays, and *Iguana* includes a line that seems to encapsulate the author's attitudes toward morality and humanity; the plays selected thus make this analysis accessible to and useful for readers at all levels of familiarity with his work. Reading these plays within law's contexts provides a new interpretation of the individual texts and introduces many of the topics central to this study.

Chapter 2, "The Power of Disgust," focuses on representations of homosexuality in the short stories "Hard Candy" and "One Arm," calling attention to the frequency of legal images, language, and situations as they were moved in and out of texts and developed from one text to another. He drafted and published these texts during the very years that attention to sexual behavior considered deviant and its proposed "dangers" were under particularly ruthless legal scrutiny and newly energized waves of prosecution. Extensive analysis of multiple drafts of "One Arm," a text containing treatments of homosexuality, prostitution, mutilation, and criminal prosecution, demonstrates his use of short prose to explore homosexuality, disgust, and law. As courts drafted legal opinions about sexuality that revealed cultural contradictions and addressed moral imperatives alongside constitutional imperatives, so did Williams.

Chapter 3, "The Fugitive Kind," begins with a focused analysis of *Cat on a Hot Tin Roof*, but the drafts amassed over two decades of work on *Battle of Angels/Orpheus Descending* prove central to my argument and are examined in detail. Although the critical consensus is that the plays from 1945 to 1961 could not/did not "place the homosexual body on stage," so to speak, offstage and oft-dead "degenerates" were common. Moreover, other types of illegal bodies, with their diverse sexual activities and law's consequences, dominated a number of the theatrical works. Indeed, the drama serves, arguably, to develop and expand focus on the legislation of sexuality by exploring male and female, homosexual and heterosexual transgression.

Chapter 4, "The Politics of Recognition," considers the cultural impact of Williams as autobiography and creative work come together in the post-Stonewall period of the 1970s. As the outrage of the 1960s became the outrageousness of the 1970s, Williams contributed to these cultural shifts, particularly with the publication of *Memoirs* and in plays that exposed wide varieties of sexual diversity. While the assumption that being "out" after Stonewall no longer exacted personal or legal cost, sodomy prosecutions did not end until the high court invalidated them in 2003. Changes in state laws prior to that decision were gradual, and public perceptions about diverse sexualities continue today to be directed by rigid moral directives; such considerations provide new insights on the reception of his late work.

Following Savran's lead, I approach the study of the work of Tennessee Williams "as an anthropologist studies cultural productions, seeing them less as individual or idiosyncratic artifacts than as instances of two distinct cultural moments, each with its implicit social hierarchy, dominant values, and symbolic code."[60] However, I am less concerned with demonstrating some particular strain of Williams's belief system than I am with situating his life and his work within the context of laws and sexual mores in order to help us make sense of what have often been seen, biographically and critically, as untenable contradictions. Williams's own experience insured that he would have equal facility with both gentility and a rougher existence. Raised partly in the Southern Episcopalian rectories presided over by his maternal grandparents, he learned the tactics of repression associated with a Christian upbringing while recognizing that the tension formed in the displacement of desire has an erotic component. He marked it with those qualities and it was changed, taking on the power of his language and the compassion of his dramaturgy. His characters spoke with silver Southern tongues forged by the parlor or the tavern, sometimes both, and he has no equal in weaving dialect and standard, even formal English, to portray the layers of experience that convey past, present, and some hint of future.

Linking history with personal and creative texts by Williams, I construct a narrative of one writer's politics, with politics defined as the narrative of an individual's lifelong project of shaping a personal identity and seeking to understand and, at times, to connect one's personal values to the societies and communities in which he moves. An exploration of the way that the private and the public meet in what we call politics, and the power that emerges from that meeting, at least in a democracy, is greatest when the balance of private and public concerns serves both the individual and the whole. With its focus on a single and singular playwright, one who lived through the majority of the century and whose life intersected with the most transformative period in modern culture, whose influence has only expanded since his death, whose multiplicity and complexity of textual production put sexual desire at the center of inquiry, we can chart the hills and valleys in progress toward rights and liberty of expression as they are connected to and bound by sexual activity and identity.

NOTES

1. Tennessee Williams, *Selected Letters, vol. II, 1945–1957*, eds. Albert J. Devlin and Nancy M. Tischler (New York: New Directions, 2004), 272–273.
2. Williams, *Selected Letters, vol. II*, 303.
3. Tennessee Williams, *Notebooks*, ed. Margaret Bradham Thornton (New Haven, CT: Yale University Press, 2006), 299.
4. Tennessee Williams, *Letters to Donald Windham 1940–1965*, ed. and with comments by Donald Windham (New York: Penguin, 1980), 35.
5. Williams, *Notebooks*, 339.
6. Tennessee Williams, *Selected Letters, vol. I, 1940–1945*, eds. Albert J. Devlin and Nancy M. Tischler (New York: New Directions, 2000), 522.
7. Albert J. Devlin, "Audrey Wood and Tennessee Williams: A Revealing Correspondence," *Tenn at One Hundred: The Reputation of Tennessee,* ed. David Kaplan (East Brunswick, NJ: Hansen Publishing Group, 2011), 85–93.
8. Edmund Wilson, "Playwright's Diary," *New York Times Book Review* 4 March 2007, 20.
9. Williams, *Notebooks*, 235.
10. Tennessee Williams, *Memoirs* (Garden City, NY: Doubleday & Company, Inc., 1975), 162.
11. Williams, *Memoirs*, 22.
12. Williams, *Memoirs*, 22.
13. George Chauncey, *Gay New York: Gender, Urban Culture, and the Making of the Gay Male World, 1890–1940* (New York: Basic Books, 1994), 301. Chauncey notes in the introduction to his chronicle that it "focuses on men because the difference between gay male and lesbian history and the complexity of each made it seem virtually impossible to write a book about both that did justice to each and avoided making one history an appendage to the other" (27).
14. Chauncey, 305–306.
15. Chauncey, 331.
16. William N. Eskridge, Jr., *Dishonorable Passions: Sodomy Laws in America, 1861–2003* (New York: Viking Penguin, 2008), 77.
17. David A. J. Richards, *The Sodomy Cases*: Bowers v. Hardwick *and* Lawrence v. Texas (Lawrence: University Press of Kansas, 2009), 8.
18. Richards, 9–10.
19. Richards, 10.
20. Chauncey, 200.
21. Chauncey, 179.
22. Allan Bérubé, *Coming Out Under Fire: The History of Gay Men and Women in World War Two* (New York: The Free Press, 1990), 98.
23. Bérubé, 99.
24. Lyle Leverich, *Tom: The Unknown Tennessee Williams* (New York: New Directions, 1995), 275.
25. Williams, *Memoirs* , 49.
26. John Lahr, *Tennessee Williams: Mad Pilgrimage of the Flesh* (New York: W. W. Norton & Co., 2014), 74.
27. Lahr, 77–78.
28. Williams, *Notebooks*, 131.
29. Williams, *Notebooks*, 133.
30. Lahr, 88.

31. Williams, *Notebooks*, 153, 152, n253.
32. John S. Bak, *Tennessee Williams: A Literary Life* (New York: Palgrave, 2013), 80.
33. Williams, *Notebooks*, 125.
34. Leverich, *Tom,* 351.
35. Williams, *Notebooks*, 132, n237.
36. Chauncey, 156.
37. Williams, *Selected Letters, vol. I,* 342.
38. John D'Emilio and Estelle B. Friedman, *Intimate Matters: A History of Sexuality in America* (New York: Harper & Row, 1988), 289.
39. Donna Penn, "The Sexualized Woman: The Lesbian, the Prostitute, and the Containment of Female Sexuality in Postwar America," in Joanne Myerowitz, ed., *Not June Cleaver: Women and Gender in Postwar America, 1945–1960* (Philadelphia: Temple University Press, 1994), 358–381, 364.
40. D'Emilio and Freedman, 290, 292.
41. Leverich, *Tom,* 398–399.
42. Jana Malamud Smith, *Private Matters: In Defense of the Personal Life* (Emeryville, CA: Seal Press, 2003), 150.
43. Malamud Smith, 153.
44. Williams, *Selected Letters, vol. II*, 155.
45. Daniel J. Solove, *Understanding Privacy* (Cambridge, MA: Harvard University Press, 2008), 144.
46. Williams, *Selected Letters, vol. I,* 305.
47. Tennessee Williams, Letter to Lucy Freeman, 8 September 1962, Box 54, folder 10, Tennessee Williams Collection, Harry Ransom Center, Austin, TX.
48. Tennessee Williams, Letter to Andreas Brown, 1963, n.d., Box 54, folder 5, Tennessee Williams Collection, Harry Ransom Center, Austin, TX.
49. Williams, *Selected Letters, vol. II,* 48–49.
50. Malamud Smith, 147–148.
51. Malamud Smith, 147–148.
52. Kevin M. Crotty, *Law's Interior: Legal and Literary Constructions of the Self* (Ithaca, NY: Cornell University Press, 2001), 93.
53. Nancy Tischler, *Tennessee Williams: Rebellious Puritan* (New York: The Citadel Press, 1961): 299, 300, 304.
54. David Savran, *Communists, Cowboys, and Queers: The Politics of Masculinity in the Work of Arthur Miller and Tennessee Williams* (Minneapolis, MN: University of Minnesota Press, 1992), 80–81.
55. Marc Robinson, *The Other American Drama* (Cambridge, UK: Cambridge University Press, 1994), 31.
56. Amiri Baraka, "Tennessee Williams is Never Apolitical," *Tenn at One Hundred: The Reputation of Tennessee Williams*, ed. David Kaplan (East Brunswick, NJ: Hansen Publishing Group, 2011), 281–282.
57. Robert J. Corber, *Homosexuality in Cold War America: Resistance and the Crisis of Masculinity* (Durham, NC: Duke University Press, 1997), 16–17.
58. "Fugitive Kind" was the title of an early Williams play (1937) that was produced by the St. Louis Mummers, an amateur activist theater group with whom he worked while still in college. "The Fugitive Kind" (1960) is the title of the film version of his play *Orpheus Descending*. In a larger sense, the phrase epitomizes one of the major thematic tensions: the need for freedom set against the impossibility of it without constant movement.
59. George Crandell, "Tennessee Williams Scholarship at the Turn of the Century," Magical Muse: Millennial Essays on Tennessee Williams, ed. Ralph F. Voss (Tuscaloosa: University of Alabama Press, 2002), 13.
60. Savran, *Communists, Cowboys, and Queers*, x.

ONE
Privacy and Identity

In April 1970, Harold H. Hart, president of Hart Publishing, addressed a letter to Tennessee Williams inviting him to submit a "piece of somewhere between 4,000 and 6,000 words" that would, as Hart says, "embrace your present thinking as to what sexual attitudes you deem valid, and what stance society should take with regard to individual sexual activity which is generally considered to be deviant." The prompt is followed by suggestions about what specific topics might be covered, with premarital sex, extramarital sex, group sex, and prostitution among them, along with such questions as "Should homosexuality among consenting adults be permitted by law?" Hart trusts that the "controversial" book that results from such queries will "represent a spectrum of present-day thinking on this vital topic," for it will contain "original pieces by well-known philosophers, psychologists, writers, religious leaders, and educators."[1] The book, *Sexual Latitude: For and Against*, was published the following year, and in its introduction Hart summarizes the question that concerns the contributors to this volume as "whether the withering away of our former morality should be approved or deplored."

Hart then quotes one of the book's contributors, Ruth Dickson, a sociologist and writer, who suggests that sexual activity, "'a simple, natural function of the body,'" has been called evil and has been suppressed by generations. Dickson argues that "'the amount of psychological damage done to otherwise normal people by this attitude is staggering to contemplate. To create guilt for doing something as natural as breathing, by instilling the notion that this act is an ugly vice rather than a beautiful and fulfilling communication between two people, is to me the worst sin of all.'"[2] No entry by Williams is included in the book— not particularly surprising given the demands on his time and the number of requests that passed across his desk. But Williams did not have to write an essay for the book, for he had submitted many opinions on the valid and deviant in the realm of sexual activities and attitudes, primarily in the form of creative texts that explored these topics. In his stories, plays, and screenplays, and in interviews, a memoir, and now-published letters and journals, he offered extended considerations of behavior regulated by law or by social norms. Williams had grappled with these issues on numerous occasions and in very public forums, and he spent much of his five-decade career debating the organizing question of Hart's book: "whether the withering away of our former morality should be approved or deplored."[3] Williams answered the question by demonstrating that what should be approved or at least not deplored are the efforts that individuals make to cultivate an honest self in the presence of others, be they family members, loved ones, or communities. What Williams acknowledges, however, is the difficulty faced by the person who risks exposure with the hope of acceptance. In two plays that roughly span his most successful period, 1945–1961, Williams expressed his compassionate views of difference; in both plays it is through the sexual history of a self-identified spinster that complicated perspectives on identity, intimacy, privacy, and freedom emerge.

The earlier of the two plays, *A Streetcar Named Desire* (1947), is probably the best known of Williams's texts, and *The Night of the Iguana* (1961) contains a line that suggests the direction of Williams's moral compass, "nothing human disgusts me unless it's unkind, violent." The reading of the two plays that follows here, concentrated as it is on issues of sexuality and law, seeks to demonstrate the connections between his representations of sexual intimacy with legal concerns about privacy and the formation of the self in the modern world. *Streetcar*'s stage premiere in 1947 secured the playwright's position at the forefront of midcentury American theater, and the first production of *Iguana* in 1961 marks the beginning of the end of Williams's Broadway years, or at least the years of assumed success and of ready access to sufficient financial backing for major productions.

In *Iguana*, Reverend Shannon asks aging spinster Hannah Jelkes: "Have you never had in all of your life and your travels any experience, any encounter, with what Larry-the-crackpot Shannon thinks of as a love-life?" In response Hannah narrates two incidents, the first an advance by a young stranger in a movie theater that ended with the stranger "arrested for molesting a minor," the second a request for her underpants made by an Australian salesman in a Singapore sampan; when she complies, he fondles them as he masturbates. She describes the latter interaction as "embarrassing, not violent" and even "rather touching." As she explains to an incredulous Shannon: "I mean it was so *lonely*, out there in the sampan with violent streaks in the sky and this little middle-aged Australian making sounds like he was dying of asthma! And the planet Venus coming serenely out of a fair-weather cloud." Shannon, taken aback by her assertion of what he calls "that, that . . . sad, dirty little episode," and what was for her a love experience, asks her, "You mean it didn't *disgust* you?" To which Hannah replies: "Nothing human disgusts me unless it's unkind, violent."[4] This exchange is quintessential Williams: a narrative of an episode many audience members would have surely judged as sordid and shocking, a response within the play that seems to support such judgments, and a rebuttal made by one of Williams's "sensitive" figures, who argues for a more human and humane assessment. Williams's texts are known for their sympathetic portrayal of difference, particularly sexual difference, and celebrated for dramatized moments of "the kindness of strangers," not to mention kindness toward the strange, and they indicate that the author concurred with Dickson's perspective that consensual sex, no matter what form it takes, can be a "beautiful and fulfilling communication between two people." What has rightly complicated such a conclusion about Williams's portrayals of romantic and erotic fulfillment, however, are his characters' persistent, even pervasive use of adjectives such as "disgusting," "dirty," "unnatural," and "degenerate," to describe acts of sexual intimacy, either others' or their own. The duality of endorsement and condemnation are presented, as we see in Hannah and Shannon's dialogue with each other, and such exchanges often end without resolution, leaving viewers or readers with ambiguities rather than answers.

Another brief consideration of the letter from Hart Publishing and the scene from *The Night of the Iguana* frame the convergence of sexual behavior, morality, and law that marked Williams's work as confluent with politics and culture. The questions posed by the query letter sent by Harold Hart might be summarized as follows: Ought consensual sex among adults, whatever its form, be legalized and even supported by our political and social systems in order to further the public good? What role do constitutional rights play in such decisions; in the case of the prostitute, for example, ought she be free to "dispose of her own body in any way she sees fit," for "although her case be deplored, no other being has a right to prohibit that choice?"[5] Moreover, how might a diverse group of experts from such fields as psychology, sociology, literature, education, and philosophy (the professions Hart lists do not, rather conspicuously in this context, include lawyers, judges, or constitutional scholars) put forth opinions and perspectives convincing enough to influence the public sphere by arguing for modifications to the current systems of morality and, one might assume, law.

In *Iguana*, similar concerns are raised, with the emphasis on sexual activity and on issues of physical intimacy, emotion, and empathy. Williams acknowledges specifically the connection between sexual impulse and legal regulation, particularly when the impulse occurs in a public space; indeed, the question of whether sexual acts take place in private or public places is raised frequently in Williams's creative texts, and this differentiation proves of paramount importance to the condemnation and punishment of transgression. So was it true in the laws of the time, if for no other reason than it is more difficult to identify illegal acts conducted in private spaces. The first example of what Hannah defines as a love experience ended with a molestation charge for the man who persisted in pressing his leg against Hannah's in the back of the dark movie theater; from a legal standpoint, the advance was unwanted. Although Hannah "jumped up and screamed" in protest, she subsequently convinced the police to drop the charges by telling them that it was a "Clara Bow picture—and I was just excited."[6] The first of her two "encounters" results in an arrest without a subsequent prosecution, and the second did not take place in the United States, but both incidents would have been considered "illicit" if not illegal; prohibitions against public masturbation, primarily but not solely designed to protect children, still exist in many jurisdictions. During Williams's time, the offense was regularly included in local or state regulations criminalizing sodomy or the "crime against nature."[7] Only hinted at here, Williams's interest in, and knowledge of, laws regulating sexuality are more fully evident in many of his creative works as well as in his notebooks and letters, his characters' and his own brushes with the law in connection with some kind of "lewd behavior" constituting the majority of the legal scenarios in his texts.

Moreover, the words used by Shannon to describe his response to Hannah's second anecdote, "dirty" and "disgusting," were, throughout American legal history, integral to the language and spirit of legislation that regulated sexual behavior considered deviant and thus detrimental to individuals and to society. The elicitation of disgust in the justification and support of such laws, many of which criminalized sodomy specifically but also included statutes against oral sex, adultery, and prostitution, is long-standing, as Eskridge notes: "Disgust Americans feel toward sensual activities remind us of our animal natures; fears of pollution, especially when sexuality, gender role, and racial identities are combined, and of predation, especially as regards our children; and self-definition that depends on creating symbolic others who are our degraded opposites."[8] The language of disgust as Shannon employs it, in the evaluation of sexual behavior, parallels the law's use of such language, and the circumstances that warrant such disgust and fear in the law's texts are often identical to the scenarios that Williams creates in his fictions.

However, in Williams's texts, the language of disgust, whether applied to transgression or disease, is deployed in ways both pointed and elusive. While his word choice projects the speaker's judgment of the deviant natures or acts of persons spoken about, such words as "degenerate" or "unnatural" are rendered determinedly vague by his narrative style. His expert application of Southern speech, with its eliding tendencies, prompted in part by propriety and delicacy, means that these terms of disgust convey the worst while the ellipses and unfinished sentences that surround them allow the details, which are too shocking for the speaker to verbalize, to remain unspoken. This "softening" effect is complicated, however, for the reader or audience member who recognizes that these words of condemnation, expressed by judgmental characters in a Southern parlor or, as in *Iguana*, by a defrocked minister on a hotel veranda in Mexico, are the same words that functioned as consensus-seeking in legal documents that regulated sexual behavior. Assumptions that Americans could and would stand on common ground about what disgusts them have been the source of heated legal debates, of course, and yet laws have been supported and passed when such assumptions could be successfully established and agreed upon as ideologically sound.

The exchange between Hannah and Shannon reveals that the expression and evocation of human compassion are also regularly linked to representations or discussions of sexuality and our responses to it. The differences between some criminal acts and others, and particularly the differences between the ways that judgment is passed upon the transgressive, coincide, as we shall see, with what legal theorists have established as a difference between acts that may disgust some but that are not necessarily reprehensible, and those that harm others and must therefore be legislated against. Martha C. Nussbaum defines what she calls the "politics of humanity" as a "politics of equal respect," noting that the "American Revolution was in that sense radical, rejecting all previous modes of social organization and opting for one entirely new, built on the idea that all persons have equal human dignity and equal natural rights."[9] The emotion that disgust elicits, furthermore, "encourages us to accept hierarchies and boundaries that are not defensible within a political tradition based on equal respect."[10] This discussion of equal respect and rights, as it pertains to Williams's treatment of Hannah's "lovelife," draws our attention to the timeliness of *Iguana*'s appearance on the stage, for the play premiered on Broadway in December 1961, at the start of a decade during which the nation was consumed with and embattled over issues of civil rights, not limited to, but including, sexual rights. As the last major "hit" for Williams, the play has been widely regarded as a moment of triumph for him at what has been considered the peak of his most potent public influence. However, this study aims to revise the narrative of his decline by demonstrating Williams's significance in a public sphere that was poised to experience an overhaul of attitudes and values about identity and rights.

Nussbaum reminds us that the American tradition grants "ample liberty to each person to pursue his or her own way in matters of conscience," and that a "world that respects conscience therefore gives equal liberty to all people to pursue its promptings in matters concerning both belief and conduct."[11] She then draws the analogy between religious and sexual liberty, acknowledging that while the pursuit of sexual happiness may in many ways differ from the pursuit of religious fulfillment, the "point of the analogy is to say that the pursuit of sexual happiness is viewed by most Americans as a very intimate and important part of the pursuit of happiness, a part that touches on the core of the self," bound up with the "core of a person's identity and personality, and with the most intimate aspects of striving and searching for meaning."[12] Seen within the context of Nussbaum's remarks, Williams's work can be considered central to American conceptions of liberty and freedom, for his regular focus on sexual activity is always connected to the issues that Nussbaum lists: "the core of the self," a "person's identity and personality," and the "most intimate aspects of striving and searching for meaning."

It is Hannah's position of compassion that tempers both Shannon's and, presumably, the audience's shock at her unusual reactions to the sexual experiences she narrates: convincing the police to drop the charges against the first man, and describing the salesman and his request as "gentle" and "apologetic, shy, and really very, well, *delicate* about it" [emphasis in original]. In her reactions and in her description of the salesman we recognize the "politics of humanity" that Nussbaum calls for, defined, she says, as the "combination of equal respect for one's fellow citizens with a serious and sympathetic attempt to imagine what interests they are pursuing." To respect another person as an equal, Nussbaum continues, "is to see that person in a certain way: as an end, not merely as a means, as a person, not merely as an object. That way of seeing requires endowing the other with life and purpose, rather than with dirt and dross, with human dignity rather than with foulness."[13] Such a way of seeing others opposes directly what Eskridge argues has long been at the root of laws prohibiting the crime against nature, fueled as such laws were by a desire for "self-definition that depends on creating symbolic others who are our degraded opposites." The way to respect that Nussbaum describes is Hannah's way, we see explicitly in Williams's text, with her proclamation, "nothing human disgusts me unless it's unkind, violent." And it is her attitude that arguably triumphs in this scene of debate between her and Shannon, that provides a maxim for living, and that even suggests, implicitly, a way that society might distinguish the morally acceptable from the legally actionable.

Another of Williams's plays provides further evidence of the centrality of sexual politics in his work as well as his interest in a politics of humanity and its importance to cultural and legal systems. In two scenes at either end of *Streetcar*, Blanche DuBois inadvertently reveals her emotional vulnerability to her brother-in-law Stanley Kowalski, and in doing so dramatizes the internal conflict that has driven many of her choices: a desire for human intimacy, coupled with her awareness of the risks of being exposed in that intimacy or by that intimacy. In scene 2, when

Stanley reaches into the bottom of her trunk and pulls out the love letters from her dead husband, Blanche cries out, "Give those back to me!" and "Now that you've touched them I'll burn them!" Stanley's confusion about her response, "What do you mean by saying you'll have to burn them?" prompts the following explanation from Blanche: "I'm sorry, I must have lost my head for a moment. Everyone has something he won't let others touch because of their—intimate nature."[14] Blanche's desire to keep her intimacies hidden is one of the text's ongoing themes and conflicts, as her equivocations about her sex life before she arrived in New Orleans become the impetus for Stanley's increasingly persistent and damaging investigation of her illicit past.

In the play's penultimate scene, Blanche and Stanley are once again alone together, and Blanche has conjured a fantasy of departing soon for a "cruise of the Caribbean on a yacht!" as the result of an invitation from an old beau that "came like a bolt from the blue!" She exclaims, "When I think of how divine it is going to be to have such a thing as privacy once more—I could weep with joy!"[15] Having shared a two-room apartment with Stanley and Stella for five months, it comes as no surprise that she would dream of having her own stateroom; given Stanley's constant barrage of probing questions and snide insinuations, however, her wish extends beyond physical privacy to the protection of her delicate psyche. In the early scene, she admits to having "lost her head for a moment" when she reacts so vehemently to Stanley's touch on her intimate items, whose hand "insults them." Later in the play, when her past has been divulged after living for months with Stanley's questions and investigations, she is unapologetic about her interest in privacy, the thought of which elicits a joy so "divine" that it may produce tears.

It is possible, however, to read Blanche's quest for privacy not only as a wish to be alone but as a wish to be left alone, to be "once more" in the position of being able to protect the sanctity of her private life and her choices. The intrusions had begun with the first meeting of Blanche and Stanley, what William Kleb calls "one of the great moments in modern world drama." When Blanche introduces herself to Stanley he responds, "'Stella's sister?'" although as Kleb notes, "What other Blanche could she be?" Thus begins, according to Kleb, a "quiet, casual, but increasingly charged interrogation that ends minutes later with Blanche about to be 'sick,' forced to speak of the central, agonizing event of her past, the death of her boy-husband Allan Grey."[16] The questions Stanley poses, "Where you from, Blanche?" "What do you teach, Blanche?" and "You were married once, weren't you?" are all seemingly innocent inquiries of general interest, but they prove no less than the very means by which he orchestrates her destruction. Indeed, John S. Bak compares the play to the infamous "Monkey Trial" of 1925, *Tennessee v. John Scopes*, arguing that "Blanche, the witness, enters the courtroom at 632 Elysian Fields, and not a moment passes before Stanley begins cross-examining her."[17] Stanley's rummaging through her trunk in scene 2 is the physical representation of the delving he does into every part of her life, and the details he gathers assist him in convincing his wife and his friend Mitch of the danger she poses to domestic tranquility. These bits of information are all linked to her status as one of Williams's "illegal bodies," for her crimes include what she calls "intimacies with strangers" without the legal protection of marriage, at least one of them with a minor, and hints of prostitution. Seeking to expel her from his home and thus reassert his *own* right to be left alone, to live without interference, Stanley invades Blanche's privacy as a prelude to his invasion and violation of her body in an illegal act of sexual violence that seals her fate. With the rape and its outcome, Blanche is unmoored from the identity-building central to American life and success: her fate is sealed and her rights revoked with her involuntary commitment to a mental institution, banished to a place whose system of operation is structured on the absence of all privacy, spatial and psychological.

The balance between the need for community and the desire to maintain individual sovereignty is, of course, a primary concern of democracy and hence much taken up in modern Western conceptions of the rule of law. Although the word "privacy" is not included in the Constitution, the Bill of Rights reflects certain specific safeguards related to privacy that have served as the legal basis for the development of privacy laws in the United States.[18] The appearance of "The Right to Privacy," an influential essay by Samuel D. Warren and Louis D. Brandeis published in the *Harvard Law Review* in 1890, marks the moment of origin for modern debates about privacy. As recently as 2010, Steven Alan Childress asserted that the Warren and Brandeis essay "changed the world" as it was "very likely the most important, game-changing piece of legal scholarship ever." Because the essay "hooked into an emotional sense of privacy that resonated with readers and lawmakers," writes Childress, "it still hits home today."[19] Indeed, Warren and Brandeis preface their argument with a capsulation of how the conception of privacy had developed over centuries: the Founding Fathers' concerns—the need to protect the physical right to life and to insure freedom from physical harm, restraint, and the theft or destruction of property—were expanded as the notion of life and its protection developed to include the spiritual dimension of the self. As Warren and Brandeis described the elaboration of the issue: "The right to life has come to mean the right to enjoy life—the right to be let alone; the right to liberty secures the exercise of extensive civil privileges; and the term 'property' has grown to comprise every form of possession—intangible, as well as tangible."[20] Blanche's concerns include both: the "intimate nature" of the letters themselves, and the secrets they represent.

During his tenure on the Supreme Court, Brandeis continued to influence modern conceptions of privacy, most notably with this oft-cited statement in his dissent of the Court's opinion in *Olmstead v. United States* (1928):

> The makers of our Constitution undertook to secure conditions favorable to the pursuit of happiness. They recognized the significance of man's spiritual nature of his feelings and of his intellect. They knew that only a part of the pain, pleasure and satisfactions of life are to be found in material things. They sought to protect Americans in their beliefs, their thoughts, their emotions and their sensations. They conferred, as against the Government, the right to be let alone—the most comprehensive of rights and the right most valued by civilized men.[21]

The modern world's embrace of privacy as significant to all persons was confirmed in 1948, while the first production of *Streetcar* was on Broadway, when the United Nations Universal Declaration of Human Rights recognized privacy as a fundamental human right: "No one shall be subjected to arbitrary interference with his privacy, family, home or correspondence, not to attacks upon his honor and reputation."[22] In *Streetcar*, Stanley's self-admitted interference with his sister-in-law (just prior to the rape, he says, "*softly*," "Come to think of it—maybe you wouldn't be bad to—interfere with . . .") might be considered not just a sexually based criminal act but the ultimate violation of Blanche's privacy, which he has invaded consistently since the opening scene.[23] The development of privacy rights in the twentieth century, particularly as those rights were bound up with and influenced cultural and legal attitudes about sexuality, suggests that the critical exploration of Williams's diverse and often illegal sexualities will provide new perspectives on the intersections of imaginative and legal texts.

The individual's right to control identity and destiny was of fundamental concern for Tennessee Williams, present and problematized in his narratives through scenarios featuring conflicting truths, damaging secrets, and failed attempts at character reformation or transformation. Solove identifies various areas of privacy concerns, and they can be read as a compendium of Williams's plot points and themes, with an eye to both common elements and apparent contradictions among them: the right to be let alone, limited public access to the self, the secrecy of certain matters, control over personal information, the protection of personhood, the creation of intimacy. While we might assume that the guarantee of the things in this list would be uncontestable, we must acknowledge that great challenges exist when persons or groups seek to balance the importance of individual rights with the need to uphold the public good. Solove argues that one of the most important dimensions of a theory of privacy is how to assess its value, for it is only in doing so that it is possible to construct a rationale of why privacy is worth protecting. Precisely because it is so often cast as an individual right, it may be undervalued when set against what may be or what may seem to be conflicting social interests.[24]

However, Solove summarizes sound arguments from multiple fields of human study to assert that individual privacy rights support the social order, with rationales that suggest its essentialness to our well-being "'physically, psychologically, socially, and morally.'" Also supporting social order, the right to privacy and its contribution to self-development enables people to "create, explore, and experiment." Additionally, privacy supports democracy as it "permits individuals to contemplate and discuss political change, create counterculture, or engage in a meaningful critique of society."[25] According to Edward Bloustein, privacy is "an interest of the human personality" that "protects the inviolate personality, the individual's independence, dignity and integrity."[26] The visible failure of protection for the "inviolate personality" is central in much of Williams's imaginative work, as is the presentation of fictional figures who strive to live with dignity in the face of great struggle, attempting to preserve their independence and autonomy in a world that seems to target them for diminishment of self and destruction.

With a focus on identity as intertwined with privacy, thus essential for self-existence, Williams considers variously what the individual is entitled to in his multiple and varied forms of human representation. When individual choice is possible without harm to others, many of his characters argue that compassion and acceptance ought to be valued above judgment, and that humanity's diversity ought to be honored: as Hannah says, nothing human disgusts her unless it is unkind or violent. The upholding of human rights demands a wide-ranging acceptance of difference and the freedom to reveal such differences without censure, but, as Blanche's concern about her letters emphasizes, it also includes the individual prerogative to keep certain thoughts or actions private. Both concepts are fundamental, Williams demonstrates repeatedly, for the stability of the subject's identity and for the success of social interactions. The need to "be left alone" is the need to be one's self without interference; the urgency of that liberty and the protection of it drove Tennessee Williams throughout his life and throughout his career, serving as one of his major sources of motivation and inspiration. He traveled widely as a means of escape, while it was not always clear what he thought he needed to escape from. The movement facilitated his creation of an autonomous life. The need to keep one's self protected from harm also required eluding restriction, in order to prevent his becoming one of those people he called "the wild at heart that are kept in cages."[27] Restriction in his fictional representations is often actual as well as virtual; containment of the soul can be both physical and metaphorical.

The relief Blanche expresses to Stanley about having privacy "once more" would seem to conflict with what Blanche has told Stella in the first scene: "I want to be near you, got to be *with* somebody, I *can't* be *alone!*" At the play's opening, it is not privacy but connection Blanche seeks, for she's "*not very well*" and needs the physical and emotional comfort of other people. The emphatic nature of the speech, indicated by Williams's use of italics, along with Blanche's emotional assessment of herself that she provides with the lines, "I must have lost my head," point to the common condition of a Williams protagonist who lives in a heightened emotional state: the contrasting desires she expresses throughout the play, the demand for connection and privacy at once, demonstrate her need for protection and contact as well as the conflicting impulse to remain unfettered and therefore safe from injury. Whether Blanche's destruction was imminent without the further blows to her personhood that she suffers at Stanley's hands is a matter of debate: her psychological deterioration over the course of the play varies according to production choice, its progression and its causes widely variable depending on interpretation. She tells Stella, for example, that she was "on the verge of— lunacy, almost" even before arriving in New Orleans, but she regularly depends upon hyperbole, magnifying the truth as it suits her.[28] In any case, the intense psychological needs that she displays as well as her performance of these needs at a high emotional pitch underscore the significance of both intimacy and privacy to human safety and sanity, and the conflict between them is regularly presented in Williams's creative work as a precarious, indeed dangerous, balancing act that is nonetheless required. As a result, his literary and theatrical works are rightly noted for their emotional potency, for their affecting language, for their highly charged personal situations. Blanche's situation is just one example of the extent to which Tennessee Williams is concerned in his work with the need for, and the threat posed by, self-revelation, with the value and danger of intimacy, with the inescapability of a vulnerability that precipitates harm, annihilation, and confinement or death.

The conception of the "emotional sense of privacy" that Childress calls world-changing, along with the spiritual dimension of self that has contributed to the perception of property as "intangible, as well as tangible," shed light on Blanche's reactions to what she considers personal invasions: the letters are her property, yes, but their value, she makes clear in her response to Stanley, is in what they represent and contain of her emotional and spiritual selves.[29] The balance between privacy and connection is a major concern in the play, not only for her but for the other major characters, and this conflict is suggested by the very setting of the action: a two-room flat with only a curtain separating the living area from the bedroom. Blanche's collapsible bed is in the common room, and Stanley and Stella's bedroom is often occupied by Blanche. She is in the apartment throughout the play, "offstage" only when she is in the bathroom; but even when she is soaking in the tub she remains present audibly, singing, making requests of Stella, and otherwise intruding on the rare time alone the couple has since Blanche's arrival.

Stanley's desire to remove her from the apartment is driven in part by his desire to regain the marital sexual privacy he had previously enjoyed; he tells Stella that Blanche's departure will permit the two of them to "make noise in the night the way we used to and get the colored lights going with nobody's sister behind the curtain to hear us."[30] With *Griswold v. Connecticut* (1965), the Supreme Court held that the Constitution preserves a "zone of privacy" for married couples that grants protection for personal decisions about sexual conduct, birth control, and health. Justice William O. Douglas delivered the opinion of the court, which argued that "specific guarantees in the Bill of Rights have penumbras, formed by emanations from those guarantees," and various guarantees "create zones of privacy." In his concurring statement, Justice Arthur Goldberg cited the Ninth Amendment in support of the Court's decision, concluding that personal liberty "embraces the right of marital privacy, though that right is not mentioned specifically in the Constitution." By reclaiming the space that Blanche occupies in the apartment, Stanley is certain that not only can they once again behave as they wish to sexually, "to make noise in the night" but that the privacy will insure the quality of their intimacy, getting the "colored lights" going. Their relationship, as he describes it, reflects the cultural ideal of the time: a marriage between a man and a woman that would not only include a fruitful sexual life that produces children, but that would satisfy both parties, with sexual intimacy and freedom key parts of the marital bond and fulfillment.

The marriage home and bed that Stanley and Stella share is the antithesis of Blanche's experience of coupling: her sexual history, which began with a fatal love affair, leads to emotional destruction and social expulsion. An early marriage when she was "young, very young," to a man who, Stella tells Stanley in scene 7, Blanche "didn't just love but worshipped the ground he walked on," ended with the revelation that the "beautiful and talented young man was a degenerate."[31] By this point in the play we have already heard the details of Allan's "degeneracy" from Blanche, and that earlier narrative makes evident how closely issues of privacy and intimacy are intertwined with sexuality. There was, she tells Mitch in scene 6, "something different about the boy," but it is not until after the honeymoon, the traditional occasion of marital consummation, that she found out exactly what the "something different" was, "in the worst of all possible ways," by "coming suddenly into a room that I thought was empty—which wasn't empty, but had two people in it . . . the boy I had married and an older man who had been his friend for years." The discovery of her husband in an illegal relationship brands him in her mind as "degenerate," but her earlier "discovery—love. All at once and much, much too completely," means that the intimacy she had hoped would bind that love to her in marriage eluded her. She discovers this by violating the men's privacy; her discovery of her husband's actions and the confrontation she forces prompt Allan to commit suicide.

In her revelation to Mitch she recalls the words she used later that night on the dance floor with her young husband, after which he breaks away from her and heads out of the casino: "'I saw! I know! You disgust me.'" The loss of privacy in Allan's case is also the exposure of self, which proves too much for him to bear. Her husband chooses self-execution in public, shooting himself just steps away from her, exposing all to the "terrible thing at the edge of the lake" that someone tells Blanche she ought not see.[32] The depiction of Blanche's husband throughout the play mirrors the cultural opinion of homosexual sex as "immoral" and "criminally harmful," the suicide confirming Allan's shame, the act of self-destruction a recognition that he cannot live with himself or with her judgment of him. Significantly, Blanche's revelations to Mitch in scene 6 briefly move this fledgling heterosexual couple closer to each other, the scene ending on a note of possibility and increased intimacy: "You need somebody," he tells her. "And I need somebody, too. Could it be—you and me, Blanche?"[33] For the audience, however, the moment is complicated by what Mitch has failed to notice: the conversation began with Blanche's complaints about her current living conditions and economic status: "It's really a pretty frightful situation. You see, there's no privacy here," and a "teacher's salary is barely sufficient for her living expenses."[34] Privacy and identity are caught up with each other in a crisis that follows Blanche into her future and stunts her own development: she cannot become anything other than a helpless girl who seeks protection, and she cannot forget the evening that she discovered the true identity of her young husband, only to condemn him for it.

Abandoned by her husband both before and after his death, "intimacies with strangers" provide scant comfort to Blanche; she herself becomes a sexual outlaw, driven to find comfort outside of the marriage bed and therefore bringing upon her the kind of dangerous exposure that her husband faced. Beyond her self-incrimination for not providing "the help he needed" when Allan tried marriage as a way of masking his sexual orientation, Blanche is guilty of breaching his right to privacy, for it is she who exposes her husband's secret and criminal behavior. *Streetcar* thus provides an illustrative example of Williams's mixed messages about transgressive sexual activity: the degradation of the homosexual who is, after death, also glorified as a sensitive poet and Blanche's one and only true love interest, as well as the condemnation of him and its connection to the eventual punishment of her own sexual transgressions, themselves illegal activities.[35] Her fragile mental condition as the play opens helps to convey both the cost of involvement with and love for Allan and the effects of her own subsequent actions, for it is after Allan's tragic death that the love that had been like "a blinding light on something that had always been half in shadow" was extinguished, and "the searchlight which had been turned on the world was turned off again and never for one moment since has there been any light that's stronger than this—kitchen—candle."[36] Beyond her description of the extinction of that light of love, the contrast between Stanley's "colored lights" and Blanche's blinding searchlight is significant: the former evokes a string of lights on a Christmas tree or at a celebration, while the latter indicates interrogation and loss of sight.

The first production of *Streetcar* coincided with the postwar sex panic described by Eskridge; the panic gained momentum from the growing body of anti-Soviet rhetoric during the period, drawing power from the perceived need to protect the American family and to maintain national security. These amorphous sites of anxiety and their connections to each other underscore the alignment of morality and safety during the years immediately following World War II, when the search for destructive "foreign" forces in society became a national obsession. The targets were "ostensibly domestic Communism and child molesters, but increasingly the focus was 'homosexuals and other sex perverts.' The paranoid domestic politics of the 1950s ultimately expended more resources in its antihomosexual witch hunts than in its anti-Communist ones (though most Americans saw them as the same campaign)."[37] The primary targets of this period were a key focus in Williams's creative texts, characters whose past or present behavior would make them, according to the mores of the time, "sex perverts." We need only recall the few characters discussed above: Blanche's young husband, Blanche and her own subsequent "intimacies with strangers," Stanley the rapist, and, a decade later, Hannah Jelkes's "molester," to recognize Williams's use of sex panic components to infuse his texts with contemporary tensions. His work has always been noted for its depictions of outsiders and misfits, for those people living bohemian lives while occupying the liminal spaces of urban centers: the boardinghouse and the bordello, the state asylum and the tubercular ward of the county hospital. But when framed by the histories and analyses of sexuality and law in the midcentury, an additional pattern for his representations presents itself: myriad and complex interrogations of the relationships forged when sexual activity and the formation of identity are inscribed and circumscribed by paranoia and then legitimatized by the criminal justice system.

By describing specific sexual acts through the language of disgust, Williams at first glance might seem to be in assent with the dominant culture of the time, for his texts regularly describe such acts as if they are deserving of condemnation. Such descriptions, however, are matched or obscured by an overarching atmosphere of compassion, textual and theatrical, that stands in striking and powerful contrast to the language of condemnation. Although the society that Williams was born into was one that used scientific and legal definitions and theories to stipulate and legislate sexual norms and behavior, with the help of an inflexible rhetoric of (Christian) morality, his representations of such rigid piety were often mixed or countered with pity. That the plays and stories presented conflicting messages about such behavior is not surprising, for such "antihomosexual witch hunts" as Eskridge describes were one (albeit influential) part of the production of conflicting opinions about homosexuality and other sexual behavior that would, over time, lead to debates and changes in law and culture during the latter decades of the century. While it is not surprising that a creative writer would represent a range of cultural viewpoints, Williams's systematic depictions of diverse lifestyles and actions conveyed important information and perspectives on his own and others' sexual behavior, doing so with thoroughness and thoughtfulness that had the capacity to influence public opinion. His creative texts frequently call explicit attention to the crime and punishment involved in all such illegal sexual behavior, while his letters and notebooks reveal his recognition of his own illegal body. The documentation that he provided to his mainstream audiences about law and sexuality was itself a form of resistance against the silence and suppression of diverse sexualities that had long existed but were marginalized or invisible in American society.

As David A. J. Richards notes in the introduction to his study of *The Sodomy Cases*, the "development and elaboration of the constitutional right to privacy is one of the most controversial interpretive issues in constitutional law," and he goes on to demonstrate that in the twentieth century this right has been at the center of a number of significant legal debates surrounding sexual activity and private life.[38] Richards argues that the narrowing of what could count as obscene speech in *Roth v. United States* (1957) was significant in "its empowering of public arguments for gay rights," for films and literary works depicting homosexuality, even when such depictions were presented "covertly, tentatively, and sometimes quite unfairly," began to make their way into theatres and bookstores in the wake of such legal loosening of speech about activities that had been considered "unnatural and therefore obscene." He mentions *Streetcar* in the short list of creative texts he provides as examples, citing the play's influence on cultural mores and its part in the gradual shift of public opinion, about homosexuality specifically, but also of other diverse sexual behaviors as Blanche exhibits. Richards calls *Streetcar* a "great play by a famous playwright and gay man," which "touched sympathetically on gay issues and brilliantly showed, in Blanche DuBois, the plight of a highly sexual straight woman whose life challenged dominant stereotypes of women's sexuality in the same way the lives of gay men challenged stereotypes of male sexuality."[39] This brief description of *Streetcar* in Richards's study of American sodomy laws is notable for several reasons. It underscores the place of Williams's play as a frontrunner in explicit and sympathetic representational treatments of homosexuality, predating as it does the other literary works in Richards's list, and it was staged ten years before the *Roth* decision.[40] Furthermore, just prior to his statement about *Streetcar*, Richards rightly notes that gay characters depicted during this period often end up dead or raped, which is true of Blanche's husband and of Blanche, respectively, even though Richards does not call attention to that fact.

Instead, he only briefly recognizes Williams's inclusion of "gay issues" in *Streetcar* before going on to describe Blanche's sexuality more thoroughly. His brief treatment of the text mirrors Williams's focus, which was to include homosexuality obliquely if persistently before delving into a more detailed consideration of a heterosexual woman's legal and moral transgressions. Richards's recognition of and repetition of Williams's subject matter anticipates a key strain of my argument: that one of Williams's strategies was to include the topic of homosexuality in many of his dramatic texts, but to situate it at the edge of the action and then explore heterosexual transgressive relationships more thoroughly. The latter did not fail to shock or repel audience members and readers, and the texts made explicit that many practices or couplings he created would be considered immoral and illegal when committed by heterosexuals; however, they would have been considered by many to be abnormal rather than abhorrent, and thus more likely to evoke sympathetic responses. In *Streetcar*, such a distinction is developed within the text itself, for Blanche and Stella condemn Blanche's dead husband as disgusting and degenerate, but they both make excuses and expect understanding when it comes to Blanche's illegal activities.

Williams drafted *Streetcar* over multiple years, with evidence of the revisions it underwent appearing in several published versions of the play as well as in draft manuscripts and fragments. Multiple drafts demonstrate Williams's ongoing interest in representations of sexual illegalities, his determination to present them with narrative and thematic coherence, and his awareness that his creative texts had cultural and political impact on values that, as we shall see, had been codified by law. As is the case with many of his works, the textual development of *Streetcar* has been the subject of scholarly analysis.[41] In 1977 Vivienne Dickson's study of the development of the play led her to suggest that Williams began with a "basic situation in mind: an unmarried teacher visiting her younger sister and brother-in-law meets a prospective husband," the teacher and her family "conscious that she has one last chance of avoiding a lonely future as a single woman." During the composition process, Dickson continues, Williams "explored the possible complications, making false starts and rejecting many resolutions, but always returning to the original idea with something salvaged from the discarded material."[42] Dickson's description of the "original idea" is significant, for Williams did indeed remain faithful to the central dramatic situation. But as Dickson goes on to explain, the multiple drafts allow scholars to see that Williams, while working within that consistent framework, tests out a variety of meanings and experiments with a wide range of possible audience expectations and responses.

In her 1987 bibliographic essay, Deborah G. Burks charts the "creation and casting" of Blanche and Stanley by focusing her research on the character and relationship of the dual protagonists, and suggesting that Williams's differing draft treatments help him decide among three tones: ironic, tragic, and melodramatic. The ultimate choice, in Burks's estimation, was tragic. Burks cites letters that Williams wrote to his agent Audrey Wood as he revised *Streetcar*; she argues that the changes he makes to the play's tone coincided with his statements to Wood that Blanche must evoke audience sympathy, and Burks concludes that since "ironic endings detracted from his heroine, Williams turned away from such conclusions and instead developed the tragic possibilities of Blanche's situation."[43] Thematically, many fragments reveal revisions to legal language or situation, thereby demonstrating Williams's obsessive interest in the regulations and restrictions imposed by law on individual identity and action. The comparison of different versions point to details that, once introduced, may ultimately be discarded, but not before having some impact on the text as Williams moves it closer to completion. Such traces of meaning are submerged during revision but they are not entirely excised: they leave residuals of significance that remain even after specific details are omitted or altered.

The penultimate scene in *Streetcar* is one that Williams worked on extensively, and that in its final version contains an illegal act: Stanley's rape of sister-in-law Blanche, a relative rarity for Williams in that it takes place during the play rather than prior to its commencement. This particular criminal sex offense is also unusual in that it crosses the boundary line that Hannah set in *Iguana* and that mirrors Williams's own philosophy: "Nothing human disgusts me unless it's unkind, violent." Stanley's trespass, despite Blanche's warning that he "stay back" and not come closer to her or "some awful thing will happen," is a violation of her body that marks her for forced expulsion from the family setting and determines the play's conclusion.[44] Moreover, by confirming the vision that Blanche has of him as "downright—bestial," the act helps to solidify the sympathetic position for many audience members, shifting them once and for all away from Stanley and toward Blanche.[45] While the "desire" of the play's title is acknowledged as a driving force for all three residents of the Elysian Fields apartment, and it has driven Blanche to multiple illegal sexual acts, the play's concluding scenes confirm that it is only Stanley whose sexual transgressions are connected to violent force.

Draft versions of the rape scene document Williams's extensive revisions of the sexual encounter between Blanche and Stanley, charting Williams's exploration of several different sexual crimes he considered before settling on rape. In one version of the scene, Ralph (the name given here to the character who would eventually become "Stanley") speaks a version of a line that will remain, with the "a" revised to "this:" "We've had a date with each other from the beginning," but in the fragment Blanche responds by repeating yes four times, implying her consent; in the printed text she says nothing in response to Stanley, but falls to her knees, inert.[46] In several fragments that show Williams working through the possibilities that Ralph/Stanley and Blanche succumb to a mutual attraction, a morning-after scene is included that would have meant a very different kind of departure for Blanche, and a very different resolution for the play.

In what Burks calls a "representative example" of such a resolution, Ralph and Blanche have had consensual sex the previous evening; they agree that Blanche must depart prior to Stella's return from the hospital, with Blanche saying that she is not worried, for she has the bus ticket Ralph gave her for her birthday, which she says she will trade in "for one that will take me in some new direction. Where I can make a fresh start." This willful and mutually criminal act of adultery, each of them acknowledging the unsurpassed quality of the encounter, had occurred just after the call has come that Stella has delivered the baby, a daughter. As Burks notes, "Stella's victimization makes villains of the other two characters, especially Blanche, who is serenely cool at the prospect of moving on, now that she has slept with Ralph."[47] Although rarely prosecuted, adultery was a crime in most jurisdictions in the midcentury when Williams was writing *Streetcar*; the offense remains a criminal act in twenty-two states. Although Williams cut this scene in order to increase sympathy for Blanche, the revision he made had another effect: it significantly alters the criminal act and its implications for blame, shifting them to Stanley. Williams's many drafts of individual works feature similar revisions, as details from his characters' sexual histories and their sexual activities are altered for a variety of reasons and with a range of thematic and legal significance.

Changes in laws governing various kinds of sexual crimes bear on the connections Williams made between sex and psychiatric confinement, a link notable to Blanche's fate in *Streetcar*. In charting the development of attitudes about sex crimes during the period of Williams's writing, Estelle B. Freedman discusses the disintegrated "Victorian ideal of innate female purity," and suggests that the development of the image of the sexual psychopath, a distinctly modern diagnostic identity, is of a man "unbounded by the controls of female purity, a violent threat not only to women, but to children as well." Freedman describes the alleged "sex crime wave" of the 1930s as a panic that extended "beyond the media and into the realm of politics and law." Between 1935 and 1965, she explains, "city, state, and federal officials established commissions to investigate sexual crime" and "passed statutes to transfer authority over sex offenders from courts to psychiatrists." As a result, "in most states, a man accused of rape, child molestation, indecent exposure, or corrupting the morals of a minor—if diagnosed as a 'sexual psychopath'—could receive an indeterminate sentence to a psychiatric, rather than a penal, institution." However, as Freedman claims, the safety of women and children was not the underlying concern of the sex crime panics; rather, "the concept of the sexual psychopath provided a boundary within which Americans renegotiated the definitions of sexual normality."[48] It is the larger issue of normative behavior that would come to affect Williams personally and would also help to determine not only the representations of his own transgressive types but also involve him in a self-designed system of adjudication, seeking to determine what kinds of sexual activities need not be the target of social concern or restriction and indeed ought to be protected as part of a private system that insures individual freedom and a level of diversity in identity formation.

Williams's texts invite consideration and commentary about crimes that ought to be punished but whose perpetrators escape legal retribution, sometimes for ideological reasons; they regularly present situations in which the structures of power deal inconsistently with transgression, providing protection for certain types of sexual criminals while exposing other kinds to criminal action. Stanley rapes his sister-in-law; she has been fired from her teaching job for having sex with one of her teenage students. From the legal perspective of the time, then, both Blanche and Stanley might be considered, according to the law, "sexual psychopaths," whose "'utter lack of power to control'" one's sexual impulses rendered the psychopath "'likely to attack . . . the objects of his uncontrolled and uncontrollable desires.'"[49] Of the two, it is Blanche who is punished by being confined to a mental institution; she is not put away for her crime against the young boy but for daring to tell her sister what Stanley had done, for making public a most grave offense that threatens the marital relationship. Rape is an act that Freedman includes in her study of the "sex crime wave" of the period, but Stanley is neither arrested for the crime nor diagnosed as a sexual pervert, even though his sexual violence also transgresses the taboo of sex with a family member. He escapes legal censure because he represents the patriarchy, with its rights of dominance. As Susan Brownmiller noted in her landmark study of rape, it has been used "from prehistoric times to the present" as a "conscious process of intimidation by which all men keep all women in a state of fear."[50] Stella's confession to Eunice that "I couldn't believe her and go on living with Stanley" is not only a choice Stella makes of husband over sister that will keep the illegal act private: it suggests that Blanche is not the only woman kept in a state of "intimidation" by the act of rape, but that Stella, too, is reminded of her need to submit.

Williams's decision to end the play with Blanche's "imprisonment" rather than Stanley's may seem difficult to fathom in a twenty-first-century legal climate, where DNA evidence would have strengthened Blanche's accusation, and where forced commitments have become as rare as state mental institutions. But within the context of the play, the conclusion is foregone; we can see as much by considering what occurs in scene 3, not long after Blanche arrives. The connection between Stanley's sex drive and his violent criminal impulses is first made during what is called the poker night scene, when Stanley strikes Stella and neighbor Eunice warns him to leave his wife be or "you'll git th' law on you," a line that immediately precedes Stella's return to the apartment and Mitch's reassurance to Blanche that all is well: "There's nothing to be scared of. They're crazy about each other."[51] Stella denies the significance of the assault on her, for she tells Blanche the next morning that "it wasn't anything as serious as you seem to take it," and this exchange anticipates the former's refusal to accept the truth about the rape.[52] But there is a difference between Stella's unwillingness to believe Blanche's story (especially since Blanche herself admits regularly to her capacity to deny or embellish truth) and Stella's choice to participate in the suppression of evidence. The draft process demonstrates Williams's attention to what might have been Stella's criminal conspiracy. The multiple revisions of the final scene when Blanche is taken away by the doctor and nurse to be henceforth dependent on the "kindness of strangers" vary in their details concerning Stella's realization and subsequent denial of the crime, and this variance proves crucial to the play's conclusion.

In a typescript version that Williams submitted to director Elia Kazan just four months before the play's Broadway premiere, Stella and Eunice discuss what happened between Blanche and Stanley. Stella insists to Eunice that Blanche's story can't be true, for if it was, "I could never touch him again," this last part of her statement crossed out with a black crayon in the script. She goes on, "I wouldn't dare to believe her!—But look at this." The stage directions have her produce Stanley's pajama top, and they describe its condition and the evidence that she has seen on Stanley's body: "*his pajamas are torn to shreds and his shoulders and back are covered with scratches as if a wild-cat had clawed him.*" When Eunice asks, "What does he say? How does he explain it?," Stella responds: "All he says is, She's crazy. Of course she must be. [crossed out: That's why I signed the papers. I had to commit her to the asylum or believe her story and] I couldn't believe her story and go on living with Stanley."[53] Although Stella seems resigned to stay, this version concludes with visual and emotional division between the couple: Stanley rejoins the poker game, while "Stella has risen from the steps and now stands in front of the building which is dim white against the fading clouds." She draws the baby close to her and "bows her head until her face is hidden by the child's blanket."[54] However, Williams was compelled to change the ending with director Kazan's influence on character development, as the script became a performance piece. Additionally and importantly, the Broadway production was cast with Marlon Brando and Kim Hunter, whose chemistry was visible, while Brando's embodiment of Stanley was powerful but boyish. What remains of the exchange between Eunice and Stella is the latter's single line: "I couldn't believe her story and go on living with Stanley."[55] The omission of the material evidence acknowledged by the women and seen by audience members de-emphasizes Stella's complicity in a criminal cover-up, and some readers and viewers miss the implication of the line that remains to mark Stella's culpability and justify Blanche's removal from the home.

Although subtle, the line does implicate Stella, infusing with tragedy Blanche's departure and the family tableau that end the play with tragedy: Stella weeps with *"inhuman abandon"* while Stanley's *"fingers find the opening of her blouse."*[56] The play closes with guilt and with moral and legal ambiguity, an all too familiar example of truth repressed and a victim blamed. In production, Stanley did not reach inside Stella's blouse, a choice that makes the embrace one of comfort rather than of sexual desire. The revisions to the ending that became the published and produced texts of the play, however, emphasize what Brenda Murphy argues is "another strong element in Stanley's character as Kazan saw it, the desire to control, to have things his way." Rather than "sitting passively as Stella and Eunice dispose of Blanche, Stanley had an active role, indicating that the decision was a mutual one, and not Stella's alone. Stanley stood and faced Blanche as she started to come out through the curtains, holding out to the end in doing what he thought was his right, protecting his life, having things his way."[57] The play's conclusion dramatizes the tension that emerges when an individual's "right to be left alone" results in harming others, and it is that very tension that has driven debates about privacy and sexual freedom to the present day. The tentative and troubling resolution that brings down the curtain on *Streetcar* is just one of many examples of the ways that Williams incorporates complex legal situations in his texts in order to examine the political issues of his age.

During the century in which Tennessee Williams lived and worked, laws legislating gender identity and sexual behavior, particularly as they related to privacy and freedom, helped to ignite some of the most contested opinions in the modern age, and judicial decisions about the right of an individual to private consensual sexual activity of her/his choosing would be debated in several Supreme Court cases in the second half of the century. Williams's literary and theatrical projects, persistent in their interrogation of the individual's right to pursue sexual freedom and to do so without fear of punishment, legal or otherwise, provide a parallel and alternative narrative of the legal journey that led to *Lawrence v. Texas* (2003), whose majority opinion affirmed the right that all individuals have to privacy for the conduct of sexual activity. The specific question that the Court faced in *Lawrence* concerned the validity of the Homosexual Conduct law: a Texas statute that made it a crime for two persons of the same sex to engage in intimate sexual conduct. The syllabus for the case states that it "depends on whether petitioners were free as adults to engage in private conduct in the exercise of their liberty under the Due Process Clause."[58] By resolving to determine the case as an issue of due process, same-sex intimate conduct was thus contextualized by previous opinions, several of which addressed the privacy of sexual freedom explicitly.

In her review of *Flagrant Conduct*, a 2012 book on *Lawrence* by Dale Carpenter, Dahlia Lithwick describes the case as a "story of sexual privacy, personal dignity, intimate relationships, and shifting notions of family in America."[59] Although the right of sexual privacy was not confirmed for all persons until the beginning of the twenty-first century, the passages from *Iguana* and *Streetcar* analyzed above confirm that Williams had undertaken to interrogate the issue fifty years earlier, and had done so with a sophisticated knowledge of the complexity of the issues involved. Blanche's attempt to maintain her personal dignity in the face of a host of onslaughts is one of the play's central concerns; she acknowledges intimacy as something to be protected, assuming that "everyone has something he won't let others touch"; she celebrates the possibility of privacy as something to "weep with joy" over, a luxury that ought to be a right. Stanley, for his part, wants to assert his rights to enjoy marital privacy and intimacy in his own home, and in doing so he calls upon a notion of "family in America" popular at the time of the play's creation: the postwar nuclear model and one that several decisions prior to *Lawrence* would uphold even when the high court refused to grant the same protection to unmarried or same-sex couples. Given that legal challenges to sodomy laws first reached the Supreme Court with *Bowers*, just three years after Williams's death, and considering the frequency with which his work reflects an interest in issues directly related to the legal opinions, his creative canon can be examined for the ways it interrogated privacy, morality, and law in the period leading up to the Court's consideration of the issue. His texts contain various legal situations for audience consideration, and they provided the citizenry multiple opportunities for weighing in on these matters.

Lithwick's review of *Flagrant Conduct* notes that the decision rendered in *Lawrence,* delivered from the pen of Justice Anthony Kennedy for the majority opinion, was in part an argument for the importance of love's physical dimension. Lithwick quotes from the opinion and then provides commentary: "'When sexuality finds overt expression in intimate conduct with another person, the conduct can be but one element in a personal bond that is more enduring.' The opinion used the word 'relationship' eleven times."[60] The "physical dimension of love" is certainly one of the most extensively considered topics in the Williams canon, particularly as it is connected to other topics he explored regularly: the need to guard one's privacy, the complexities of intimacy, and the development or destruction of the self. His plays and stories regularly dramatize or narrate situations in which characters seek out but often fail to locate a safe place from which to fulfill pressing carnal desires; such desire and its consummation is essential for the pursuit of happiness, but we see that without the protection that privacy provides, many varieties of physical love prove dangerous or impossible. Lacking financial means or a permanent residence, many of his most sympathetic figures are prosecuted and persecuted, threatened with public exposure in the form of verbal censure or arrest, legal or extralegal punishment, and their actions are labeled disgusting, unnatural, and immoral. Thus condemned and ostracized, they are prevented from realizing their potential or exercising their freedom.

Bowers had upheld the long-standing opinion that fundamental rights to privacy ought not to apply to homosexual acts, even private, consensual ones; in that decision the Supreme Court had overturned the U.S. Court of Appeals decision to uphold the right of privacy for homosexual partners. According to the majority opinion in *Bowers*, the Appeal Court's case citation did not adequately support the "claimed constitutional right of homosexuals to engage in acts of sodomy," maintaining that no connection between "family, marriage, or procreation on the one hand and homosexual activity on the other has been demonstrated." The Court of Appeals had erred, in the high court's opinion, by seeking "to identify the nature of the rights qualifying for heightened judicial protection."[61] The lower court's appeal to fundamental liberties as "'implicit in the concept of ordered liberty,'" citing *Palko v. Connecticut* (1937), and *Moore v. East Cleveland*, as a right "'deeply rooted in this Nation's history and tradition,'" did not find support in the high court. The *Bowers* decision determined that neither formation, either of "ordered" liberty or of a "'deeply rooted'" liberty, extends "a fundamental right to homosexuals to engage in acts of consensual sodomy."[62]

The argument in the *Bowers* majority opinion for the lack of connection to "family, marriage, or procreation" is noteworthy, especially when considered within the context of earlier rulings on sexual privacy, such as the 1965 *Griswold* decision to protect marital privacy with regard to issues of birth control. Significantly, *Griswold* "gave privacy a constitutional guarantee," suggests Deborah Nelson in *Pursuing Privacy in Cold War America*, with the majority opinion crafting its warranty out of what Justice Douglas called the penumbra of specific amendments of the Bill of Rights. Furthermore, as Nelson explains, with *Griswold* the court made the home a zone of privacy and, "in so doing, the right to privacy became firmly associated, not with the wiretapping or surveillance cases that surround it, but with domesticity and family, with rights of child rearing, procreation, and sexual expression."[63] To some extent, then, the *Griswold* decision had delineated the right to privacy while perhaps covertly establishing grounds for the *Bowers* argument, specifically that "Georgia's sodomy law rationally reflected the 'presumed belief of a majority of the electorate in Georgia that homosexual sodomy is immoral and unacceptable.'"[64] If the sacrosanct nature of the home as a zone of privacy depends upon the presumption of a marital contract, it suggests that sexual activity that takes place without the legal protection of marriage may be subject to censure despite its execution within a private domestic space.

As we have already seen, issues of morality and acceptability are at the center of Williams's literary and dramatic investigations of human relationships, but the legal context helps to illustrate the extent to which his work challenged not just attitudes, but policies, particularly as the two converge. In support of the majority opinion in *Bowers*, Chief Justice Burger wrote separately but in concurrence with the majority in order to "underscore" the view that there is no fundamental right to commit homosexual sodomy. Burger argues that the "proscriptions against sodomy have very 'ancient roots'" and that the crime against nature was described by eighteenth-century British jurist Sir William Blackstone as an "offense of 'deeper malignity' than rape," calling this consensual same-sex activity a heinous act "'the very mention of which is a disgrace to human nature.'"[65] The dissenting judges argued that the case is not about a "fundamental right to engage in homosexual sodomy," but rather about "'the most comprehensive of rights and the right most valued by civilized men,' namely, 'the right to be let alone.'" The case thus implicates both the "decisional and the spatial aspects of the right to privacy"; that is, the right to privacy with reference to certain decisions that ought to be under an individual's purview, and the interest of privacy with regard to certain places and the activities that take place therein.[66] We see the tension about what was deemed immoral and illegal sexual activity during Williams's time in a new light, keeping in mind that such determinations were not limited to homosexuality but in many jurisdictions decided the morality and therefore legality of all sexual behavior, with the possible exception of consensual procreative sex within marriage. Thus contextualized by judicial arguments about rights and morality (particularly as they are concerned with producing individual and common good), representations and reactions to a variety of sexual behavior in Williams's personal and creative texts become a complex, ongoing adjudication of human lives as they exist, often of necessity, beyond the boundaries of the rule of law.

Furthermore, the four dissenting judges in *Bowers* relied heavily on the case's implications for the sanctity of personal relationships, using language that echoes several decades of popular and critical insight into Williams's imaginative work. The judges expressed their view, quoting from another recent case, *Roberts v. United States Jaycees* (1984), that privacy is the "'ability independently to define one's identity that is central to any concept of liberty,'" and that this privilege cannot be "exercised in a vacuum," for "we all depend on the 'emotional enrichment from close ties with others.'" That "individuals define themselves in a significant way through their intimate sexual relationships with others" suggests, they continue, "in a Nation as diverse as ours, that there may be many 'right' ways of conducting those relationships, and that much of the richness of a relationship will come from the freedom an individual has to *choose* the form and nature of these intensely personal bonds."[67] The "acceptance of the fact that different individuals will make different choices" is part of recognizing "the fundamental interest all individuals have in controlling the nature of their intimate associations with others." Such a "fundamental interest" in "controlling the nature" of intimate associations has been noted by literary critics as imperative for understanding Williams and his work: as C. W. E. Bigsby wrote, the same year that the *Roberts* case was decided, the playwright "was concerned with morality, though not with moralism," and the "only morality that he could sanction was that deriving from personal relationships."[68] That this need for Williams is often a desperate one makes it more visible and, therefore, more subject to judgment and less likely to be sustainable. As Blanche confesses to Mitch, after "the death of Allan—intimacies with strangers was all I seemed able to fill my empty heart with."[69] The statement is both confession and justification at once, and it echoes the section of Hart Crane's poem "The Broken Tower" that Williams used as the epigraph for the published text of *Streetcar*: "'And so it was I entered the broken world/To trace the visionary company of love, its voice/An instant in the wind (I know not whither hurled)/But not for long to hold each desperate choice.'"[70] The transitory nature of the connections made by Williams's characters render them socially unacceptable; the same is true for much sexual conduct prosecuted by law.

When *Lawrence* struck down the prohibition of homosexual sexual conduct conducted privately between consensual adults, it ended the "proscriptions against sodomy" which have had a long and expansive history in the American government's legislation of diverse sexuality. Imported by the colonies as a common law felony originally specific to anal intercourse between males, sodomy statutes were generalized and expanded in most state and local jurisdictions to include multiple offenses covering a range of what was considered deviant sexual behavior. Between the colonial period and the present, laws restricted many such acts performed in heterosexual couplings, even some committed consensually by wife and husband. As late as the 1950s, many states did not distinguish between consensual and nonconsensual acts, but the Council of the American Law Institute's Model Penal Code, developed over a decade from 1952 to 1962, reflected a shift toward codified freedom for consensual sexual partners. The recommendations that the council made begin with the group's confirmation of a "fundamental departure from prior law in excepting from criminal sanctions deviate sexual intercourse between consenting adults." The changes allowed that consensual partners, including unmarried and same-sex partners, should be free from the threat of criminal penalty for activities conducted in private among willing parties. In fact, the *Lawrence* decision quotes from the MPC, reminding the Court that the ALI went on record to decry "'criminal penalties for consensual sexual relations conducted in private,'" as a way, the Lawrence opinion argues, of maintaining that "liberty gives substantial protection to adult persons in deciding how to conduct their private lives in matters pertaining to sex" and that this "emerging recognition should have been apparent when *Bowers* was decided."[71]

Indeed, the decision in *Lawrence* makes plain that its predecessor had been decided on the basis of a belief system intertwined with historical precedent, but that it could no longer stand as either. In his dissenting opinion in *Bowers*, Justice Stevens had come to a similar conclusion. First, "the fact that the governing majority in a State has traditionally viewed a particular practice as immoral is not a sufficient reason for upholding a law prohibiting the practice." Second, "individual decisions by married persons, concerning the intimacies of their physical relationship, even when not intended to produce offspring, are a form of 'liberty' protected by the Due Process Clause" and "this protection extends to intimate choices by unmarried as well as married persons."[72] As the *Lawrence* decision concludes, "*Bowers* was not correct when it was decided, and it is not correct today. It ought not to remain binding precedent. *Bowers v. Hardwick* should be and now is overruled."[73]

In her analysis of *Bowers*, Anne B. Goldstein argues that five beliefs about homosexuality contribute to the decision and its dissent; beyond the list's usefulness as the social context of a legal decision, the list connects the case to Williams's representations of homosexuality and demonstrates that his work engaged in an ongoing cultural commentary about diverse sexual activity. Goldstein claims that her examination of the judges' commentary reveals evidence of the following perspectives on homosexuality: "that it is (1) immoral, (2) criminally harmful, (3) a manifestation of illness, (4) an identity, (5) a normal variation of human sexuality."[74] In many rich and individualized multiplicities, all these perspectives are narrated or dramatized in Williams's texts and, as they are in *Bowers*, presented in conflict with each other in debates about rights and morals. The range of sexual variance and the reactions to that range echo similar variance and attitudes in laws and judicial opinions; furthermore, Williams uses the language and tropes of law with precision and frequency, thus further aligning his work with the work of law, and indicating his persistent interest in the interrogation of policies that circumscribed such behavior in his lifetime.

Although sodomy laws criminalized many types of sexual acts, homosexual and heterosexual, the legislation against and the prosecution of homosexual acts were the most common, and in many cases laws that limited the criminal behavior to homosexual acts remained on the books after acts committed in heterosexual relationships had been revised or overturned. Williams's depictions of and his attitudes about homosexuality have been analyzed from a variety of perspectives for several decades, and the essays and books on the topic are one of several strains of scholarship that have contributed to the construction of an ever more nuanced portrait of the writer's work. Williams's own homosexual activity is an important consideration as well, for, as we shall see, copious evidence exists that demonstrates his keen awareness of the illegality of acts that he engaged in regularly. Williams's career-long documentation and interrogation of the connections between sexual transgression and disgust include his exploration of both natural and unnatural punishments for such transgression: his texts feature characters who have contracted tuberculosis or venereal disease, or who are threatened with castration or cannibalism, and these "punishments" are often suffered by those who have committed illegal sexual acts. Their fates are tied to their "unnatural" and "disgusting" behavior.

Literature, and art more generally, have been sites of emotion throughout their long histories, and Williams's work has a reputation of illustrating emotion writ large. His texts make plain, in language and in syntax (lots of exclamation points!), his concerns with the emotional lives of his characters and the impact that systems, formal or informal, that propose to operate on reason exert on those who prefer to embrace the cultural values associated with the arts to direct their course. By creating whole lives, albeit fictional ones, through which to witness the human cost of discrimination against and punishment for certain kinds of behaviors, Williams contributed to a more complex understanding and acceptance of the many manifestations of sexual identity in his life and in his work. As legal scholar Terry A. Maroney notes, the law has always taken account of emotion, to the extent that articulation of the connection seems "almost banal"; however, the relationship has been "a rocky one," in part because of an often assumed or imposed separation: "A core presumption underlying modern legality is that reason and emotion are different beasts entirely; they belong to separate spheres of human existence; the sphere of law admits only of reason; and vigilant policing is required to keep emotion from creeping in where it does not belong."

This theoretical model has persisted "despite its implausibility as a model of either how humans live or how our law is structured and administered."[75] It is only recently, Maroney continues, "that scholars have begun to speak deliberately about the role of emotion *per se* and to self-consciously reckon with the myriad ways in which the law reflects or furthers conceptions of how humans *are*, or *ought to be*, as emotional creatures."[76] By the mid-1990s, he reports, "the outlines of a distinct law-and-emotion jurisprudence were forming," and the development of this interplay led to new interpretations on multiple areas of legal theory and practice, including the function of victim impact statements, shaming punishments, emotion in the language of judging, the nature of disgust, and the role of sympathy in legal judgment.[77] Maroney notes a high-water mark of this development in the publication of a collection published in 1999 called *The Passions of Law*, which included essays from scholars in philosophy, political science, and critical legal studies and was organized around general topics that echo many of Williams's foremost representational concerns: disgust and shame; remorse and revenge; forgiveness.[78] A shortcoming of the collection, Maroney notes, was its failure to include perspectives from social and life sciences, despite the fact that the connection between emotion and cognition had been ongoing in other disciplines and empirical research on law and emotion had been following a similar trajectory of increased interest.[79]

As Nelson suggests, "No concept in the late twentieth century proved more generative or more volatile in more domains of social, political, and aesthetic life or for longer duration than 'privacy' . . . the terms 'public' and 'private' became essential, maybe even mandatory categories of evaluation." While some critics predict privacy's demise, others foresee privacy rights threatening safety in the public sphere; for Nelson, the two are "twin anxieties and ought to be considered adjacent rather than opposed."[80] Williams's work regularly does just that: represent the public and private as "twin anxieties" that are "adjacent rather than opposed." Furthermore, privacy issues, in Williams's time and in our own, have often been theorized and practiced in conjunction with judicial decisions about and legislations of sexuality. On a larger scale, particularly when it comes to the treatment of sexual activity and identity, legal perspectives on privacy have continued to proliferate throughout the twentieth century; such perspectives provide numerous avenues for a detailed examination of Williams's literary and theatrical texts. His construction of sexual diversity is a commonplace of the critical commentary that has established him as a major literary and theatrical figure, but there are myriad ways that the existing scholarship on Williams can be advanced with the addition of issues raised here. Bringing the law to bear on his work yields new insights on his texts and their enduring legacy in the cultural and political landscape of the twentieth century.

NOTES

1. Harold H. Hart, Letter to Tennessee Williams, 1 April 1970, Tennessee Williams Papers, Rare Book and Manuscript Library, Columbia University Library.

2. Quoted in Harold H. Hart, "Introduction," *Sexual Latitude: For and Against* (New York: Hart Publishing, 1971), 7.

3. Hart, Letter to Tennessee Williams.

4. Tennessee Williams, *The Theatre of Tennessee Williams, vol. IV* (New York: New Directions, 1972), 363–364. All subsequent references to *The Theatre of Tennessee Williams*, eight volumes, 1971–1992, will be identified by volume number and page number.

5. Hart, Letter to Tennessee Williams.

6. Williams, *The Theatre of Tennessee Williams, vol. IV*, 361.

7. Eskridge, *Dishonorable Passions*, 3, 17, 18.

8. Eskridge, *Dishonorable Passions*, 3.

9. Martha C. Nussbaum, *From Disgust to Humanity: Sexual Orientation and Constitutional Law* (Oxford: Oxford University Press, 2010), 32.

10. Nussbaum, *From Disgust to Humanity*, 20.

11. Nussbaum, *From Disgust to Humanity*, 38.

12. Nussbaum, *From Disgust to Humanity*, 40.

13. Nussbaum, *From Disgust to Humanity*, 50.

14. Williams, *The Theatre of Tennessee Williams*, vol. I, 282–283.

15. Williams, *The Theatre of Tennessee Williams*, vol. I, 393, 396.

16. William Kleb, "Marginalia: *Streetcar*, Williams, and Foucault," *Confronting Tennessee Williams's* A Streetcar Named Desire: *Essays in Critical Pluralism*, ed. Philip C. Kolin (Westport, CT: Greenwood Press, 1993), 30.

17. John S. Bak, "Tennessee v. John T. Scopes: 'Blanche' Jennings Bryan and Antievolution," *Tennessee Williams Annual Review* 8 (2006), 73–94, 88.

18. The First, Third, Fourth, Fifth, and Ninth Amendments of the Bill of Rights address the necessity of safeguarding the autonomy of person and the protection of the individual's possessions and domicile, and these amendments are the basis for developing the legal parameters for privacy. The First Amendment protects the privacy of beliefs, the Third protects the individual's home against unlawful occupation by soldiers, the Fourth prevents unreasonable searches that violate the right of the people to be secure in their persons, houses, and possessions, and the Fifth establishes protection against self-incrimination, thus protecting certain kinds of personal information. In addition, the Ninth Amendment, which states that the "enumeration of certain rights" in the Bill of Rights "shall not be construed to deny or disparage other rights retained by the people," has been interpreted as justification for broadly reading the Bill of Rights and the value of privacy in ways not specifically provided in the first eight amendments. "Bill of Rights," *The Charters of Freedom*, http://www.archives.gov/exhibits/charters/bill_of_rights.html. Accessed 13 November 2012.

19. Steven Alan Childress, "Foreword," in Samuel D. Warren and Louis D. Brandeis, *The Right to Privacy* (New Orleans: Quid Pro Law Books, 2010), Kindle edition.

20. Samuel D. Warren and Louis D. Brandeis, *The Right to Privacy* (New Orleans: Quid Pro Law Books, 2010), Kindle edition.

21. *Olmstead v. United States* 277 U.S. 438 (1928), http://supreme.justia.com/cases/federal/us/277/438/case.html#478. Accessed 3 May 2013.

22. "The Universal Declaration of Human Rights," *United Nations Website*, accessed 3 May 2013, http://www.un.org/en/documents/udhr/.

23. Williams, *The Theatre of Tennessee Williams*, vol. I, 401.

24. Solove, *Understanding Privacy*, 78–80.

25. Solove, *Understanding Privacy*, 79–80.

26. Edward J. Bloustein, "Privacy as an Aspect of Human Dignity," 39. *New York University Law Review* 971 (1964).

27. Tennessee Williams, *Stairs to the Roof* (New York: New Directions, 2000), v.

28. Williams, *The Theatre of Tennessee Williams*, vol. I, 254, 257.

29. Childress, "Foreword."

30. Williams, *The Theatre of Tennessee Williams*, vol. I, 373.

31. Williams, *The Theatre of Tennessee Williams*, vol. I, 364.

32. Williams, *The Theatre of Tennessee Williams*, vol. I, 355.

33. Williams, *The Theatre of Tennessee Williams*, vol. I, 356.

34. Williams, *The Theatre of Tennessee Williams*, vol. I, 351.

35. I use the terms "transgress," "transgressor," and "transgressive" in their various definitions. To transgress is literally to go beyond a limit or boundary—to exceed or overstep. That literal connotation is then often applied to both legal and moral acts that cross the boundaries of propriety or sin, or both. Thus the transgressors in Williams's texts are the ones who commit acts that were illegal in many jurisdictions at the time that Williams wrote. Because of the nature of the crimes that are being focused on here, and because of Williams's Christian upbringing, both connotations of

the definition are applicable. The transgressors in Williams's texts are both male and female, married and single, gay and straight. They may be new to transgression or they may have been shaped by it, but in both cases the transgression haunts them and is often the subject of narratives about the past that are repeated or alluded to throughout the work.

36. Williams, *The Theatre of Tennessee Williams, vol. I,* 355.
37. Eskridge, *Dishonorable Passions,* 75.
38. Richards, *The Sodomy Cases,* 1.
39. Richards, *The Sodomy Cases,* 18–19.
40. The staged version of *Streetcar* makes it clear to audiences that Blanche's husband was homosexual, for as she tells Mitch: "I found out. In the worst of all possible ways. By coming suddenly into a room that I thought was empty—which wasn't empty, but had two people in it . . . the boy I had married and an older man who had been his friend for years" (Williams, *The Theatre of Tennessee Williams, vol. I,* 355). However, the film version released in 1951 does not contain this section of the text, which is replaced by Blanche's description of her dead husband as "weak."
41. See the entry *"A Streetcar Named Desire"* in Philip C. Kolin, ed., *Tennessee Williams: A Guide to Research and Performance* (Westport, CT: Greenwood Press, 1988), 51–79. Also, see Vivienne Dickson, *"A Streetcar Named Desire*: Its Development through the Manuscripts," *Tennessee Williams: A Tribute,* ed. Jac Tharpe (Jackson: University of Mississippi, 1977), 154–171; Deborah G. Burks, "'Treatment Is Everything': The Creation and Casting of Blanche and Stanley in Tennessee Williams' 'Streetcar,'" *Library Chronicle of the University of Texas at Austin* 41 (1987): 16–39.
42. Dickson, *"A Streetcar Named Desire*: Its Development though the Manuscripts," 154–155.
43. Burks, "Treatment Is Everything," 23.
44. Williams, *The Theatre of Tennessee Williams, vol. I,* 401.
45. Williams, *The Theatre of Tennessee Williams, vol. I,* 322.
46. Tennessee Williams, "A Streetcar Named Desire," draft fragments, n.d. Harry Ransom Humanities Research Center, University of Texas at Austin.
47. Burks, "Treatment Is Everything," 23.
48. Estelle B. Freedman, "'Uncontrolled Desires': The Response to the Sexual Psychopath, 1920–1960," *Journal of American History* 74 (June 1987): 86–87.
49. Freedman, "Uncontrolled Desires," 83–84. Freedman cites legal codes here that used such terminology, and notes that almost every state included the phrase "utter lack of power to control his sexual impulses" (84n2).
50. Susan Brownmiller, *Against Our Will: Men, Women, and Rape* (New York: Simon and Schuster, 1975), 15.
51. Williams, *The Theatre of Tennessee Williams, vol, I,* 306–308.
52. Williams, *The Theatre of Tennessee Williams, vol. I,* 312.
53. Quoted in Burks, "Treatment Is Everything," 37.
54. Quoted in Burks, "Treatment Is Everything," 38.
55. Williams, *The Theatre of Tennessee Williams, vol. I,* 405.
56. Williams, *The Theatre of Tennessee Williams, vol. I,* 419.
57. Brenda Murphy, *Tennessee Williams and Elia Kazan* (Cambridge: Cambridge University Press, 1992), 57.
58. *Lawrence v. Texas,* 539 U.S. 558 (2003).
59. Dahlia Lithwick, "Extreme Makeover," Books, *New Yorker,* 12 March 2012: 76.
60. Lithwick, "Extreme Makeover," 76.
61. . *Bowers v. Hardwick,* 478 U.S.176 (1986).
62. *Bowers v. Hardwick,* 478 U.S.176 (1986).
63. Deborah Nelson, *Pursuing Privacy in Cold War America* (New York: Columbia University Press, 2002), 2.
64. Quoted in William N. Eskridge, Jr., *Gaylaw: Challenging the Apartheid of the Closet* (Cambridge, MA: Harvard University Press, 1999), 149.
65. *Bowers v. Hardwick,* 478 U.S. 176 (1986) (concurring opinion).

Privacy and Identity 55

66. *Bowers v. Hardwick*, 478 U.S. 176 (1986) (dissenting opinion).
67. *Bowers v. Hardwick*, 478 U.S. 176 (1986) (dissenting opinion).
68. C. W. E. Bigsby, *A Critical Introduction to Twentieth-Century American Drama*, Vol. 2 (Cambridge: Cambridge University Press, 1984), 128–129.
69. Williams, *The Theatre of Tennessee Williams, vol. I*, 386.
70. Williams, *The Theatre of Tennessee Williams, vol. I*, 239.
71. *Lawrence v. Texas* 539 U.S. 558 (2003) (opinion).
72. 478 U.S. 176 (1986) (dissenting opinion).
73. *Lawrence v. Texas* 539 U.S. 558 (2003) (opinion)
74. Ann B. Goldstein, "History, Homosexuality, and Political Values: Searching for the Hidden Determinants of *Bowers v. Hardwick*," in *Homosexuality and the Constitution, Volume 1: Homosexual Conduct and State Regulation*, ed. and with introduction by Arthur S. Leonard (New York: Garland, 1997), 50.
75. Terry A. Maroney, "A Proposed Taxonomy of an Emerging Field," *Law and Human Behavior* 30 (2006): 119–142, 121.
76. Maroney, "A Proposed Taxonomy," 121.
77. Maroney, "A Proposed Taxonomy," 122.
78. Susan A. Bandes, ed. *The Passions of Law* (New York: New York University Press, 1999).
79. Maroney, "A Proposed Taxonomy," 122.
80. Nelson, *Pursuing Privacy*, 1.

TWO
The Power of Disgust

Tennessee Williams's short story "The Vengeance of Nitocris" was published in pulp magazine *Weird Tales* in 1928, when he was just seventeen. He continued to write short fiction until the end of his life, and by the 1980s, when his *Collected Stories* appeared, his prose works had begun to garner critical attention beyond their significance as source material for his stage plays and screenplays. Friend and peer Gore Vidal wrote in his introduction to the volume: "These stories are the true memoir of Tennessee Williams. Whatever happened to him, real or imagined, is here. Except for an occasional excursion into fantasy, he sticks close to life as he experienced or imagined it."[1] Central to "life as he experienced it" was his identity as a homosexual in an era defined by its social and sexual conformity; Vidal's comment that Williams's stories stick "close to life as he experienced or imagined it" suggests that the stories are likely to treat homosexuality or depict homosexual lives during the period in which he wrote, and indeed some of them do.

The fact that Williams began his career with stories, with a private form of writing, is in keeping with the ways that he shielded himself personally as he began to formulate his identity; such an approach was not necessarily consistent, for it is possible to see in some of the early stories the kinds of successful or less than successful negotiations that his personal papers have revealed above. His apprentice work, including the voluminous letters and notebooks from the early years, might be seen as part of his identity-building. As he tried on personal personas in the documents he sent to family and friends, he also tried on a type of writer's identity and a writer's relationship with sexuality and sexual behavior that of necessity, for a homosexual coming of age in the period, was conducted privately, tentatively, experimentally, and with the law very much in mind because it had to be. It could not be done without careful negotiation.

As gender studies critics David Savran, John Clum, and others rightly note, Williams's stories represented homosexuality more openly and sometimes even more positively than did his plays of the 1940s and '50s; several of the prose pieces, Savran argues, are "avowedly and almost jubilantly gay." In contrast, Savran continues, the "pre-Stonewall plays and films, written for a much larger and more popular audience, are more cautious and, to use Williams's word, 'oblique.'"[2] In 1989, John Clum noted that Williams's presentation of homosexual persons in his theatrical and cinematic texts remained oblique until "public tolerance allowed a candidness in drama which Williams had previously restricted to his stories and poems."[3] Claude J. Summers, in his book *Gay Fictions*, asserts that Williams "fills his fiction with grotesque characters and situations, and homosexuality in his work also often reeks of decadence." But, he continues, Williams's gay fictions "are never designed merely to shock," for they "present homosexuality straightforwardly and unapologetically," and they are "actually strong and healthy contributions to the literature of compassion."[4] Such recent re-assessment of Williams's prose work has helped to expand a critical reputation that had been bound for decades to what was considered to be his apolitical Southern sensibility and a conception of him as a poet of the stage. When Williams's public homosexual identity and his frank depictions of homosexual lives have been considered from political perspectives, they have not also been considered legally—that is, within the context of midcentury laws that criminalized sodomy and other nonprocreative sex acts. This apparent critical blind spot has persisted, despite the fact that his creative texts frequently called explicit attention to the illegality of such behavior in others, and his letters and notebooks, as we have seen, revealed his recognition of his own illegal body.

Summers argues that Williams's "gay fictions" of the 1940s and the 1950s are "never designed merely to shock, even when they contain undeniably sensationalistic incidents." They focus on "individuals who have been bloodied by life, but who are still actively contending as they struggle against loneliness and isolation. Often heroic in their persistence and commitment, they arouse pathos and compassion." Summers adopts the common perspective on Williams's work with this statement, with its focus on "individuals" and their struggles, on characters that nonetheless persist in a quest for happiness, and the combination of struggle and persistence that elicits compassion in readers. His study of selected gay fiction takes as its overall purpose an exploration of "attitudes expressed through literature that culminated finally in a mass movement for reform," the fictional representations he analyzes contributing to the "change from conceiving homosexuality as a personal failing or social problem to a question of identity and the change from viewing sexual identity as an indispensable element in the wholeness of personality and the acceptance of erotic interest as a distinguishing individual and social characteristic."[5] Although Summers does not propose that Williams was more interested in "social context or explicitly political issues in than particular dilemmas," he acknowledges that the work "documents the cruelty and oppression suffered by gay people in mid-century America." Exploring the possibility of accepting the human in all its variety, and regularly espousing a philosophy that condemns only willful cruelty and mendacity, Williams "wrote about homosexuality with a naturalness that was highly unusual in the 1940s and 1950s."[6]

Williams's first story collection, *One Arm and Other Stories,* was published in a limited edition in 1948, the same year Kinsey's *Sexual Behavior in the Human Male* reported that 40 percent of the men interviewed had engaged in homosexual activity. Richards notes the mixed reaction to the Kinsey report, which "surprised and shocked Americans" but "prepared the way for a freer discussion of sexual matters."[7] Cultural dialogue about sexual diversity had pros and cons, for as Corber notes about the Kinsey report, one of the ways the Cold War "discourses of national security tried to contain the impact of these findings was by using them to justify the construction of homosexuality as a security risk," for if gay men did not differ significantly from straight men, "then they could infiltrate the nation's cultural and political institutions and subvert them from within."[8] He further argues that in "promoting fears about the potential illegibility of the gay male body, the discourses of national security sought to contain the increasing visibility of gay men."[9] Williams's first prose collection, with its titular story's interrogation of same sex desire and prostitution, made visible to an American readership that he was not afraid of depicting transgressive behavior, and that he was willing to risk doing so at a time when cultural constructions of homosexuality were being debated, openly and covertly. His treatments of the topic, and public reactions to them, are equally ambiguous.

Most early critical assessments of Williams's stories discussed them primarily as source material for the plays, and many of the short prose texts, in fragments or complete and published, certainly served that purpose. The early and persistent emphasis on his career in playwriting deflected attention away from his prose: as Dennis Vannatta, editor of the first book-length study of the short fiction reported in 1988, scholarly pieces on Williams's plays outpaced that on his short fiction by roughly fifty to one. Such neglect is sufficient justification for Vannatta's book, but he cites at least one other: the charge made in the 1960s and '70s that Williams failed to deal "honestly and directly" with the issue of homosexuality in his plays. Vannatta argues that as early as 1941, Williams was writing "sensitive and interesting short fiction in which homosexuality is an issue; and the subject becomes more frequently and directly treated throughout the remainder of his short-fiction career. If we wish, then, to see how a great writer dealt artistically with this very personal, often painful, part of his life, we must turn to his short fiction."[10] Echoing the connection Vidal makes between the personal and the literary in Williams's prose, Vannatta's argument indicates the potential usefulness of linking fiction and biography, but the book also adds social and political context that expands Williams's critical reputation and demonstrates the significance of the short fiction.

While scholarly attention may have come belatedly to his fiction due to the (rightful) lionization of Williams as playwright, popular consumption of his prose texts proceeded regularly throughout his long career. His stories appeared in multiple *Best American Short Stories* annual collections, often after they had been published in the *New Yorker*, *Esquire*, *Vogue*, *Playboy*, *Story*, as well as in several volumes published prior to the *Collected Stories* edited by Vidal. Near the end of his study, Vannatta's attempt to assess Williams's legacy to the genre includes mention of the Southern locale and grotesque, his work's relationship to that of William Faulkner and Flannery O'Connor, and also his place among other American modernists. Additionally, Vannatta discusses the resurgence in popularity of the short form in the 1970s. He proposes that "transitional Southern homosexual" might be "what we are left with" when attempting to place Williams within the short story tradition.[11] Although he acknowledges both the truth and the limitations of such "pigeonholes," it is the truth we might glean from such categorizations that has been a central focus in much of the critical conversation to date.

In a 1955 review of the reissue of *One Arm and Other Stories*, *New York Times* critic James Kelly wondered if these short pieces were but "quick notes about the defeated, the directionless, mutilated, bereft, diseased people living in cribs and boarding houses," recorded in brief for later appearances in "mature work." This assessment suggests the stories are apprentice work that serve as thematic place-holders for future use; although many of the scenarios were subsequently reworked for "later appearances," Kelly's summary suggests the kind of dismissal that Vannatta's study challenges. But the review does recognize in Williams's first volume of stories a trio of elements that reflect and connect to what Kelly identifies as the title story's single theme of desire, here quoting Williams, as "'something that is made to occupy a larger space than that which is afforded by the individual being.'" The reviewer then asserted that, for the author, "imagination, violence and surrender of self to others are simply the means for overcoming the guilt of incompletion."[12] This last remark suggests that there is more to the stories than Kelly himself has given them credit for, but more importantly, it points out an issue that relates to privacy and law: the implications of the "surrender of self to others."

Insights in a 1964 essay by William H. Peden first published by *Studies in Short Fiction* and reprinted by Vannatta provide additional direction for this examination of key stories and their manner of depicting illegal sexuality: the best stories from Williams's first two collections are "those concerned with basically non-exceptional characters" depicted with "understanding, sympathy and compassion."[13] Peden focuses on a subset of stories that "center around characters who are pathological or societal outcasts and rejects" and who represent Williams's "almost obsessive preoccupation with homosexuality, decay, and degradation." Peden calls "One Arm" the best of these stories, but his analysis is most notable for its word choices, which echo the legal language of disgust used to define and condemn homosexuality: "degeneration," "deterioration," "deviates," "hereditary taints." They are also words used by Williams in the works themselves in order to describe his characters, and it is significant to note that such language can be adapted from legal to literary to critical usage, and done so ubiquitously. The power of such language, particularly as it was applied to the shaping of public attitudes about sexuality in the postwar period, indicates Williams's place, front and center, in debates about social and political difference, as the midcentury's cultural and judicial containment transitioned into the contemporary shift toward equality and tolerance.

In *Tennessee Williams: A Tribute* (1977), Edward A. Sklepowitch focuses his attention on the "image of the homosexual" in Williams's fiction, proposing that the author's homosexuality ought to be considered as central to the literary achievement of his prose. For, as he suggests, the biographical information provides the critic "with an important way of understanding and perhaps of evaluating that vision so frequently labeled grotesque, decadent, and neurotic," particularly because Williams's vision "is at many points related to homosexuality."[14] In 1998, in a survey of the criticism to date, Jürgen C. Wolter summarized notable and recent critical perspectives for their arguments that "Williams used the 'privacy' of the genre of fiction for a more straightforward elaboration of his major theme, the destructiveness of desire, than he could ever achieve or dare on the stage."[15] Despite the fact that Williams described a wide variety of experiences in his prose texts, the perception of secrecy about certain matters, a key component of one of the most common understandings of privacy, may remain intact when images are made with words rather than with theatrical tableaux.[16] With his focus on the "generic" differences between story and play, Wolter argues that the form of the prose text allows Williams to "take the risk of being less oblique" in the fiction "about personal matters." The parallels between this literary assessment and Solove's discussion of how legal privacy is conceived are considerable, for beyond the secrecy of certain matters, and control over such matter, Solove notes that privacy can be constituted as "limited access to the self," the protection of personhood, and as the right to be let alone.[17] Williams's depictions of diverse sexuality address all of these privacy matters within the stories themselves, but the acknowledgment that

Williams's fiction was regularly self-revelatory underscores the extent to which his work represents the negotiation with his own self and with privacy and revelation in his own life.

Wolter identifies one of the major problems that have confronted the critics in their assessment of the quality and significance of the short fiction: that they "have to accept homosexuality as a serious and genuine expression of humanity"; if he is correct, then Williams's work in this area is a strategy of self-realization and self-exposure.[18] In his 2012 book, Michael S. D. Hooper claims that Williams used the short story form in the early 1940s to capture the details of his life at the time, for writing prose "may have offered greater freedom at a time when the freshness of Williams's experiences of the gay underworld would have made them compelling material upon which to draw."[19] Two kinds of exploration, Hooper seems to suggest, are occurring simultaneously: one at the level of experience, as Williams moves back and forth between the world and the "gay underworld," and one at the level of expression, as he attempts to convey his discoveries in suitable forms. Savran and other critics have explained Williams's representations of homosexuality by identifying a tension of opposites that defined the writer's attitudes toward, and attempts at, resolution. John Clum argues that "the constant in Williams's career is the dual vision that shaped his presentation of the homosexuality he was always impelled to write about" and notes Williams's own "sense of a split personality which separated the homosexual artist from his work," citing the latter's often-quoted interview statement: "'I never found it necessary to deal with it [homosexuality] in my work. It was never a preoccupation of mine, except in my intimate, private life.'"[20] Williams's assertion suggests that he conceived of the split between public work and personal life as a rather clear and uncomplicated one, but Clum takes issue with the simplicity and the accuracy of Williams's assessment.

At a semantic level, Clum suggests, Williams may not have found it "necessary" to deal with homosexuality in his work, but he does so regularly. Moreover, Clum argues that the "theoretical separation of his homosexuality" is in conflict "with his many assertions of the highly personal nature of his work and of the close relationships with his characters." The essay goes on to focus on the frequency with which Williams references split personality and split vision in his work and in his personal documents, noting its connections to the "problematics of Williams's stance as homosexual artist and of the gulf between private art (poetry and fiction) and public art (drama), and the corollary gap between private homosexual and public celebrity."[21] Elsewhere, Clum argues that Williams "paradoxically managed in his most successful work to make homosexuality an insistent presence while keeping it an absence."[22] The tensions of private and public, visible and absent, that have been pointed to in Williams's life and work direct this consideration of the personal and the professional, the biographical and the literary, as they have intersected with the legal environment in which they were created.

The conflicts between secrecy and fame, between the protection of limited access to the self and the desire for public recognition were personal, occupational, and political challenges that Williams faced throughout his adult life, and some of the earliest manifestations of these tensions are visible in his short fiction. Savran, for example, argues that the opposition in Williams's work comes about as the need for obscurity in conflict with a compulsion for revelation, and he compares Williams's style "to that of his ideological and spiritual forebear, Hart Crane." Borrowing a term from a study of Crane called *Hart Crane and the Homosexual Text* by Thomas E. Yingling, Savran explains Williams's transmutation of his own sexual orientation: Williams wrote "'under a number of screens and covers' that would allow him to represent his homosexuality in other guises: as a valorization of eroticism generally and extramarital desire, in particular; as an endorsement of transgressive liaisons that cut across lines of social class, ethnicity, and race, and violate mid-century social prescriptions; and as a deep sympathy for the outsider and the disenfranchised, for the 'fugitive kind.'"[23] Although both Clum and Savran are attuned to the tensions between private and public, between cover and exposure, and they acknowledge Williams's split vision and dual purpose, they fail to connect these strategies to the legal aspects of privacy and their implications for the self, generally, and the homosexual or sexually transgressive self, in particular. They emphasize what they seem to consider involuntary compulsion on Williams's part, the tension emerging from an internalized sense of self, although they recognize that social norms shaped the author's perceptions. But there is another level of constraint to consider, one that is not just socially imposed, but legally imposed. For when the life and work are contextualized by a long-developed set of narratives of law, the paradox is more striking and, arguably, more necessary. The time and place that produced the work create a particular postwar climate, and the man and his individual creative nature were shaped by it.

Historians and literary critics agree that during the pre- and postwar years of modernity, sexual representations in a book were considered less dangerous (for writer and audience) than such scenarios would have been on the stage or on the movie screen. The privacy of fiction is conceived of through the image of the closed book: what can be presented through words on pages allowed greater social latitude than what was performed on a stage, where real bodies and other realistic elements existed in three dimensions. As Nicholas de Jongh suggests, the "theatre is public, open and corporate, where the novel is private, closed and personal." However, all writers working with illicit subject matter, no matter the genre, had to consider the consequences to their reputations while attempting to reconcile their own lives or their own conceptions of homosexuality with acceptance and success. As de Jongh argues, the "dramatists of the inter-war years, who managed to secure productions for plays contending with homosexual desire, adapted some of the strategies of subterfuge already employed by novelists brooding upon similar themes."[24] Moreover, there were legal considerations for homosexual writers that no doubt inhibited free expression, whether on stage or in print.

In 1989 John Clum suggests that Sklepowitch was the "first critic to deal intelligently with this aspect of Williams's work," this "aspect" being the treatment of homosexuality.[25] Assuming Clum is correct, there was a three-decade lag between the publication of Williams's first collection of stories and the first thoughtful scholarly consideration of this important theme in Williams's work. While Clum asserts that homosexuality was a topic that Williams could not treat satisfactorily, attacked as he was "from all sides for his treatment or nontreatment" of the issue, he does not agree, however, with Sklepowitch's argument that Williams developed his homosexual characters in a progression from mystical to realistic.[26] Rather, Clum argues, Williams displayed a consistent attitude toward homosexual acts—that the playwright chose to be "privately open about his sexual orientation, but publicly cautious, in the employment of what Williams himself calls 'obscurity or indirection' to "soften and blur the homosexual element," and he expressed "a complex acceptance of homophobic discourse, which he both critiques and embraces."[27] Although Clum acknowledges the relative candidness of the prose, his study of the fiction suggests a split vision of privacy and publicity in Williams's short prose texts, which might be one more way to think of them as apprentice work—not in the typical sense of unpolished or immature, but as a means for constructing the author's platform from which to explore strategies of both exposure and indirection.

Calling "Hard Candy," a story published in 1954, "characteristic of Williams's fiction in dealing with homosexuality and its evasions," Clum asserts its embodiment of "Williams's split vision and attendant manipulation of language."[28] Like most other critics who have analyzed "Hard Candy," Clum notes a key passage in which the narrator warns the reader that in "the course of this story, and very soon now, it will be necessary to make some disclosures about Mr. Krupper of a nature too coarse to be dealt with directly in a work of such brevity." Clum quotes Williams's explicit self-direction woven into the text: in order to explain what befalls the main character on the day of his death, the narrator must seek to convey the indelicacy by utilizing in fiction "'the same, or even approximate, softening effect that existence in time gives to those gross elements in the life itself.'" If Mr. Krupper's sexual encounters are described as "'*mystery*,'" the narrator claims the possibility of discussing such matters "*without a head-on violence that would disgust and destroy and which would only falsify the story*" [emphasis Clum's].[29] Such narrative equivocation allows Williams to exhibit sympathy and understanding toward his readers' sensibilities, according to Clum, and in doing so the writer develops the narrator's position as someone who will reveal the "'place where the mysteries of his nature are to be made unpleasantly manifest to us.'" The narrator's delicacy of treatment may originate in the author's conscious manipulation of his readers, but its end result is to convey the complexities of public perception about what details can be shared and what must be obscured.

The "dual vision" works variously, with Clum's attention to it as "the split between the physical grotesqueness and disease of the subject" and the "shadowy beauty of the object of that desire" (the handsome young vagrant) relevant to my examination of Williams's prose fiction.[30] The tension between what we are drawn to and what repels us emerges as something quite common to the human experience as represented by Williams, and it is central to his depictions of sexuality. Ren Draya argues that "lack of purpose in life is the sad corollary to lack of identity. Williams knows that we all seek 'someone or something'; ultimately, we seek love—it is the something that gives life purpose." More exactly, "he is concerned with the need for love and with the various relationships possible between love and sex."[31] This need for love does, however, expose the individual to harm, be it emotional, physical, or, in the case of homosexuality, social and legal, and so a search for purpose is both the draw to fulfillment and the fear that such fulfillment will be the source of condemnation or destruction. Legal scholars have defined privacy as a form of intimacy, and as Solove claims, this theory "appropriately recognizes that privacy is essential not just for individual self-creation, but also for human relationships."[32] In Williams's many explorations of intimacy, then, we can identify a network of concerns that include the connections from sexuality to privacy to law.

The relationship between "disease/ugliness and homosexual desire" is a significant part of the dual vision Clum defines, as is the text's "intense consciousness of the split between the public persona and the private actor central to Williams's treatment of homosexuality."[33] Considered together, the two are pertinent to this analysis of selected short fiction: the disjunction between the disease of the subject and the shadowy beauty of the object creates a space for sympathy, sometimes conflicted, but nonetheless effective and affective. One strain of sympathy emerges from the readers who identify with the diseased subject, the he or she who becomes unclean in desiring the beautiful love object, assuming that such desire is culturally forbidden. The desired object is likewise tainted, exposed to risk as the gaze descends and implicates it because of its own attractiveness. Both the subject and object face the split between public and private, and Clum anoints only the "gay reader" with immediate recognition of the significance attached to Mr. Krupper, found dead and on his knees in the balcony of the theatre with sticky candy wrappers littered on the floor around him.

In his explication of "Hard Candy," Corber argues that the narrator's circumspection about the purpose and details of Mr. Krupper's visits to the balcony of the Joy Rio movie theatre is an attempt to avoid having the reader "come to the reductive conclusion that Mr. Krupper is a dirty old man who preys on innocent young boys, even though there is ample reason for the reader to do so."[34] Indeed, the language of the story provides the ample reason, as we shall see. Unlike critics who assessed this avoidance as evidence of Williams's homophobia or self-hatred, however, Corber's argument is a significant variation of Clum's: that the semiotic challenges the story offers, the extent to which the reader must look for signs of meaning, compel that reader to master the "gay male reading practices" and require "her/him to occupy a gay male subject-position."[35] Furthermore, he says, Williams's equivocations about Krupper's homosexuality "have the paradoxical effect of rendering it visible." As "the mystery of Mr. Krupper's identity continues to elude us, forcing us to acknowledge that we can never fully know him," his homosexuality becomes a sign "not of his corruption but of his subject-hood, thereby discouraging us from positioning him as sexually other."[36] Corber's argument underscores the complexity of Williams's representation, for although the nature of Krupper's desire might be partially obscured, the obscurity is called attention to in the narration and is therefore, ultimately, revealed.

Although Corber allows for what he calls the "political limitations" of shrouding Krupper's homosexuality in mystery, he notes that "Williams's strategy of attributing to Mr. Krupper a form of selfhood that in capitalist social formations is usually reserved for white, middle-class, heterosexual men seriously challenged the dominant understanding of gay male identity in the fifties" and bespeaks Williams's unwillingness to "compromise his project by making his representation of gay male experience more palatable for straight middle-class readers."[37] Savran's claim about the story also emphasizes its narrative strategies: the text, he writes, provides a "guide to the possible ways of reading a Williams text and, more specifically, to the way that homosexuality, described by the story's narrator as a '"certain mystery in the life of Mr. Krupper,' is coded and decoded in his writing for the most public of literary arenas, the theater," thus guiding the most astute readers to recognize the various and complex ways we make meaning when we read and write.[38]

While all three critics succeed in countering the most problematic and limiting approaches to the homoerotic in Williams's texts, thus furthering a more complex understanding of the author's postmodern and culturally astute aesthetic than had been widely considered before the 1990s, there is another explanation of the public/private split identified in Williams's prose. If we add a consideration of the legal history of sexual practice during the period, then privacy, disgust, and shame become visible as interconnected and integral to any thorough understanding of Williams as a major cultural force. In his book, Savran includes a brief discussion of the legal persecution of gays, a period of persecution that coincides with and follows World War II, but he does so primarily as a prelude to his overview of what he calls the "homosexual rights movement" that gains momentum during this period.[39] The discussion that follows will expand this narrow focus, using information and context about the war and postwar periods, and specifically the circumstances that led to the persecution and prosecution of homosexuals, in order to relate them to Williams's literary production of the same time.

With its opening sentence, "Hard Candy" establishes merchant Krupper as "a man of gross and unattractive appearance and with no close family connections," a description that may appear to be of no consequence other than to define him as both unappealing and unattached.[40] The candy he uses to attract boys to him as he sits in the dark recesses of the movie theater's upper balcony sometimes "accumulated in the paper bag till it swelled out of his pocket like a great tumor," a simile that implies the diseased nature of what we come to recognize as his sexual arousal, and lends cause to the "'faugh' of disgust" that his fat cousins utter when he leaves their shop and heads to the town square. Despite the narrator's assertion that as a sick old person Krupper has developed a lack of sensitivity to dislike and even hatred, the man "knows that he is fat and ugly" and "that he is a terrible old man, shameful and despicable even to those who tolerate his caresses, perhaps even more so to those than to the others who only see him." Both Corber and Savran comment on the language of disgust that Williams uses in his description of Mr. Krupper, and both acknowledge its relationship to representations of or at least intimations of homosexuality.

Savran notes the "many adjectives in the text that mark Mr. Krupper as degenerate and diseased, gross, unattractive, sick, detested, yellow-toothed, dangerous, sad, unhealthy, terrible, shameful, despicable, and so on," but argues that "the force of this list is ingeniously undercut by two factors," the narrator's wry tone and what he calls the "curious and elaborate metanarrative intrusion near the beginning of the story" remarked upon above.[41] Corber asserts that Williams's "unflattering descriptions of Mr. Krupper, which threaten to reduce homosexual desire to a form of bodily corruption," have been in large part responsible for the charges of internalized homophobia against Williams that has troubled even the critics who make them. But Corber then quickly moves to a focus on what he sees as Williams's deliberate evasions that work to encourage the "reader's pornographic interest and thus implicate the reader in Mr. Krupper's activities." He argues that "Williams's mockery of the reader is not limited to encouraging a pornographic interest in Mr. Krupper's sexual activities"; the obscurity of the language, he says, "reduces the reader to engaging in the sort of reading practices that negotiating the gay male subculture often necessitated in the Cold War era" in which the text was published.[42]

Corber's assessment of this strategy is, not surprisingly, mixed: he argues that by reproducing the "epistemological structures of the closet," Williams renders Krupper's homosexuality a "sign not of his corruption but of his subjecthood, thereby discouraging us from positioning him as sexually other." He complicates his own reading, however, by acknowledging that "Williams's attempt to establish Mr. Krupper's subjecthood by shrouding his homosexuality in mystery is highly problematic from a political point of view."[43] And here he links the closet to the tensions between private and public that marked the era: for, "to avert the possibility that the reader's interest in the story will remain pornographic," Krupper's homosexuality remains a secret. For although his encounter with the youth "occurs in the public space of a movie theater, it is a private act" that "not even the reader is allowed to witness."[44] In *The Anatomy of Disgust*, William Ian Miller notes the connection between morality and disgust as long-standing, as crucial to community building, and as significant in "punishing certain kinds of behavior." His claim that "to the extent that the moral involves matters of purity and pollution it generally involves disgust" is followed by his assertion that disgust "is especially useful and necessary as a builder of moral and social community" for it and indignation "unite the world of impartial spectators into a moral community, as cosharers of the same sentiments, as guardians of propriety and purity." Furthermore, indignation "forces disgust to aid in the cause of justice by motivating action against the offender."[45] The role disgust plays in midcentury politics of difference are significant to an understanding of both law and literature of the period, as well as to my argument about how disgust and morality combined to exert a powerful influence on social and cultural attitudes about sexuality in the midcentury, all of which are reflected in Williams's texts.

If the text, its use of the language of disgust, and its tension between public and private are framed within a discussion of the restrictive sex laws of the period, the story and its features may be less problematic politically than Corber asserts. The contempt that the cousin and family have toward their relative, staring at his departing back with "the sort of look that you turn to give a rock on which you have stubbed your toe, a senselessly vicious look turned upon an insensibly malign object," is ameliorated by the fact that narrator makes clear that they do not really know Krupper. If he is "insensibly malign" in their eyes, it is due to their own ignorance and blindness, not because of any human qualities that the narrator reveals about him. He may be of "gross and unattractive appearance," but the cousins themselves are so fat they cannot fit in the store's doorway together, and their daughter is "already fatter than either of her fat parents and developing gross, unladylike habits."[46] The projection of their own grotesqueness onto the other is telling, and because they are not astute or curious enough to know of his activities at the Joy Rio, their assessment of him as an object of disgust is self-incriminating and reflective of their own fear of the body. Furthermore, the use of the word "gross" to describe both Krupper and the cousin's daughter, the product of the sexual union of "fat parents," suggests that Williams attaches the language of disgust and its sexual implications to a variety of persons, including heterosexual and married couples and their children. In his work, the possibility of repulsion is rarely missing in acts of sexual intimacy; as William Ian Miller argues, all love involves the "suspension of disgust," and Williams's creative work manifests the challenges of this suspension regularly. Overcoming disgust in the process of experiencing care and intimacy is a requirement, Miller continues: it involves the "notion of privileging another to see, touch, or otherwise experience you in a way that would be disgusting, shameful, or humiliating to you if that person were not so privileged," for "sexual desire depends on the idea of a prohibited domain of the disgusting." In Krupper's case, his own apparent suspension of disgust for his cousins, as well as his "insensibility" to his cousins' ill feelings might be seen, in this regard, as a sign of kinship and connection that define "intimacy between rough equals."[47]

A more compelling case for the way the narrative deflects the readers' judgment of disgust against the aging merchant and promotes tolerance for diverse sexual practices is evident in the story's denouement. Although "Hard Candy" touches only briefly on the disgust Krupper's family feels about him, it explores more fully the dangers, emotional and legal, of both rejection and success that Krupper recognizes are part of his particular way of forging connections with those outside his family. In the movie theatre, he carefully seats himself next to his object of desire, a "shadowy youth" who has retreated to the dark balcony and "who does not have the price of a hotel bedroom" and is therefore "in terror of being picked up for vagrancy."[48] With the latter detail Williams conveys that the youth's outward attractiveness is not sufficient to keep him safe in the eyes of the law, for his financial insufficiency, particularly as it limits his options for securing housing, is cause for arrest. Williams's invocation of vagrancy laws alternate between descriptions of homelessness and instances of lewd actions, suggesting quite rightly that they are connected: those who cannot afford a residence lack a space for sexual intimacy.

The theme of risk is developed further, as Krupper strains to make out the details of the young man in the dark whose odor is "captivating," knowing that "sometimes it is possible, in the dark, to make very dangerous mistakes" and that "even the most cautious man must depart from absolute caution if he intends at all to enjoy them." He emphasizes care in every other area of his life, the narrator tells us, "to compensate for those necessary breaches of caution that were the sad concomitant of his kind of pleasure."[49] Lighting a match to get a better look at the boy, he realizes that "never in his thirty years' attendance of matinees" has he discovered beside him "any dark youth of remotely equivalent beauty."[50] The climax of his sexual life has come, it would seem. As the almost silent negotiations commence, which begin with the offer of hard candy, Krupper, who "knows that he is fat and ugly," understands that he must offer payment for services rendered, and so he shakes the six quarters in his pocket to signal as much.[51] Finally, at the very moment when Krupper is about to withdraw his hand from contact with the hand of the youth, "that hand turns about," as the coins "descend, softly, with a slight tinkle, and Mr. Krupper knows that the contract is sealed between them."[52] At each stage of the elaborate exchange, he experiences the panic of failure, or worse, indictment, for although Krupper has assured "the usher's neutrality with a liberal tip," what occurs between the men in the dark balcony could result in arrest for both parties, and the youth's fear of a vagrancy charge (or worse) might be realized.

The need on both sides, the boy's for food in the form of hard candy and for a transfer of some silver to his pockets, and the man's for the consummation of his attraction, draws them together in an act that is illegal in part because it is deemed disgusting and fit only for darkness. Yet the exchange has the effect of elevating Krupper, lifting him up and away from disgust, both the self-recognition of his own repulsiveness and the isolating condemnation of his relatives. There is the sexual communion itself, serving the needs of both parties, but the story closes with a report of Krupper's death notice, which is marked by irony and sympathy. For the narrator goes on to explain that the dead man is discovered "in the remote box of the theater with his knees on the floor and his ponderous torso wedged between two wobbly gilt chairs as if he had expired in an attitude of prayer." The genuflection, the gilt of the chairs, and the apparently prayerful death connote saintly supplication rather than sordid sex. Williams's sensibility is clearly in play here, for the notice "was composed by a spinsterly reporter who had been impressed by the sentimental values" that she identifies in the dead man's presence at the cowboy thriller with hard candies in his pocket. But in so misreading the situation, the presumably virginal reporter conveys a comic naiveté that protects the dead man from postmortem charges of deviance.

Although the "notice of the old man's death was given unusual prominence for the obituary of someone who had no public character and whose private character was so peculiarly low," the public account of his demise does not expose him as someone with a low private character. Rather, as the narrator conveys it: "the notice contained no mention of anything of such a special nature," leaving the private character of Mr. Krupper "anonymous in the memories of those anonymous persons who had enjoyed or profited from his company in the tiny box at the Joy Rio."[53] Public exposure after death excludes the possibility of criminal prosecution, but this passage nonetheless carries a certain weight of judgment alongside the more obvious relief. The words "special nature" become particularly complex in this context, as does the "spinsterly" nature of the sentimental reporter. The reporter is unaware of Krupper's "special nature" because of a presumed sexual inexperience that could be considered dangerous for someone who works in the public sphere, and while the appeal of "sentimental values" to which she succumbs in her assessment of the circumstances of Krupper's demise is sad and funny, it suggests a humanity in her judgment that softens the sobering effect of Krupper's isolation and loneliness.

It is the daughter of Krupper's "distant" cousins, who had at age five been dubbed by her father "The Complete Little Citizen of the World," who saw the death notice in the newspaper and shared the "astonishingly agreeable" news with her parents, and it was she who exclaimed, "*Just think, Papa, the old man choked to death on our hard candy!*" (emphasis in the original).[54] His high blood pressure killed him, not choking, but the girl's assumption, connecting the demise to the hard candy, has the effect of implicating the callous relatives in Krupper's secret sexual life. They have all along provided him with the candy that he used as bait for the young men whose services he contracted, and their ignorance about him works primarily to make them look foolish. If the reader is savvier than the story's characters, it is because the narrator has not withheld the necessary details of Krupper's exploits at the Joy Rio theatre, and if we compare ourselves with the cousins, it is to feel superior to them. While Williams's story does not overtly present Krupper as an attractive or sympathetic figure—indeed, there is much in his character and behavior that might put off readers—it is because of the cousins and because of the sentimental obituary that we consider him with compassion, if not fondness. Although this story does not focus overtly on the legal ramifications of its protagonist's sexual behavior, it demonstrates Williams's concerns with obscurity and exposure and is but one example of the way he weaves issues of disgust complexly through his texts.

There is arguably no better example of a prose text by Williams that demonstrates his work's complex negotiations with sexuality, disgust, and law than the short story "One Arm." The story explores the fate of Oliver, a male prostitute convicted, sentenced to death, and executed after being found guilty of murdering one of his wealthy johns. "One Arm" is representative of much of Williams's work in its extended history, its extensive evolution, and its existence in multiple versions and forms. Adapted for the screen by Williams although the film was never made, the full-length screenplay is included in the volume *Stopped Rocking and Other Screenplays* (1984). In 2004, playwright and director Moisés Kaufman developed and directed a stage version that drew upon the short story and the screenplay. Kaufman and his Tectonic Theater Project produced *One Arm* at Steppenwolf Downstairs Theatre in Chicago in 2004, and in 2011 at the New York City's New Group. As we shall see, the history of the text, not an uncommonly complex one for Williams, provides a means for examining Williams's move from the privacy of prose to the public nature of the cinematic or dramatic performance, and in this case the journey is one that covers multiple decades.

Some of the story's elements are familiar ground for Williams: a French Quarter setting in the opening section, depictions of street life and prostitution, a damaged protagonist, a sudden act of violence. Also familiar is Williams's documentation of his composition process. In May 1942, he left a note for Donald Windham at the New York City YMCA that he "today wrote new story 'One Arm' about the 1-armed blond hustler in New Orleans—I want to show to you."[55] A notebook entry written the following year while Williams was in Santa Monica finds him working on the text again: "Yesterday was foggy so I stayed home and went back to work. Worked well on short story about the 1-armed youth in N.O."[56] In subsequent entries dated over the next few weeks he mentions his story revisions in passing multiple times, and on November 14 he writes that he was "working on 'One Arm'—read it over and discovered that I had destroyed it."[57] While it is unlikely that the latter was the case, his anxiety about revisions is clear in this notebook entry, as is the extent of his changes: that they were, in his opinion, substantial enough to completely alter the quality of the text.

The story follows Oliver, a former sailor and light heavyweight champion who loses his arm in an automobile accident and leaves the hospital "to look about for destruction," taking up street life and male hustling before murdering a client who had paid him to act in a pornographic film.[58] It is the act of murder, not the act of sodomy, that makes Oliver an extreme version of Williams's many illegal bodies, and although he commits sexual crimes for a living, when he is arrested, the text's narration makes the distinction that it is "not on an ordinary charge of lewd vagrancy, but for questioning in connection with the murder."[59] With what the story's narrator calls "the mechanical cruelty of the law," Oliver's life ends in state-sanctioned execution after a period on death row during which he receives love letters from former johns, and the missives coax him out of the detachment that defined his life after the accident.[60] Brian M. Peters analyzes "One Arm" and "Desire and the Black Masseur" for their "images of subverted male-male desire," arguing that Williams's use of figurative language in the two stories "reflects the impact of society's often limiting approach to non-conventional romantic options," and that the story is "an articulation of homosexuality that reveals the downfall of the queer character."[61] The presumption that Oliver is homosexual has gone unchallenged; although Peters acknowledges that "during his boxing career Oliver is not (to the reader's knowledge) gay," he suggests that once Oliver loses his arm, he "assumes a new 'calling'" as his "heterosexual past is exchanged for a homosexual present."[62] Such an exchange is debatable, but perhaps the question of Oliver's homosexuality is significant precisely because it cannot and should not be answered. To do so would be to delve into a matter that Williams chose to obscure: although the story contains explicit references to Ollie's homosexual activity, it is coy about his homosexual identity.

The story's obliqueness serves to expose the complicated nature of Williams's gay fiction. The indirection of "One Arm" begins in the title, which persisted through many drafts; it points to an absence via a presence, for by referencing the arm that remains, it calls attention to the missing one. This strategy does not, however, shield us from the tragedy of Oliver's situation, for the title is shockingly graphic. The visibility of the missing arm has determined his life since he "left the hospital to look about for destruction," for as a "broken statue of Apollo" he has become "unforgettable."[63] The narrator tells us that with the arm "had gone the center of his being," but Oliver does not "consciously know" the full impact of the "psychic change which came with his mutilation."[64] His true self is hidden from him and only hinted to us, even as his illegal actions, beginning with transient prostitution and ending with murder, are in plain sight, like the mutilation. The striking contrast of the external injury with the mysterious interiority of its effect suggests that explicit physical desire, when prohibited by cultural norms, can result in an obscuring of the self. With "One Arm," Williams created a fiction that depicted an extreme version of the reality many Americans faced in the mid-twentieth century, when norms of culture and law had not progressed to match changes in demographics and lifestyles. Oliver represents an individual who has lost "the center of his being;" the accident is the occasion for that loss.

The loss does not keep him from doing but from being, and the story explores the idea that with the concealment of identity one may be temporarily free from public scrutiny, but cannot long survive. Williams's own struggles to maintain the integrity of identity in a society that condemned many of his personal and professional choices found their way into his work, which stuck "close to life as he experienced it" and become visible to us with "One Arm": in the published text, in its revision history, and in Williams's own comments on the story and its composition. The question of Oliver's homosexuality is an open one because his center has gone but only the "speechless self knew it." Who he is, including his sexual orientation, is unknowable, even to him; with few exceptions, the story's revelations emerge from action rather than reflection. The mystery of Oliver and the necessity for the mystery reflect the legal and political climate of the postwar period, when the question of "are you now or have you ever been?" destroyed private and public lives. To be named homosexual was a form of social suicide; masking the self was a survival tactic. The open question of Oliver's identity relies upon an obscurity of narrative, but it reflects the self-masking that many Americans used to keep themselves safe.

"One Arm" provides an excellent example of Williams's interest in the interrogations and assaults on identity that came with heightened attention to sexual criminal activity, for the narrative focuses on law's power to determine not only Oliver's life, but his death. Another letter to Donald Windham dated July 28, 1945, which Williams wrote from Laredo, Texas, documents his work on "One Arm" while in Mexico, and demonstrates his fears about its subject matter being made known to officials. According to the report he makes about his border crossing, a customs official confiscated all his manuscripts at the border and he was delayed in Laredo waiting for them to be cleared. Upon receipt of them, he writes Windham, "I discovered one was missing, the story 'One Arm' which I had just gotten into final shape when I left Mexico. Of course I suspected it was being held because of its subject matter."[65] The custom officials denied confiscating it and Williams was driven back to his hotel to check for it in his trunk. He found it there, having mislaid it under a pile of shirts, but he did not report the discovery and as a result the story was never inspected by border officials. This anecdote provides evidence of Williams's fears that his materials might be seized because of their illicit content, and reports the ongoing process of textual revision that took place steadily over the first half of the 1940s. Both his worry and his commentary about revision are pertinent to this analysis: the former demonstrates the restrictive climate of the period, while the latter provides a framework of the time investment and the process of development he committed to so many of his texts.

His concern about the dangerous subject matter of "One Arm" continued, for prior to the 1948 publication of the story collection, Williams wrote to New Directions Press editor James Laughlin to express his nervousness about the book's advertising: "I don't think the book should be publicized and sold through the usual channels. We agreed to have it sold on a subscription basis. This is mostly because of consideration for my family, and because only a few of us will understand and like it, and it is bound to be violently attacked by the rest."[66] Williams's fears about violent attacks on the work by critics and readers were not unwarranted, and although the attacks he expects are verbal, his use of the word "violently" recalls the physical attacks on homosexuals during the period. Furthermore, "One Arm" was published just as vice squads around the country stepped up their focus on homosexual activity and the Truman administration launched investigations of government employees believed to be homosexual. In 1949, Eskridge reports, "sodomy or solicitation of sodomy generated almost sixty percent of the arrests" made by the city morals squad in Philadelphia, and in 1950 the squad "was hauling two hundred homosexuals into court each month."[67] The upswing in arrests also coincided with the Truman administration's investigations of government employees believed to be homosexual. The legal restriction of homosexual lives and activities included the possession of homosexual texts and writing about homosexuality without disapproval, and the letter demonstrates Williams's keen awareness of the cultural climate and its impact on his literary production and reception.

Leverich reports that the story "created a furor when it was first published, because of its ruthlessly honest treatment of male prostitution and capital punishment."[68] The trepidation that Williams had about publicizing and distributing his first story collection was echoed in Laughlin's letter to Audrey Wood, in which the editor assures the agent that the release of the volume would involve "no advertising" and "no review copies." "You may be sure," he wrote, "that I don't want any scandal any more than you do."[69] In another letter to Laughlin in October 1948, Williams reiterates similar concerns: "Please remember not to let 'One Arm' be displayed for sale in bookstores. When I heard that Miss Steloff had ordered 200 copies, I became alarmed with visions of you and I pinned up like our one-armed hero. I hope that the book will be distributed as we planned, entirely by subscription. Let me know how you plan to distribute it."[70] Williams's awareness of the raids and arrests targeting homosexuals is reflected in references contained within his letters and notebooks; in them he alternates between coded reference and candid revelation, between earnest concern that his confessions might be held against him and the desire to shield his family and the need to pursue his art wherever it takes him.

Hooper summarizes the conflict Williams faced, arguing that "on the one hand, Williams's attitude to the marketing of his books would suggest that he was prepared to tread carefully and avert controversy;" on the other, he continues, "the very writing of such stories, at a time when he was enjoying commercial success in the theatre, represents a determination to address gay experiences without being gagged."[71] As Hooper notes, the legalities of the 1873 Comstock Act would have allowed authorities to stop the distribution of material considered obscene.[72] Indeed, Williams's prose of this period, by its very existence, was a challenge to intersecting sets of laws: laws governing individuals and their acts, and laws governing texts, the common purpose to protect society from "undesirable" elements. The need for caution was in contest with the pull of freedom. In the prose texts discussed in this chapter, we see another version of this kind of negotiation, as well as a movement outward as the author releases material into a published textual space of short fiction. In doing so, his letters above demonstrate, he was aware of the cost to his family and his reputation, and yet he was determined to put diverse forms of sexual activity on display in sympathetic and complex ways.

But he absorbed more than just conflicting sets of values, for his work demonstrates his awareness that people might be publicly exposed and prosecuted for acts that were deemed "degenerate" and therefore criminal, the revelation and censure of sexual transgressions among his work's constants. "Unnatural" and "lascivious" acts were legislated at the state and local levels as "crimes against nature," with many of the statutes in place since colonial times, but with population growth throughout the nineteenth and into the twentieth centuries came the expansion of such laws, particularly in cities. These changes in the legislation of sexuality were framed, as were the sex panics, by new freedoms on one side and new fears on the other; Eskridge notes that as the country was transformed through industrialization and other factors, "demographic changes produced new patterns of sociability and sexual behavior, with sexual variety openly flourishing."[73] Chauncey depicts the development of an unlawful sexual sphere in New York at the eve of the twentieth century; much of what he describes is useful for understanding the urban underworlds that Williams discovered as a young man and budding writer. These spaces were sometimes bars, but Chauncey also reports that much of the gay world took shape in streets and parks, "where many men—'queer' and 'normal' alike—went to find sexual partners, where many gay men went to socialize, and where many men went for sex and ended up being socialized into the gay world."[74] D'Emilio and Freedman argue for a shift "toward consumption, gratification, and pleasure" that resulted in the "commercialization of sex, previously an underground, illicit phenomenon," moving somewhat into the open.[75] In most jurisdictions, sexual activity other than marital intercourse consummated in private, with the intention of or the possibility of procreation, was prohibited by law, and men and women who violated sodomy laws, which included all forms of solicitation, were deemed sexual deviants. Peters argues that by linking homosexuality with prostitution in "One Arm," Williams proposes "that queer desire is tantamount to sexual deviancy"; however, the history of sexuality demonstrates that the playwright was, rather, representing a connection already established by the laws of the period.[76]

Although the homosexual sex in "One Arm" is the primary focus for Williams's representations of illegal acts, the texts in draft and in finished form include multiple transgressive sexualities and their legal regulation. Whether or not Oliver is homosexual, his body is a lure for men interested in sex and willing to pay for it, and it is therefore significant to Williams's wide-ranging interrogations of sexual illegality. Oliver is identified at the story's opening as one of "three male hustlers" loitering on Canal Street in New Orleans. Of the three he is the "unforgettable youth," and before we know what will become of him, we hear of his singularity. He attracts attention from potential johns with no effort on his part, "staring above the heads of passers-by with an indifference which was not put on."[77] Raymond-Jean Frontain argues that Oliver "has been reduced to prostituting himself to other men in order to survive financially," emphasizing economics above sexuality.[78] This reading is in keeping with Chauncey's assertion that sex workers could make more money than young men in many other occupations; the story reports that when Oliver joined the southern migration of hustlers and vagrants who wintered in Miami, he "struck it rich."[79] Williams's decision to have Oliver turn to prostitution after the accident would appear to be an economic consideration as well as a reflection of sexual deviancy, and the protagonist's relationship with his johns reveals complex and contradictory attitudes about his livelihood.

Once damaged, Oliver enters a liminal space that is both exposed and secretive, and thus does the narrative call attention to Williams's textual strategies, which rely on tension between the private and the public. The story implies that Oliver attracts attention because of his physical mutilation, and his decision to support himself through prostitution determines his transient life of little or no privacy, meeting his johns on street corners and retreating to their private spaces whenever possible. For despite his need for exposure to potential clients, he must keep his activities hidden. His mutilation limits his employment options while expanding his sexual desirability; however, the story hints at his pre-accident disposition for engaging in acts of "unnatural ardor." Prior to leaving Arkansas to enlist, he hauled lumber for a living while conducting a "coarse and startling affair" with the wife of the man he worked for— this adulterous relationship was the "first to make him aware of the uncommon excitement he was able to stir."[80] There are moral and legal prohibitions against all his couplings, save, perhaps, for the "tentative knowledge of girls" that had "suddenly exploded" into the illicit affair; what few details we have about Oliver's former life reveal a transgressive and illegal heterosexual past.

The details of his past take up less than a paragraph in the published text, but they are crucial for underscoring the ubiquity of what would have been considered deviant desire during the period of composition and publication. In one of many examples of Williams's inclusiveness, the boy who becomes a mutilated murderer began his life as a strapping farm boy from Arkansas, who was all too quick to reject the "emotional adventures" with culturally appropriate potential mates for acts of "unnatural ardor" with an older, married woman. Thus does this imaginative text seem to confirm what Kinsey's studies exposed: that American men and women lived sexual lives more diverse than the era's social norms suggested. The details of the adulterous affair in Arkansas included in the published version are few but significant, for they reveal Oliver's proclivity for sexual criminal activity before mutilation, and before the psychic change that came with it; furthermore, they underscore the ambiguity of his sexual identity. Oliver's sexual orientation is less significant than his sexual activity, for whether violating the legal sanctity of another's marriage or hazarding arrest for lewd vagrancy on Canal Street, it is through sexual transgression that the text presents Oliver as a figure of "uncommon excitement," and it is in the paucity of information that the text conveys the need for secrecy in an age when the law may prosecute all that is considered deviant.

Quickly acclimated to a life on the street that involved being passed from "one wealthy sportsman" to another, however, Oliver finds fleeting pleasure in fast money and anonymity until one night, while drunk on a yacht in Palm Beach and "for no reason that was afterward sure to him," he strikes his client's inclined head with a copper book-end and kills him. Picked up by the police a few months afterward for questioning in connection with the murder, Oliver lands on death row after a short trial during which "everything went against him."[81] "One Arm" is unusual in that it "dramatizes" the crime and punishment of the sexual outlaw more directly than many works, particularly those that narrate scrapes with the law as part of a character's past, not present. Frequent mentions of having been arrested for "lewd vagrancy," or of leaving town before such an arrest could take place, is often how law is treated in the works, whereas in the case of "One Arm," the story's plot is the arrest, conviction, and execution of Ollie. These details, offered in rapid succession in the narrative's opening paragraphs, chart an explicit geography of sex and violence while providing an early example of one of Williams's mutilated and illegal bodies; with the plot and its denouement in place, the story shifts focus to Ollie's psychological journey, whose sexual needs or behavior are tied up with disgust and loathing for self and others, in parts equal to and in contest with self-acceptance and the craving for compassion.

In "One Arm," the disgust expressed is primarily self-disgust that is both physical and sexual. Although at first glance it would appear that the connection between sex and disgust is connected only to homosexuality, there are indications that other types of transgressive sex are repulsive to Oliver. Indeed, Oliver reacts with revulsion to both his male and his female sexual partners; his reaction seems to emerge from the surprise he experiences in being physically desirable after the accident, but there is also an element of legal prohibition in all of his couplings that is consistent with Williams's complex interplay, often manifested at the individual level, between transgressive sexual activity and legislated morality. Although he becomes a prostitute only after losing his arm, Oliver's sexual history prior to enlisting in the service had prompted him to flee the scene, for as the narrator goes on to explain, it was "to break off this affair that he left home and entered the navy at a base in Texas."[82] Although his earlier sexual experience was heterosexual, it was with another man's wife, and Ursula Vogel has documented the history of laws prohibiting adultery as "the vestiges of a long and powerful legal tradition which has created 'adultery' as an offence of different quality and consequence for women and men." In multiple ancient and modern systems, she explains, a "double standard exists or did exist in which "a wife's (but not a husband's) adultery strikes at the order of property and, as a direct consequence, at the foundations of civil society itself."[83]

American legal codes bear up this double standard, for there are considerable variations in state adultery statutes, a good number of which remain in place today: as Posner and Silbaugh report, there are two issues that arise in legal definitions of adultery, and the first is "whether only a married person can be guilty of adultery or whether an unmarried person is also guilty of adultery for engaging in sex with a married person." In at least one state, Minnesota, only a married woman can be charged with adultery, and the other party, married or not, is also subject to prosecution; however as the statute goes on to specify, there is "no prohibition against sex between a married man and an unmarried woman."[84] This differentiation is no doubt related to long-standing notions of wife as property; in this context, and because he has violated the marriage of another man, Oliver is legally guilty of sexual theft. Furthermore, as Vogel notes, adultery prohibitions are concerned not only with the sanctity of marriage and "the property right of a private person that is at stake," but "adultery counts as a punishable offence under the criminal law, which will exact retribution for the violation of the public interest."[85] A 1942 draft version of the story makes no mention of this affair, and instead describes Oliver's prior sexual experience as follows: "He was eighteen then and had only known work in the sun in the Arkansas cotton country tiredness at night and fooling around with the fellows and just the bare beginning of knowing girls and a few months of training and then some time at sea where he'd taken up boxing."[86] The addition of the illicit affair adds weight and a pertinent history to his story, but, more significantly, it establishes him as a criminal prior to the accident.

This background also helps to connect adultery and other sexually transgressive acts with immorality intrinsically challenging the common good, with public and private concerns in tension and in concert alternately, with civil and criminal law sharing jurisdiction over a relationship that serves individual and community interests. Occurring as it does before the accident, Oliver's affair and its sexual and moral stains are a precursor to the loss of innocence and optimism that disappeared when his arm did, an event that ironically only increased his desirability in the eyes of other sexual outlaws. Conveniently, with the arm "had gone the wholesome propriety that had made him leave home. . . . Now he could feel no shame that green soap and water did not remove well enough to satisfy him."[87] He is, at once, stained and cleansed, or at least he has found a way to absolve himself of shame, with an outward sign of imperfection that has heightened his appeal to others. In Williams's complicated representation of mutilation, sin, crime, punishment, and absolution, the author crafts a view of sexuality that suggests its importance for fulfillment, freedom, and character formation.

While Oliver's physical escape from the small town removed him from the site of his first illicit sexual experience, followed by the amputation that "dulled his senses" and erased his capacity for any kind of lasting shame, the specifics of his damaged physical condition cannot help but continue to align him and his body to the anatomy of disgust, for as Miller argues, there are "few things that are more unnerving and disgust evoking than our partibility." While psychoanalysis has predisposed us to a kind of hierarchy of partibility, with castration reigning as the most horrific, Miller suggests that severability is "unnerving no matter what part is being detached, castration merely being one instance of many and not especially entitled to stand as an emblem for any instance of separation."[88] It is misogyny that "raises the stakes for castration as against other maiming, mutilation, and deformities which do not require misogyny to account for their uncanny and disgusting qualities."[89] While limb loss is often seen as an emblem of castration, "One Arm" seems to suggest quite the opposite, for Oliver's success as a hustler does not come until after the accident: he "left the hospital to look about for destruction," but upon landing in New York he "learned the ropes of what became his calling" after "another young vagrant . . . wised him up to his commodity value and how to cash in on it."[90] Economics is implied by the "commodity value" mentioned here, but made even more explicit in the May 1942 draft, which includes the following sentence: "After he left the naval hospital, honorably discharged from the service, Oliver took to knocking around the country, first with sufficient money in his pocket—then as a penniless vagrant."[91] His turn to prostitution is implied as need-driven, but it is always also connected to his unique yet shocking physical desirability.

Although the murder he commits is described as one that occurs "for no reason that was afterward sure" to Oliver, the published text does provide an additional smattering of detail about what preceded and therefore what seems to have precipitated the murder. Like other pieces of the story, it points to disgust while connecting several illegal acts. The filming of a "blue movie" on the yacht, with Williams describing the movie "as a privately made film of licentious behavior among two or more persons," in this case Oliver and a female prostitute, who each "had been given a hundred dollars each," caused Oliver to "suddenly revolt," to strike the girl and kick over the camera. While the complex negotiation of mutilation, disgust, and sexual attraction, all of them connected to either money or law, is apparent throughout the first several pages of the published version of "One Arm" in prose form, the screenplay, with its expanded length and in its greatly developed sections of dialogue, provides important additional evidence of Williams's interest in these topics and his great attention to them throughout the years of composition.

The development of Williams's representations of such material, as it reflected the culture and politics of the age, and the revisions he makes to

"One Arm" during the multiyear drafting process, indicate his interest in and commitment to exploring issues of disgust, law, and emotion. Draft versions that demonstrate the differentiation of these elements do not reveal a linear progression of Williams's treatment of his subject matter; rather, we see an ongoing negotiation and renegotiation of how these themes and this language are shaped and how they are emphasized. His transformation of the story into a screenplay presents an additional opportunity to see what happens when he returns to the narrative two decades after its publication in his first collection of stories.

In the introduction to the published volume of screenplays that includes *One Arm*, Richard Gilman writes that although the dates of the four works contained within cannot be definitively stated, it is likely that Williams wrote the film text of *One Arm* in the 1960s.[92] He wrote all four screenplays without having secured a director or a studio, and at the time of publication of this volume, in 1984, one year after Williams's death, none had been produced.[93] This twenty-year gap between story and screenplay composition covers a crucial time of cultural transformation in the area of sexual norms, but the *One Arm* version arranged for film provides substantial evidence that Williams's concern with law and sexuality had not abated in the 1960s; indeed, this version of the text offers a unique addition to my argument about his political engagement and an example of his adaptation of a (private) prose text to a text meant for performance. Precisely because the screenplay was not produced as a film and was not published immediately, it occupies a space between the private and public: that is, Williams intended it for mass consumption during the years of sexual liberation, but it remained hidden from view, not even available in print form.

The screenplay considerably expands the scope of the short story while maintaining the latter's plot, main characters, and central concerns. Dramatizing what was narrated in the prose text while adding additional characters and situations, it retains the use of a narrative voiceover, thus providing insight on perceptions of sex and law in American life. In an author's note published with the screenplay, Williams stipulates that a producer would have to offer him a choice of directors, noting the following: "I don't think I'm mistaken in thinking that (the director) should be an American. There is so much of (allegorical) American life in the script, whose story, basically, is not a limited one."[94] While he points to the allegorical, as was his way, analysis here of the legal and political aspects of the film script, interwoven with selected details from draft versions of "One Arm" and the published prose text will focus on disgust and identity formation.

Nussbaum's interrogations of the relationship between disgust and law include her challenges to the ideas of two theorists, one Williams's contemporary and one her own, both of whom defended a society's right to regulate actions in connection with disgust. Lord Patrick Devlin, a

British lawyer whose influential tracts on disgust and law appeared in the 1950s, and Leon Kass, an American bioethicist who has written primarily about human cloning, both concluded, Nussbaum tells us, "that widespread disgust at a practice is sufficient reason to forbid that practice through law, even if it involves only consenting parties and does not violate the rights of the nonconsenting."[95] Devlin found insufficient John Stuart Mill's principle "that only the imminent prospect of harm to others licenses restrictive laws," Nussbaum notes, and relies instead upon what prompts an average member of society to "feel disgust at the thought of some behavior that does not directly affect him" to conclude that such conduct is 'a vice so abominable that its mere presence is an offence.'" For his part Kass believes that, as Nussbaum explains, "disgust is a reliable warning sign, steering us away from atrocity."[96] Nussbaum acknowledges that the arguments of Devlin and Kass have weight not because they are well-reasoned, necessarily, but because they resonate with "prominent aspects of people's emotional lives." She continues: "People do feel deep disgust with certain practices and, by extension, the groups that engage in those practices. They believe that these practices threaten the social fabric, and they are usually eager to make law in response to that perceived threat."[97] Ultimately, in her demonstration that "it is inappropriate for a liberal democratic society to rely on this emotion as a source of law," she seeks to influence constitutional law and its perspectives on sexual orientation.

In the screenplay's version of the yacht scene with the female prostitute, Ollie has a private conversation with the girl he has been paired with for the "blue movie," during which he describes his hesitation to be used for a "freak show" once he realizes that the filmmaker "wanted a man that was mutilated! . . . A beautiful girl doing things to a mutilated man, a man with one arm and the other a stump, a flipper."[98] As to what the couple is being required to do together, Ollie asks her, "You don't feel disgust?" and tells her that he hates hearing the director "tell you to do unnatural things to me like he tells you in his oily voice with his fat wetmouth grin."[99] Despite his hesitation, Ollie goes through with it, as he does not in the published version of the prose text. In the screenplay scene, the girl convinces him that the money will be worth it and that he should not think about it because, as she says, "It's me that does it to you. I like doing it, so you don't have to think."[100] Oliver's aversion to himself and to those he attracts appears to be rather universally applied to his experience with sexual contact, perhaps not born out of but certainly heightened by what the story refers to as the loss of "wholesome propriety" that comes with his amputation, separating him "from his development as an athlete and a young man wholly adequate to the physical world he grew into."[101] Oliver might be considered the American version of Devlin's average person, averse to what society would consider "unnatural," the ardor that the coarse older woman had introduced him to, for example; while the mutilation, also a source of disgust, takes his "natural" compass with it, according to the narrator, the text first aligning this outlying criminal with the conservative majority of the midcentury and then moving him to a position beyond caring. His participation in what he himself considers disgusting activities results in an internal tension that, for Oliver, is released through violence against the person he considers to be the site of the unnatural behavior. In a survey conducted by the Kinsey Institute in 1970 that was not published until 1989, the authors report that "with regard to many forms of sexual expression, our respondents were extremely conservative," with a majority disapproving of "homosexuality, prostitution, extramarital sex, and most forms of premarital sex," with masturbation disapproved of by 48 percent of respondents.[102] In social science, then, we detect a similar kind of contradiction: the studies of the Kinsey Institute consistently bore out the gap between what American men and women said they believed was normal sexual practice and the diversity of acts in which they engaged. Oliver exemplifies such contradictions.

Although Williams does not explicitly use the word "moral" when he describes what has transpired in Oliver's short life, the text describes it as an unmooring:

> He knew that he had lost his right arm, but didn't consciously know that with it had gone the center of his being. But the self that doesn't form words nor even thoughts had come to a realization that whirled darkly up from its hidden laboratory and changed him altogether in less time than it took new skin to cover the stump of the arm he had lost. He never said to himself, I'm lost. But the speechless self knew it and in submission to its unthinking control the youth had begun as soon as he left the hospital to look about for destruction.[103]

The destruction comes, fittingly, with his turn to an amorality that is much more blatantly and dangerously sexual and illegal than the affair that drove him from his home place, for prostitution becomes his way of supporting himself now that he has been "abruptly cut off" from the kind of adulthood he had expected. When he moved from one normalized sphere, the farm community of his youth, to another, the navy boot camp where he took up boxing and "all that he had to deal with was the flesh and its feelings," he remained contained by the limits imposed by community morals or institutional parameters. Once he is forced to leave those contained spaces of existence, he is "lost," but he is also free to wander and to test out extreme ways of being in the world.

A passage that was removed from the printed story at Williams's request makes clear the connection between Ollie's life before the accident and after, although it also demonstrates the character's move from subject position to object and other. In a letter to James Laughlin dated 18 May 1948, Williams asks his editor to make "one very important change" to the story "One Arm," his justification that both he and Donald Windham "feel that it cheapens the story." What Williams calls for is the removal of all references to the "blue movie" that prompts the murder; what is omitted, however, is a not the entire section but only a passage that describes Oliver's previous experience viewing a pornographic film:

> Oliver had seen one in Marseilles when he was in the navy. It was exhibited in a room in a fancy brothel, projected on a sheet torn off a whore's bed, while the audience of sailors and girls gasped and giggled and under the inflaming influence of the erotic images flickering on the silk sheet, the gathering had turned into a circus of lust. But that was before his reserve had gone with his arm. The spectacle and its influence on his shipmates had sickened the seventeen-year-old sailor. He had slipped out of the brothel and vomited behind it and the disgust of the experience had made him chaste for weeks. But that was the last voyage before the loss of his arm and two years later he found himself and a girl prostitute performing some of the very scenes that he had witnessed in the blue movie at Marseilles.[104]

In witnessing a pornographic film, before the accident, he had not felt excitement but disgust, which brought on physical illness and a determination to remain chaste. But it was not the film alone that had triggered his revulsion; the "influence on his shipmates" had also had its effect. As we shall see in other draft versions of the prose text, he is repelled primarily by displays of sexual excitement rather than by the acts that elicit it. One way, then, to consider his reaction is as a rejection of the intimacy and subsequent loss of privacy that results from sexual activity, as individuals are exposed to one another, physically and emotionally, through the power and rawness of bodily desire.

In a seminal 1941 article, psychoanalyst Andras Angyal defines disgust as a reaction to unwanted intimacy, a definition that can be applied to Williams's texts in an attempt to identify the logic that drew the author to this topic and held him for a lifetime. His literary and theatrical projects were, in part, a test of the boundaries of self and the limits of human relations, for he created many fictional scenarios in which his characters seek out connections to others, and sometimes to the other. The need for safety is outweighed by the desire to make contact and to demonstrate the possibility of a shared humanity. But that contact carries with it a hefty price: the possibility of destruction. When they present themselves, the opportunities to be one's true self in the presence of other people must be ventured, but the danger of exposing oneself to derision, condemnation, or rejection infuses such decisions with fear. The feelings of disgust and accusations of disgust expressed in Williams's work indicate his awareness that caring for others is fraught with a base danger that must be guarded against, for when disgust is used as a barometer of behavior, moral judgment is interwoven with a visceral assessment.

This reflection suggests the intricate link that is the point of coherence and the point of tension in much of Williams's work, between a draw toward spiritual contact and an aversion to bodily contact. The specific act of intimacy is important, of course, but it is also worth noting that disgust has been theorized as having a specific source that can then take on numerous associations. As Angyal notes, disgust is bred by the threat of being soiled by excreta, and the more "intimate the contact, the stronger the reaction."[105] The more this threat can be masked or diminished during the act of contact, the more likely it is that the reaction will be controlled as well. But if a central focus on intimacy and its challenges meant that Williams generated and coped with the emotion of disgust, it also meant forging another connection as well: to the law. For whether or not he intended to stage and narrate chronicles of crime and punishment, they found their way into his texts regularly. The connections between law and disgust about sexuality that Williams draws upon are ones that he finds embedded in the social and political fabric of his era. He needed to look no further than law's language for sources of tension, for in it he discovered a complex lexicon for exploring the domestic and foreign crises of the postwar era. Although Cold War threats, real or perceived, were global in nature, they were often defined in the national imaginary in terms of individual identity and conformity, and thus do such national security issues coincide with his concerns about the self and its search for pleasure, for fulfillment, and for freedom.

Although Oliver's limb loss does not allude to castration or sexual impotency, but rather heightens his sexual attractiveness, it does transform him into an emblem of disgust; he represents a combination of revulsion and desire, and his expressions of disgust about others would seem to emerge from a strain of self-loathing. The outward sign of his disfigurement attracts attention to him, but the lifestyle he adopts is one that requires privacy, so his post-accident existence is one of both exposure and obscurity. This duality is often a feature of sexual intimacy, for coupling requires decisions about whether to publicize the liaison or keep it private. Illegal trysts are fraught with this dilemma, and Williams's texts make the complication explicit. One of the opening scenes of the *One Arm* screenplay depicts Ollie on the street attracting interest from what the narrator tells us in a voiceover is a "middle-aged homosexual" who is in town "for business other than this dangerous business of cruising," and who worries that the "boy is employed by the police to attract imprudent homos." In an earlier draft of the screenplay, Williams includes the following details: "Yes, he's almost certainly a male prostitute, yes, but he's still waiting for the boy to give him a sign of interest. Now Ollie gives him, at last, the sign that the wisely prudent 'John' was waiting for. Ollie still doesn't look at him but he jingles a bunch of keys and coins in his pocket."[106] When Ollie makes an almost imperceptible move to signal assent, the "middle-aged man with a hunger for boys is as reassured as he can be in a city, a world, so dangerous to the pursuit of his kind of pleasure, which is an ancient pleasure, but never out-of-date."[107] Williams points here very specifically to the political conundrum of transgressive desire: its physical dangers and legal consequences set against its historical ubiquity.

Oliver's mutilation is linked to homosexual attraction and desire, but perhaps more pointedly to the illegal nature of Oliver's life, connecting the body and the criminal activity to each other and calling attention to the physical nature of the sex crimes he commits and the financial benefits he reaps. A draft version of the short story provides specific details about the instant education he received on the streets and the confirmation of his success: "He learned the ropes at once. The second night in New York he was standing in front of Diamond Jim's at forty-second and Broadway—picked up at once, he held out for several dollars and they were paid him. After the summer he went away from New York. Hitchhiking was easy. Nobody was afraid to pick up a one-armed boy with such a friendly smile."[108] He reaps these benefits both because he has been genetically gifted and circumstantially altered by the accident; he is perceived complexly but positively. With fascination, surely, and possibly with disgust, along with what seems in this passage to be an acknowledgment that he is, literally, unarmed and therefore harmless. With a life of hitchhiking come additional social marks of transience, freedom, and reliance upon strangers. His post-military profession moves him outside the borders of law and propriety while opening him up to acts of intimacy that he resisted prior to the accident.

Ollie's self-regard is variable, and the wrestling that he does with both self-promotion and insecurity is more available to readers in the screenplay format, both because of its length and development of details and because we hear much more direct speech from the protagonist. The challenges he faces in this regard are tied to identity, for the accident and the loss of the arm took suddenly from him his occupation (sailor) and passion (boxing), and he is left to forge not only a new life but a new self-conception. He does so by recognizing that his body, now visibly different, has cut him off from normalcy while opening to him an outlaw life that provides him a very different kind of existence, one that is also tied to physicality but that admits him into a dark world of conflicting emotions. In the screenplay, Ollie's arrest is foreshadowed by a gypsy fortune teller, the shadow she sees behind him "as dark as a crime" and the shadow in front "payment for the shadow behind." When he asks her why he does not run from the shadow in front as she bids him do, she replies, "You despise yourself."[109] In another scene prior to his arrest he attempts to help an ailing older man on the street who, despite Ollie's assistance, is run over by a speeding ambulance. A long speech by the narrator makes Williams's interest in connecting his chronically afflicted characters to the society that has rejected them: "There were so many of them, the queer, the mutilated, the not-so-young anymore with their loneliness a terrible cry in their throats, muted, or stifled to dumbness by the iron hand of bigotry and law. We can't play back all their voices or deal out all their photos like a gypsy's deck of filthy, dog-eared cards, telling always almost the same fortune both to them and the boy." The next section of the speech makes plain that Ollie's strength against such forces is temporary: "Oh, he must have known, he must have realized with God knows how much—dread? Yes, dread, even terror—that the game could only be won the way that he played it for a little while and then—well, he'd have to surrender a bit, and then a bit more, and more and more and more, till finally—well, he couldn't think about that without feeling sick to his stomach."[110]

Because of the mutilation, he would also be very readily recognizable by a witness, victim, or collaborator in crimes that he might commit. He conveys the complexity of his situation when he tells his john in the first of two scenes from the screenplay:

> I guess I've got no regular work, unless hustling is regular work. I think it's irregular work. Oh, I keep busy at it but it's not a thing you could call regular work. It's too irregular from a society point of view to be called regular. It's an illegal, outlaw occupation, so I got to be well-paid for it. You can understand that. I used to think nobody would want a hustler with one arm. But I was wrong. It don't throw them off me. [*Then, bitterly.*] A mutilation attracts them.[111]

A later scene finds Oliver, after the murder but prior to arrest, in a penthouse apartment in New York City talking to a john about his upbringing in Idaho.[112] In setting his price for the evening, Ollie reminds the client of his "special endowment of a mutilation." "I have one arm," he says repeatedly, and then adds, "It took me a while to find out that johns like a mutilation, as long as it's above the belt." But when this particular john attempts an additional act of intimacy in the form of a kiss, Ollie is quick to refuse it by covering his mouth and then saying, "Les, I'm not gay trade. In three years of hustling I've never let a man kiss me."[113] While the prohibition against kissing suggests his aversion to intimacy, the distinction he makes between hustling and "gay trade" demonstrates a denial of homosexuality, stipulating in his own mind, at least, the difference between desire and work, between sexual orientation and a business relationship.

Based on the careful delineation of his sexual role and his actions, it is possible to conceive a resultant avoidance of the emotional response to disgust, both physical and sexual, that Nussbaum and others have traced in their examinations. The passage above from the *One Arm* screenplay, when Ollie speaks privately with the female prostitute about his disgust for the blue movie, belies that assumption, but since that section is not developed until Williams adapts the short story for filming, one might argue that it was only in the later version that he attributed to Oliver a conflicted attitude toward the transgressive desire to which he was subject. However, the May 1942 draft of the story contains a very different and much more detailed treatment of the homicide, one that demonstrates Williams's early explorations of desire and disgust. This version never appeared in print, but it is useful for illustrating Williams's exploration of disgust in this narrative. In it, Williams constructs an extreme and graphic portrayal of his protagonist's disgust in response to the desire that he elicits in an illegal and homosexual setting; in this scene, however, the disgust is not connected, as it is elsewhere, to Oliver's mutilation.

The section is quoted here at some length for several reasons that are significant to my argument, not the least of which is that contains some very explicit sexual description that is unusual for Williams. It begins by describing when Ollie hitches a ride outside of Phoenix, Arizona, with "a queer who acted very excited;" the two travel out into the desert and park, where

> the man undressed so roughly he tore his clothes: his penis stood up scarlet as a dog's in the glaring desert sunlight. Oliver felt disgusted and undressed slowly, lingering deliberately over the trouser-buttons and clasp of the belt. The man came up impatiently behind him and began to run his hands along Oliver's back, cupping them over the massive, tight-muscled buttocks with frenzied, panting sounds and rubbing himself up against him.

Oliver is repulsed, and thinks to himself that he cannot go through with it, but he gets undressed and stares at the "purplish mountains while the dark little man crouched midget-like with his busy tongue and fingers between the columnar limbs of the former boxer." The mountains were like "spectators, austere and shocked, and the sky seemed to be full of eyes that looked down at the beastliness on the desert." After thinking to himself that he ought not to be bought this way, Ollie "suddenly kicked at the man whose mouth had just fastened leech-like upon his groin." He then planted one foot "on the prostrate belly before him: the other he brought down fiercely on the man's face and he ground the heel around on the mangled features until the man quit squirming." He returns to the car, taking the victim's pants and his money, and he drives off "with a clean, elated spirit, into the purplish mountains which now seemed friendly."[114] The passage is remarkable for several reasons: its use of nature, and specifically the desert; its graphic language; and, in connection with the published version of the story, its use of Oliver's thought process to inform the reader about the young man's emotional response to the experience.

The specific use of the language of disgust is much in evidence, and it is very clearly connected to his john's "dirty" body, his erect penis, the sounds and physical expressions of his desire, and, as we have already seen elsewhere, the connection of this desire to his role as prostitute: "I'm not to be bought like this and used by people to satisfy dirty instincts."[115] Shockingly, it is the violent act he commits, in this case a very physical one that might engender more disgust in a reader than does the sexual description that precedes it, that frees Oliver of his negative feelings. And nature agrees with him, for while the mountains had been "shocked" by the oral sex and the sky "full of eyes" that condemned it, the murder and subsequent robbery of the excited "queer" renders him a "clean, elated spirit" and the mountains "friendly." It is important to note that consensual sodomy and lewd or lascivious acts were not decriminalized in Arizona until 2001 (although reduced to a misdemeanor in 1977) and the statute describes the offense as follows: "A person who knowingly and without force commits, in any unnatural manner, any lewd or lascivious act upon or with the body or any part or member thereof of a male or female adult, with the intent of arousing, appealing to, or gratifying the lust, passion, or sexual desires of either of such persons, is guilty of a misdemeanor."[116] Whether or not Williams was aware of the specifics of the state law in which he set this version of the murder, the contrast he develops here between the condemnation of the sex act and the purity of the post-homicidal Oliver suggest the author's recognition that oral copulation, even consensual, may prompt extreme but nonetheless warranted (at least within the tale's context) repulsion.

The section of this draft that describes Oliver's confession also differs quite substantially from the printed text: in the latter version, it takes up no more than an utterly unrevealing sentence: "'I knew when they left him alone with me that he would be sorry,' Oliver said in his statement to the police."[117] The draft typescript, on the other hand, expands the details of the arrest and includes Oliver's extended account: "Sullenly he said, 'Yes, I killed the man. I guess I wanted his money.—Why?—I was broke that's why.—But that's not all the reason.—The son of a bitch was dirty. Sure, you get accustomed to people being dirty. But this was worse on account of it was right out there in the open, the sun still up, the light showing every goddamn detail of it!—It got me sore and I kicked him and let him have it! That's about all I can say."[118] It is legally and linguistically useful to connect Oliver's response to his lascivious john with prevailing cultural attitudes about the preservation of morality in the age of sex crime panics. Some concerns for public safety may have been warranted (the prevention of perversions that might harm children, for example), but paranoia paired with issues of national security made for unnecessary policies designed to prevent the "infiltration" of individuals or groups deemed dangerous or unpatriotic.

While the draft versions of the story "One Arm" include Oliver's revulsions about pornography and his condemnation of homosexual sex, especially when it is animalistic and anonymous, the published version of "One Arm" broadens the scope of Oliver's own transgressions before the accident while cutting sections that reveal his attitudes about them. These changes result in the recession of parts of Oliver's identity, sexual or otherwise, for the final narrative, stripped of many details, render a more private Oliver: by removing many of the references to his character's emotions, Williams performs an editorial amputation that makes the protagonist as unknowable to the readers as he is to the johns he attracts and the detectives who arrest him. "I knew when they left him alone with me that he would be sorry" is enough to establish premeditation for murder, but it does not reveal his motivation or the disgust that moves him to violence. The drafts do provide these details, however, and thus serve as a back story, not only for Oliver but for Williams's thematic explorations during his composition process. It is not possible to make a definitive argument about the extent to which the previous passages represent Williams's own views or the pressure he felt to uphold social norms, and indeed ideological clarity does not often befit creative texts that are ripe with ambiguity.

If we look beyond his imaginative texts, we find evidence in one of his letters from roughly the same period that his attitude about homosexual sex was anything but the kind of disgust he has Oliver express. A letter that Williams wrote to friend Donald Windham in 1940 includes a long description of the relationship that Williams had begun with dancer and model Kip Kiernan in July 1940 in Provincetown, Massachusetts. Though brief, the love affair with Kip was for Williams a significant emotional experience, and more than two decades later he dedicated the 1967 paperback reissue of *One Arm and Other Stories* to Kip's memory.[119] The letter to Windham is striking in the ways that it describes the physical intimacy between the two men in explicit and then loving terms, ending a passage that describes their sexual act in graphic details that include sounds and odors, but ends with an atmospheric expansion and connection to nature that is similar to the "One Arm" draft of Oliver's desert getaway. Williams describes the post-coital scene as follows: "The bed seems to be enormous. Pacific, Atlantic, the North American continent.— A wind has blown the door open, the sky's full of stars. High tide is in and water laps under the wharf." The shame described this time results from Kip's declaration of affection, "I like you, Tenny," Williams describing his lover as "hoarse—embarrassed—ashamed of such intimate speech!—And I laugh for I know that he loves me!—That nobody ever loved me before so completely. I feel the truth in his body." The letter ends, however, with the recognition that all he has described to Windham exposes him in a way that could be dangerous: "Please keep this letter and be very careful with it. It's only for people like us who have gone beyond shame!"[120] Windham published the letter in 1976 in a privately published limited edition in Verona, Italy, then commercially in the United States one year later. Williams granted permission for the first publication without realizing that he had signed over all rights, and the two old friends became embroiled in a public feud. Although Williams was most upset by what Lahr calls Windham's "sour critical commentary" about the creative work, this series of events speaks volumes to the tension between private and public experience and expression.[121]

Malamud Smith contends that you "can't understand privacy without understanding shame."[122] Speaking even more specifically about the connections among shame, sex, and privacy, she argues that the paradox involved in revealing details about one's sex life is that "you cannot declaim your sexual truth because the very quality that endows it with sexiness is that it is veiled, held away from language and public exposure—private."[123] By cataloging one's sexual fantasies or preferences, not to mention histories, they lose their personal meaning. Furthermore, she argues, that "fiction preserves privacy, and by so doing allows us to expose our most personal experiences without harming them."[124] These suppositions would seem to render any easy assessment of Williams's attitudes about sexuality and privacy difficult if not impossible, but one of the goals here is to problematize previous attempts to determine his personal relationship with shame about his own homosexuality.

Malamud Smith's discussion also connects the topic of shame to identity, claiming that "shame is an early warning system we carry within that alerts us when we are in danger of cutting an important tie," telling us "loud and clear when we are at risk of revealing something about ourselves we fear will harm a connection with others important to us—isolate us from the group on whom our survival depends."[125] Her argument helps to contextualize the previous assessments of Williams's own attitudes about his sexuality in several ways. The assertion, for example, that Williams concerned himself with success and public acclaim has merit, of course, but it is too simple to say that because he wanted to be produced, published, and popular as a writer, his work often seemed to condemn the sexual outlaws he created. However, if he perceived that the cloak of "fiction" would not keep his life and his sexual activities private, it could be that shame would be an appropriate response of recognizing the "risk of revealing something" that might "harm a connection with others." The very real possibility that the law might also contribute to this shame by imposing the legal isolation of arrest, jail, and publication of offense, is another element in which the fear of being ostracized from society might play a part.

In the published text of "One Arm," the story moves to its resolution by reminding readers of the many men Oliver impacted during close encounters on the streets and hotel rooms of America's cities: after the arrest, the "face of the one-armed youth was shot from newspapers into the startled eyes of men who had known him in all those places Oliver had passed through in his aimless travels."[126] But the 1942 draft infuses the reference with more detail and more emotion, which signals the shift in the story from Oliver's alienation to the communion and intimacy he will experience in prison: "In all the cities he'd been in his picture and crime were published. In other places, smaller, which he'd passed through, a man who was drinking coffee and reading the news would suddenly find a tightness around his heart as he saw that face and remembered where he had known it. A man on a train would gasp and look again. A man in his office, in some big city building, would look and brood and shake his head in sorrow."[127] As the men react with emotion to the news about Oliver's arrest, with brooding, a gasp, tightness around the heart, the reader is pointed to something unexpected—emotional connection with one of Williams's most disturbing of illegal bodies: a maimed murderer without a moral center. After Oliver has arrived on death row, when the law can do no more to him than carry out his sentence, "One Arm" moves toward personal revelation and narrative resolution. His private life is made public, and he is suddenly connected, his "face" with their "startled eyes," to all the men he has known. This passage also raises the question of whether the "tightness" or the "gasp" reflects feeling for Oliver or fear, this previous association reminding them of their own sexual practices and the exposure they may be subject to because of past association with a convicted criminal.

As Oliver awaits execution, his former sexual companions reach out to him in letters written on "fine white paper, some of them faintly scented," communications that illustrate the shift among his admirers from sexual attraction to a search for a more meaningful connection. There was "something about him, they wrote, not only the physical thing, important as that was, which had made him haunt their minds since."[128] For some the search was spiritual, for "he became the archetype of the Savior Upon the Cross who had taken upon himself the sins of their world to be washed and purified in his blood and passion."[129] The idea that sins could be "washed and purified" in "blood and passion" resonates in this context, for it recalls the sex act, alluding to the public discourse of the "crime against nature" with its dependence on moral and religious tropes of filth and purity. The following section from the 1942 draft version has Oliver continuing to keep his distance from the men, even as the passage casts them in a sympathetic light: "Once he said to a jailer, Did you ever have anything to do with queers? The man replied Hell, no!—An I don't associate with rattlesnakes neither!—Well, said Oliver, they're a funny bunch!—What are they like? asked the jailer." He begins to tell the jailor the "crazy things" that men have asked him to do, but then stops, for it "seemed to him now that he ought to keep their secrets. Gradually in his powerful, ox-like heart a feeling of human warmth, of something like gratitude had begun to appear."[130] The unpublished section makes explicit Oliver's complex attitudes about the men who allowed him to make a living and who have now reached out to him, and this passage shows his movement from considering them as his meal ticket to thinking of them as human beings whose sexual secrets he ought to keep. Even as he decides to protect their privacy, he reveals himself to them, and in the published text, the focus is on Oliver's revelations about himself.

Oliver responds to the men who have written him, "at first with a laborious stiffness," but we see him quickly transformed into one of Williams's compassionate artist figures: "the sentences gathered momentum as springs that clear out a channel" and "began to flow out almost expressively and to ring with the crudely eloquent backwoods speech of the South, to which had been added salty idioms of the underworld he had moved in, and the road, and the sea." His language thus retains the color of his experience and even its illegality and transience, but what was formerly "crude" is now "crudely eloquent." Most significantly, however, an internal mental and emotional change occurs, for "as a stone gathers heat when lain among coals, the doomed man's brain grew warmer and warmer with a sense of communion."[131] His confessions to them include his acknowledgment that the identity he had forged as a transient was as a prostitute, not as a homosexual: "I picked up strangers in every city I went to. I had experience with them which only meant money to me and a place to shack up for the night and liquor and food." The letters, he tells those who have written to him, prove that he "meant something important to hundreds of people" and that he had "run up a debt of some kind. Not money but feelings." This recognition offers him a revived sense of his own self and purpose: "If I had known then, I mean when I was outside, that such true feelings could even be found in strangers, I mean of the kind that I picked up for a living, I guess I might have felt there was more to live for."[132] The published story reminds the reader that it is Oliver's ultimate detachment from life, living out his endgame on death row, that brings about the change that once again makes him whole—if not physically, then emotionally. It is striking that he is both surrounded by law and free of it: "In his stifling cubicle there was very little to do while waiting for death and time enough with the impetus of disaster for the boy's malleable nature to be remodeled still again, and the instrument of this process became the letters."[133] One final opportunity for identity formation and community connection presents itself to him.

That his former johns may represent the man he has murdered means that the correspondence serves as atonement for the crime of murder even as it psychologically decriminalizes the sexual acts they performed together and elevates those physical actions to a level of equality and respect that was not previously available to Oliver. Before imprisonment he had thought of his maimed body as something that, being broken, "was only fit for abuse," and the "excitement he stirred in others had been incomprehensible and disgusting to him." But the letters from men "who couldn't stop thinking about him" had "begun to revive his self-interest." Armed with the compassion of others, Oliver begins to adopt an attitude of self-love. "Armed" again, at least figuratively, with the compassion of others, Oliver adopts an attitude of self-love which, fittingly, takes an erotic and ironic turn as his "one large hand made joyless love to his body." We are reminded, however, that loss looms large and unyielding on death row: "too late, this resurrection."[134]

It is at this point, resurrected too late, that Oliver receives a visit from a young Lutheran minister whose attraction to Oliver is matched only by his fear of it. In this encounter we come close to seeing who Oliver is, not just what he does, as he seeks to use the visitor in his self-initiation into feelings and sexual desire. He asks the visitor for a rubdown, first with a towel, and then, as Oliver lowers his shorts, he directs him to proceed softly and to rub with his hands. But what might seem to be the first acknowledgment of Oliver's homosexual desire is complicated by his repetition of what he had written to his johns: that it is not desire but indebtedness that motivates him, the letters on the shelf reminding him of "bills from people I owe. Not money, but feelings." He goes on, however, to say that for "three whole years I went all over the country stirring up feelings without feeling nothing myself. Now that's all changed and I have feelings too. I am lonely and bottled up the same as you are."[135] When the minister flees, Oliver hopes that perhaps he will return. He does not, and the narrator explains that "Oliver died with all his debts unpaid" but with "a good deal more dignity than he had given his jailors to expect of him."[136] He expires with the letters closed between his thighs "in a desperate vise," a macabre embrace of the compassion that has been shown him.

Although the short fiction provided a creative space for Williams to explore homosexuality with considerable candidness, this discussion of "One Arm" demonstrates that his prose from this period is not without its opaqueness. Indeed, ambiguities about sexual identity create textual interest, but they also point to Williams's awareness of a complex cultural and political climate that valued clear delineations of sexual identity at a time when such delineations were being exposed as simplistic and unrealistic. In 1977, Ren Draya described "One Arm" as an "early catalogue of Williams's concerns: an openly homosexual theme, the fascination with mutilation and its attendant psychic loss, the power of words (represented by the letters) to effect change, the theme of guilt and atonement, and the importance of sex both as a means of human communication and as a channel to awaken acceptance of one's existence."[137] Two decades later, Jürgen C. Wolter reiterates Draya's assessment by noting one of the major problems that had confronted the critics in their assessment of the quality and significance of Williams's short fiction: that they "have to accept homosexuality as a serious and genuine expression of humanity."[138] But "One Arm" also reminds us that law's attempts to regulate sexual activity and sexual identity have all too often resulted in assaults on privacy, and that the need to keep identity shielded from the very communities we inhabit can cripple our development and our social integration, leading to real or figurative imprisonment or death.

We might newly see the tension in Williams's texts as an exploration of what Martha Nussbaum calls for: a commitment to the respect of fellow citizens that "requires endowing the other with life and purpose, rather than dirt and dross, with human dignity rather than with foulness"; a "shift in the imagination" that that will mean that the "person who practices the politics of humanity never retreats to a position from which the equal humanity of others can't be seen."[139] Nussbaum's very recent argument for a "politics of humanity" promotes the transformation of current laws in the area of sexual orientation, the advance of the "piece-meal and local" non-discrimination law with the adoption of "a federal nondiscrimination statute that will do for sexual orientation what Title XI did for gender."[140] In her conclusion she argues that the law has been relatively slow-moving in this area, and that to date, the impetus toward a politics of humanity has come "perhaps above all, from the arts, which have given us models of dignity, equality, and joy that can hardly fail to work upon people's insides in ways that prompt change."[141]

Williams's many texts, featuring characters not easily dismissed or rejected as "other," challenged the public discourse of disgust that supported the criminalization of diverse sexual activity. His work confirmed that compassion and acceptance are not easy, and that fear and loss all too often close us off from human communion. But it also demonstrated to readers and audience members that the pathway to mutual respect, when carved out by sympathy and imagination, can lead to a change of heart and mind, shifting the balance of opinion toward a change in law. He consistently challenged the public discourse of disgust that supported the criminalization of diverse sexual activity by reminding his readers and his theater audiences that compassion and acceptance are not always easy, and that fear and loss all too often close us off from human communion. But by creating situations and characters who cannot ultimately be rejected as "other," he insists that we stay in the fight for liberty and equality for all.

NOTES

1. Gore Vidal, "Introduction" to *Collected Stories* by Tennessee Williams (New York: New Directions, 1985), xx.

2. Savran, *Communists, Cowboys, and Queers*, 83.

3. John Clum, "'Something Cloudy, Something Clear': Homophobic Discourse in Tennessee Williams," in *Displacing Homophobia: Gay Male Perspectives in Literature and Culture*, eds. Ronald R. Butters, John M. Clum, and Michael Moon (Durham, NC: Duke University Press, 1989), 150.

4. Claude J. Summers, *Gay Fictions Wilde to Stonewall: Studies in a Male Homosexual Literary Tradition* (New York: Continuum, 1990), 15, 17.

5. Summers, *Gay Fictions*, 15, 17.

6. Summers, *Gay Fictions,* 24.
7. Richards, *The Sodomy Cases,* 16.
8. Corber, *Homosexuality in Cold War America,* 11.
9. Corber, *Homosexuality in Cold War America,* 64.
10. Dennis Vannatta, *Tennessee Williams: A Study of the Short Fiction* (Boston: Twayne Publishers, 1988), x.
11. Vannatta, *Tennessee Williams,* 81.
12. James Kelly, "Madness and Decay," *New York Times Book Review,* 02 Jan 1955, reprinted in Vannatta, *Tennessee Williams,* 113–114.
13. William H. Peden, "Mad Pilgrimage: The Short Stories of Tennessee Williams," *Studies in Short Fiction* 1 (Summer 1964), reprinted in Vannatta, *Tennessee Williams,* 116–123.
14. Edward A. Sklepowich, "In Pursuit of the Lyric Quarry: The Image of the Homosexual in Tennessee Williams' Prose Fiction," in *Tennessee Williams: A Tribute*, ed. Jac Tharpe (Jackson: University of Mississippi, 1977), 526.
15. Jürgen C Wolter, "Tennessee Williams's Fiction," in *Tennessee Williams: A Guide to Research and Performance*, ed. Philip C. Kolin (Westport, CT: Greenwood Press, 1998), 223.
16. Solove, *Understanding Privacy*, 12–38.
17. Solove, *Understanding Privacy,* 15–29.
18. Wolter, "Tennessee Williams's Fiction," 227.
19. Michael S. D. Hooper, *Sexual Politics in the Work of Tennessee Williams: Desire over Protest* (Cambridge, UK: Cambridge University Press, 2012), 97.
20. Clum, "'Something Cloudy,'" 150.
21. Clum, "'Something Cloudy,'" 151–152.
22. John Clum, *Still Acting Gay: Male Homosexuality in Modern Drama* (New York: St. Martin's Press, 2000), 121–22.
23. Savran, *Communists, Cowboys, and Queers,* 83.
24. Nicholas de Jongh, *Not in Front of an Audience: Homosexuality on Stage* (London and New York: Routledge, 1992), 16.
25. Clum, "'Something Cloudy,'" 149.
26. Clum, "'Something Cloudy,'" 149.
27. Clum, "'Something Cloudy,'" 152.
28. Clum, "'Something Cloudy,'" 154.
29. Clum, "'Something Cloudy,'" 154.
30. Clum, "'Something Cloudy,'" 155.
31. Ren Draya, "The Fiction of Tennessee Williams," *Tennessee Williams: A Tribute*, ed. Jac Tharpe (Jackson: University Press of Mississippi, 1977), 654–655.
32. Solove, *Understanding Privacy*, 34.
33. Clum, "'Something Cloudy,'" 155.
34. Corber, *Homosexuality in Cold War America,* 107–108.
35. Corber, *Homosexuality in Cold War America,* 110.
36. Corber, *Homosexuality in Cold War America,* 112.
37. Corber, *Homosexuality in Cold War America,* 113.
38. Savran, *Communists, Cowboys, and Queers,* 113–114.
39. Savran, *Communists, Cowboys, and Queers,* 84–88.
40. Tennessee Williams, *Hard Candy: Collected Stories* (New York: New Directions, 1985), 335.
41. Savran, *Communists, Cowboys, and Queers,* 113.
42. Corber, *Homosexuality in Cold War America,* 108.
43. Corber, *Homosexuality in Cold War America,* 112–113.
44. Corber, *Homosexuality in Cold War America,* 113.
45. William Ian Miller, *The Anatomy of Disgust* (Cambridge, MA: Harvard University Press, 1997), 194–196.
46. Williams, "Hard Candy" *Collected Stories*, 336–337.
47. Miller, *The Anatomy of Disgust,* 136–137.

48. Williams, "Hard Candy," *Collected Stories*, 341.
49. Ibid., 342–343.
50. Williams, *Hard Candy*, 343.
51. Ibid., 345.
52. Ibid., 345.
53. Ibid., 345.
54. Ibid., 346.
55. Williams, *Letters to Donald Windham*, 27.
56. Williams, *Notebooks*, 399.
57. Williams, *Notebooks*, 405.
58. Tennessee Williams, "One Arm," *Collected Stories*, 176.
59. Williams, "One Arm," *Collected Stories*, 177.
60. Williams, "One Arm," *Collected Stories*, 179.
61. Brian M. Peters, "Queer Semiotics of Expression: Gothic Language and Homosexual Destruction in Tennessee Williams's 'One Arm' and 'Desire and the Black Masseur'" *Tennessee Williams Annual Review* 8 (2006), 109–121.
62. Peters, "Queer Semiotics of Expression," 113.
63. Williams, "One Arm," *Collected Stories*, 175–176.
64. Williams, "One Arm," *Collected Stories*, 176.
65. Williams, *Letters to Donald Windham*, 175–176.
66. Williams, *Selected Letters, vol. II*, 139.
67. Eskridge, *Dishonorable Passions*, 98, 100.
68. Leverich, *Tom*, 424–425, 453.
69. Williams, *Selected Letters, vol. II*, 139n.
70. Williams, *Selected Letters, vol. II*, 211.
71. Hooper, *Sexual Politics in the Work of Tennessee Williams*, 103.
72. Hooper, *Sexual Politics in the Work of Tennessee Williams*, 98.
73. Eskridge, *Dishonorable Passions*, 41.
74. Chauncey, *Gay New York*, 179.
75. D'Emilio and Freedman, *Intimate Matters*, 172.
76. Peters, "Queer Semiotics of Expression," 113.
77. Williams, "One Arm," *Collected Stories*, 175.
78. Raymond-Jean Frontain, "Tennessee Williams and the 'Arkansas Ozark Way,'" *Tennessee Williams Annual Review* 9 (2007), 80.
79. Williams, "One Arm," *Collected Stories*, 177.
80. Williams, "One Arm," *Collected Stories*, 176–177.
81. Williams, "One Arm," *Collected Stories*, 178.
82. Williams, "One Arm," *Collected Stories*, 176.
83. Ursula Vogel, "Whose Property? The Double Standard of Adultery in Nineteenth-Century Law," in *Regulating Womanhood: Historical Essays on Marriage, Motherhood and Sexuality*, ed. Carol Smart (London: Routledge, 1992), 147–148.
84. Richard A. Posner and Katharine B. Silbaugh, *A Guide to America's Sex Laws* (Chicago: University of Chicago Press), 103, 106.
85. Vogel, "Whose Property?" 148–149.
86. Tennessee Williams, "One Arm" [story], May 1942, Tennessee Williams Collection. Harry Ransom Research Center, University of Texas at Austin.
87. Williams, "One Arm," *Collected Stories*, 176–177.
88. Miller, *The Anatomy of Disgust*, 27.
89. Miller, *The Anatomy of Disgust*, 105.
90. Williams, "One Arm," *Collected Stories*, 176.
91. Williams, "One Arm" [story].
92. I use italics to indicate the expansion of the short text into a full-length screenplay.
93. Richard Nelson, "Introduction," in *Stopped Rocking and Other Screenplays*, Tennessee Williams (New York: New Directions, 1984), vii. An adaptation of the prose

version of "One Arm" was one of the first off-off-Broadway theater productions at Ellen Stewart's Café La MaMa in 1961.

94. Tennessee Williams, "One Arm," in *Stopped Rocking and Other Screenplays* (New York: New Directions, 1984), 197.
95. Nussbaum, *From Disgust to Humanity*, 8.
96. Nussbaum, *From Disgust to Humanity*, 10–11.
97. Nussbaum, *From Disgust to Humanity*, 10–11.
98. The film version lists the protagonist as "Ollie" rather than Oliver, and uses the short version of the name throughout.
99. Williams, "One Arm," in *Stopped Rocking*, 216.
100. Williams, "One Arm," in *Stopped Rocking*, 216.
101. Williams, "One Arm" [story], 176.
102. Albert D. Klassen, Colin J. Williams, and Eugene E. Levitt, *Sex and Morality in the U.S.: An Empirical Enquiry under the Auspices of The Kinsey Institute*, ed. and with an introduction by Hubert J. O'Gorman (Middleton, CT: Wesleyan University Press, 1989), 17.
103. Williams, "One Arm" [story], 176.
104. Williams, "One Arm" [story].
105. Andras Angyal, "Disgust and Related Aversions," *The Journal of Abnormal and Social Psychology* 36.3 (1941): 394.
106. Tennessee Williams, "One Arm," screenplay draft, Tennessee Williams Collection, Rare Book and Manuscript Library, Columbia University Library.
107. Williams, "One Arm," in *Stopped Rocking*, 202–203.
108. Williams, "One Arm" [story].
109. Williams, "One Arm," in *Stopped Rocking*, 228–230.
110. Williams, "One Arm," in *Stopped Rocking*, 253.
111. Williams, "One Arm," in *Stopped Rocking*, 220.
112. Williams, "One Arm," in *Stopped Rocking*, 243. The location change of Ollie's birthplace from Arkansas to the Mountain West is an unusual one for Williams, and while there is no direct evidence that the insertion of Idaho was done purposely to call attention to the state's complex legal history concerning consensual sodomy during the 1960s, it is worth noting how Idaho lawmakers dealt with changes to the state's sodomy laws during the period. During the 1950s, the American Law Institute in Philadelphia created a Model Penal Code whose final draft was adopted in 1962 and that included a recommendation to states for decriminalizing consensual sodomy. Idaho's Legislative Council, through the work of a special subcommittee, turned its attention to criminal code revisions in the years following Stonewall. The committee recommended adopting the Model Penal Code with only minor modifications, and with few objections and in a short amount of time, both chambers had approved the changes and Governor Cecil Andrus signed them into law in March 1971. Idaho was the third state to decriminalize consensual sodomy; however, a subsequent challenge that occurred soon after the new code went into effect prompted the legislature to repeal the new code and reinstate the old one. Although the challenge had originated with members of the Church of the Latter-Day Saints and their specific objection to the legalization of fornication, adultery, and "homosexuality," the revised code included provisions regulating firearm possession, bad checks, and the theft of animals. As Eskridge tells it, "Once gun owners, prosecutors, ranchers, and Mormons came together, there was tremendous pressure on the legislature to revisit the new criminal code" (182). Also see Eskridge, *Dishonorable Passions*, 176–177, 182–184.
113. Williams, "One Arm," in *Stopped Rocking*, 247–249.
114. Williams, "One Arm" [story].
115. Williams, "One Arm" [story].
116. Quoted in Nussbaum, *From Disgust to Humanity*, 62.
117. Williams, "One Arm," *Collected Stories*, 178.
118. Williams, "One Arm" [story].

119. Kip broke it off with Williams within weeks of their first meeting, not long after Kip had introduced Williams to a girlfriend who had warned Kip that he was in danger of "turning" homosexual and that Kip himself "had seen enough of the world to know that he had to resist it." From Williams, *Memoirs*. Kip went on to marry but he was diagnosed with a brain tumor in 1944 and died at the age of twenty-six.
120. Williams, *Letters to Donald Windham*, 10.
121. Lahr, *Mad Pilgrimage*, 546. Also see Williams, *Letters to Donald Windham*, 10.
122. Malamud Smith, *Private Matters*, 119.
123. Malamud Smith, *Private Matters*, 121.
124. Malamud Smith, *Private Matters*, 121.
125. Malamud Smith, *Private Matters*, 123.
126. Williams, "One Arm," *Collected Stories*, 178.
127. "One Arm" [story].
128. Williams, "One Arm," *Collected Stories*, 178.
129. Williams, "One Arm," *Collected Stories*, 179.
130. "One Arm" [story].
131. Williams, "One Arm," *Collected Stories*, 180.
132. Williams, "One Arm," *Collected Stories*, 181.
133. Williams, "One Arm," *Collected Stories*, 179.
134. Williams, "One Arm," *Collected Stories*, 182.
135. Williams, "One Arm," *Collected Stories*, 187.
136. Williams, "One Arm," *Collected Stories*, 188.
137. Draya, "The Fiction of Tennessee Williams," 648.
138. Wolter, "Tennessee Williams's Fiction," 227.
139. Nussbaum, *From Disgust to Humanity*, 50–51.
140. Nussbaum, *From Disgust to Humanity*, 208.
141. Nussbaum, *From Disgust to Humanity*, 205.

THREE
The Fugitive Kind

In 1937, Williams's paternal aunt, Isabel Williams Brownlow, wrote to him about her aspirations for his writing career. Acknowledging her faith in his talent and her certainty that he would go on to achieve success as the "world" defines it, she urged him to focus on his ability to "lift me—to purer living—to noble ideals—to be constructive—in a word, to be successful as God estimates success." In her opinion, "there is so much that is sordid and unclean in the literature of today," and there is "nothing sadder than to see a real gift dragged in the muck and mire of the present day."[1] Eight years later, with the debut production of *The Glass Menagerie*, her prediction about his success as the world defines it came to pass, for he would never after need to supplement his writing income with other work. His aunt died in 1938, so she did not live to witness either the success or his subsequent preoccupation with what she very likely would have considered the "sordid and unclean." His aunt's evocation of God's estimation of success was her attempt to encourage her nephew to honor and support the Christian values he was raised with; although his preoccupation with the sordid would most likely have displeased her, there is ample evidence that he was always greatly concerned with it.

In an interview conducted by Don Ross in 1957, originally published in the *New York Herald Tribune* on the occasion of the Broadway debut of *Orpheus Descending*, Williams took up the issue of morality and, specifically, his attitudes about the "sordid." When responding to the reporter's question of whether he filled his plays with sordid characters, he hissed the word "sordid" as if, the reporter noted, "he didn't think much of the word." "I don't think deeply troubled people are sordid," Williams claimed, and it became clear to Ross that "the more Mr. Williams thought of the word sordid as applied to his people, the more preposterous it became." Williams explained: "I think pettiness and meanness is sordid. I would never choose a person of that sort for a main protagonist because they don't interest me." When asked if he is a moralist, he continued the distinction that he had begun to make between those who are "troubled" and those he considers "mean": "I'm not polemical, but I have a distinct attitude toward good and evil in life and people. . . . I think I regard hypocrisy and mendacity as almost the cardinal sins. It seems they are the ones to which I am most hostile. I think that deliberate, conscienceless mendacity, the acceptance of falsehood and hypocrisy, is the most dangerous of all sins. . . . But I don't want to pretend that I'm a great moral evangelist. I'm an entertainer and a playwright."[2] Trusting a writer's self-assessment (or anyone's self-assessment on moral positioning, for that matter) is complicated, but Williams's comments here are quite defensible when we look at the record of his work. Nancy Tischler calls Williams an "amoral moralist, suggesting that he believes in God, but makes fun of organized religion and of the Puritan ethic"; Christianity is "a source of his symbolism, and often the key to his story." But "Christianity, in his treatment, acquires Williamsian features," and, as "the Old Testament was for his grandfather, the Bible, as a whole, is to him an allegory; but unlike the old clergyman, he has no world view." In her conclusion she states what she considers to be a summation of his value system:

> His ultimate ethic is *sympathize*. In a universe that rolls on its inevitable way, living in a society that we cannot change, we are powerless to influence or even understand our fate. The best we can do is face our doom with fortitude and reach out our hands in sympathy to our doomed fellow-beings.[3]

As for his political engagement and its relationship to a moral vision, it would become commonplace to acknowledge that although many of Williams's most compelling characters resided on society's margins and raged against injustice, their trauma and tragedy were conceived as personal and psychological, not cultural. Although the troubled people he creates are often destroyed by violence, perpetrated by themselves or by others, the judgment that such violence might seem to impose is often itself open to judgment within the context of the work, for Williams is masterful at exposing the shades of words and actions that often render them ambiguous. In "One Arm," the violent murder that Oliver commits is punished by lawful execution, but the community he finds among the "lawless" men he associated with before his arrest eases his journey to the electric chair, and the story's conclusion is one more deeply tied to human connection than to human extinction. Oliver's unclaimed body becomes experimental fodder for medical students, but not before those who will cut him open are "somewhat abashed" by his physical nobility and purity, even in death. Such is the expression of morality's value in

Williams, for the evocation of sympathy for people or things labeled as sordid often signals moral redemption.

Tennessee Williams: A Tribute, a large volume of essays published in 1977, marks a transitional period in Williams studies: it presented a wide range of critics and perspectives and what the preface calls "a renewal of interest in the work of Tennessee Williams;" significantly, it reveals the increased complexity of critical viewpoints and the expansion of attention to his prose and poetry. But although this tribute volume includes study of a wider range of primary material than the narrow selection of texts that had up to that point been the main focus of scholarly study, an emphasis on the early major plays is still evident, as is the conception of the personal, the poetic, and the universal qualities that Williams was already known and valued for. For example, Esther M. Jackson identifies the "dramatic world" of Tennessee Williams as "the symbolization of a personal vision of reality, the concretization of the singular imagination of a poet," while S. Alan Chesler reaffirms the universality of the work:

> Another reason for Williams's popularity is his plays' direct appeal to basic human emotions. This appeal results from both Williams' concentrated treatment of man's purely emotional response to his environment and the original, often symbolistic, means he employs to dramatize this concern. In communicating his conception of modern man's existential problems, Williams has utilized a wide range of theatrical and literary techniques which convey underlying human feelings that traditional, realistic drama could not present.[4]

While these assessments are certainly accurate, the volume's attention to the personal, the poetic, and the emotional elements in Williams's creative works meant that the range of perspectives on his work would remain limited and that his canon of valued texts would remain quite small.

However, the "renewal of interest" that marks the appearance of *Tennessee Williams: A Tribute* coincided with a wave of biographical and autographical material that found its way into print during this period and that began with his *Memoirs*, which was published in 1975 and turned a spotlight on him that had never been extinguished but had dimmed in intensity during the late 1960s. In a period marked by civil strife nationally and internationally, the impulse to define oneself or others in political terms was powerful, and Williams and his reputation developed in new directions in part because of the context in which the personal documentation appeared. His apparent lack of interest in positioning himself in relationship to party politics or affecting election results at the polls is supported by anecdotes throughout his *Memoirs*, for his claims of political and even revolutionary interest in the transformation of society are always vague; he describes a visit from a German television crew intent on interviewing him, describing how he "cut through the prepared questions to talk about the atrocity of the American involvement in Vietnam, about Nixon's total lack of honesty and of a moral sense," and of his "devotion to the cause of Senator McGovern."[5] In an interview with George Whitmore in 1976, the playwright himself insists that "all good art is essentially revolutionary."[6] Such claims of political interest and commitment are not necessarily contestable, but they are also not demonstrable examples of political intention or action.

In *Memoirs* he wrote of his political past, claiming to have voted only once, when he came of age while working at the International Shoe Company in St. Louis in the early 1930s, and when he had already embraced socialism. It was to socialism with a small "s," however, that he attributed whatever faithfulness he felt toward a particular political leaning. As Leverich writes, "Tom considered himself a socialist and believed all his life that capitalism must inevitably give way to some form of enlightened socialism."[7] The vagueness of this description, as well as its ascription to the man (Tom), not the artist (Tennessee), is noted by Hooper, who remarks that Williams's abysmal voting record is countered by the fact that the Federal Bureau of Investigation was "sufficiently interested in his potentially transgressive politics and sexuality" to keep a file on him.[8] While it was not unusual for an author of the postwar period to have an FBI file, Hooper's statement connects Williams's "potentially transgressive politics" to "sexuality," suggesting that if Williams's life and work aroused suspicion sufficient for the FBI to keep track of him, his legal transgressions were likely to be sexual in nature, his influence on the age related to identity politics rather than to issues of state.

Other personal texts found their way into print not long after *Memoirs* was published, and helped to round out the self-portrait that sparked renewed interest in the man and his work, interest that has not since wavered but only grown. In 1977, Windham edited the collection of letters he had received from Williams in the years 1940–1965; another friend, Richard Leavitt, published his photo-biography, *The World of Tennessee Williams* in 1978 (revised and updated in a new version in 2011). Also that year, his selected essays were collected in a volume titled *Where I Live: Selected Essays* by New Directions (updated and released as *New Selected Essays: Where I Live* in 2009). Williams's own work—plays, stories, poetry, screenplays, and essays—has been published by New Directions, individually and in collections, at a rate that has seemed in some ways, since his death, to deny his demise, especially with a tradition of publishing "new texts." On its website, New Directions claims Tennessee Williams as a "cornerstone" of the firm, which publishes "everything he wrote of his storied career. He is also our single bestselling author."[9] As such, then, he has continued to challenge his reviewers and critics to reassess his prodigious output and to contextualize him in new ways. His death in 1983 brought a new wave of works about him, both personal and scholarly: *Tennessee Williams: An Intimate Biography*, written by brother

Dakin Williams and Shepherd Mead; an entry in the *Dictionary of Literary Biography* in 1984; and the first complete and authorized biography of his life, *The Kindness of Strangers: The Life of Tennessee Williams*, by Donald Spoto, in 1985.

Scholarly work in several areas of cultural studies sparked an increased interest in Williams among a new generation of scholars looking to understand his place in shaping and reflecting midcentury American life and theater. The parameters that had been so useful in determining his significance and that had shaped a critically coherent perception of his work as lyrical, symbolic, and universal, however, continued to influence the teaching and stage productions of his work, even as the expansion of topics to be considered marked increased diversity of theatrical and scholarly perspectives. In 1984, British critic C. W. E. Bigsby, in the second of his three-volume survey of twentieth-century American drama, was among the first to push for a more comprehensive analysis of Williams; he did so, paradoxically, by drawing on the previous generation's dichotomous comparison of Williams to his prolific and successful midcentury companion, Arthur Miller. Bigsby begins by aligning the postwar legacies of Williams and Miller, whose periods of apprenticeship as "political playwrights" in the 1930s were transformed by the war, as the "pieties of pre-war America no longer seemed capable of sustaining the individual or the culture—though both writers were capable of invoking them, ironized by their own deepening sense of unease."[10] By adhering to the formulation that earlier reviewers and scholars had used to position Williams and Miller in opposition with each other, Bigsby argues for the distinction between the respective political investment each brought to his work: while Williams "largely turned away from a direct concern with social structures, seeing them simply as images of the facticity which threatened the necessary fictions of his characters," Miller was "stung into a defense of liberal values by the political persecutions of the 1950s."[11] Although Bigsby goes on to say that it is "hard to know just how deep Williams's radicalism went," he concludes that what is there is very personal: "there seems little in the way of an ideological conviction in his work" and his sympathies "are certainly with the outsider, the bohemian, the underclass, but not because they represent a revolutionary potential."[12]

On the other hand, Bigsby plants the seeds of what would become an important strain of criticism about Williams, for he argues that the early work came directly out of the tensions in his own experience," and that "it was in a sense the public dimension of a series of private conflicts." Then Bigsby continues, "For some years, perhaps a decade, these tensions seem to have addressed a similar ambivalence in the American sensibility. Certainly the political persecutions of the 1950s were in part a debate about national identity" as they were equally an attempt to "accommodate older models of private and public behavior to the new realities of post-war existence." Bigsby concludes this section of his analysis with a statement that suggests the through line of his claims, made three decades ago, to my own. For a particular period of the playwright's career, "not merely did Williams's own private debates generate a drama luminous with his own psychic, sexual, social and spiritual contradictions but he also touched a nerve in the national sensibility in a way that only Miller otherwise succeeded in doing." Williams had confessed to "feeling a deep chasm between himself and all other people, even deeper than the relatively ordinary ones of homosexuality and being an artist, but that condition of 'alienation' was scarcely unfamiliar in a culture in which the word was used with some abandon in the 1950s and 1960s."[13] Bigsby alludes to something that we can now recognize as quite political in Williams's engagement with the transgressive. What we find in his work, Bigsby claims, "is an account of the collapse of morality and morale, and his awareness of that distrust of the deviant which took public form in the shape of domestic and foreign policy but private and symbolic form in the persecution of the non-conformist." As a homosexual and an artist Williams "scarcely needed economic and political theory to justify his sense of exclusion and even persecution."[14]

As for Williams's confluence of politics and morality, both emerge from the playwright's life-long negotiation with sexuality, private and public. As David Savran argues for the "politics of masculinity" in Williams, he rightly notes that historically, the "characterization of Williams as a revolutionary is at odds with the portraits offered by Williams's critics." It is Bigsby, Savran writes, who provides the most incisive and historically rigorous portrait of Williams, "one of the very few that addresses the social implications of a character's deterioration and credits the 'subversive' quality of sexuality in Williams's early plays." Too cautious is Bigsby, however, according to Savran, for even as the former acknowledges the link between the sexual and the political, he "rigidifies the two categories, erecting a set of congruent binarisms" that "oppose the political to sexual, public to private, center to margin," and "privileges the first in each pair." John M. Clum's study of homophobic discourse in Williams, Savran continues, is "one of the more carefully considered studies of the textual implications of Williams's homosexuality," but it is "based on an analogous set of assumptions." As Savran pushes against the limits of what Bigsby and Clum will allow, he argues that the back and forth between the "political and the sexual" that is consistently apparent in Williams's work emerges from the anxiety of masculinity that marked the Cold War era and "offers an urgent challenge to the stubborn antitheses between the political and the sexual." Savran continues by arguing that Williams's plays "redefine and reconfigure resistance so that it is less the prerogative of rebellious individuals than a potential always already at play within both social organization and dramatic structure."[15] But the destabilization of the binary oppositions between political/sexual, public/private, center/margin, particularly when they are concerned with transgressive behavior in the middle decades of the twentieth century, must be considered within the context of law. Williams does so in his prose, as we have seen, and he does so in his plays.

The most frequently analyzed of Williams's early plays on the topics of sexuality and politics is *Cat on a Hot Tin Roof*; the reasoning is primarily, if not wholly, because it is one of the most open treatments of homosexuality in Williams's dramatic works of the 1950s. Williams himself thought highly of the play and its achievement, for as he wrote two decades after its premiere: "I believe that in *Cat* I reached beyond myself, in the second act, to a kind of crude eloquence of expression in Big Daddy that I have managed to give no other character of my creation."[16] Also, as Clum notes, the play contains Williams's "most interesting attempt at measuring his characters' troubled relationships against the potential of an abiding love between two men," despite what Clum considers the playwright's failure "to forge a positive language for the homosexual love the play tries to affirm."[17] At the same time he argues that Williams was "the great dramatist of the closet, a master of the tactic necessary to present homosexuality at all in a particularly repressive period in American society, the era of John Wayne."[18] His assessment that Williams fails "to forge a positive language for the homosexual love the play tries to confirm" is only partly right, for he does not fully consider what Williams may have accomplished, paradoxically, by utilizing the legal system with its judgmental language of disgust to interrogate laws and mores prohibiting at least the physical and public expressions of homosexual love. Indeed, one of the biggest challenges to the theory that *Cat* is a homophobic text is the representation of the estate's former owners, Jack Straw and Peter Ochello, who took in Big Daddy the drifter and willed their plantation to him. It is in the exchange between Big Daddy and Brick about the relationship of the plantation's former owners, an exchange that takes place in the bedroom Straw and Ochello once shared, that we can explore Williams's acknowledgment of legal prohibitions and his description of transgressive love that not only skirts legal prosecution but that represents the most enduring love relationship in the play.

Clum acknowledges that "the legacy of these two lovers lies at the heart of the play," and their love both "stands as a counter to the compromised heterosexual relationships we see played out" and does not "carry the freight of negative stereotypes other Williams homosexuals carry."[19] But he all too quickly dismisses their significance by maintaining that Big Daddy's defense of his surrogate fathers is "interrupted by the appearance of Reverend Tooker," which "allows Brick's homophobic discourse to dominate the scene." Brick does indeed couch the relationship of the former plantation owners in the language of disgust, for his descriptions of them include "unnatural," "dirty old men," and "queer." However, Tooker's interruption is brief, Big Daddy continues his narrative about his own past after sending the preacher on his way, and the patriarch's allusions to his colorful if not illegal history of sexual behavior can be better understood within the specific legal history that Big Daddy confesses to, as can Brick's violent reaction against it.

John S. Bak places Brick's homophobia within the Cold War politics of masculinity; he argues that Kinsey's 1948 study *Sexual Behavior in the Human Male* "may have done more to damage the psyche of Cold War heteromasculinity than it did to transfigure it," for the question Kinsey's report quickly generated was not *who* was homosexual but *what* constituted homosexuality and, by extension, heterosexuality." Bak summarizes the effect of the Kinsey report as follows: "Kinsey publicly assured the gay community that they were not perverted or isolated, privately persuaded some closeted homosexuals to emerge and join the body politic, openly alarmed a bigoted and conservative community of the prevalent 'feminizing' of the American male, and thoroughly confused heterosexual society, male and female alike, as to what caused, shaped, or even defined homosexuality."[20] What Bak's analysis helps us to see, as he points us to the confusion in society as a way of reading the ambiguity in the play, is that the relative certainty of law, both actual and that which is represented by Williams, would have provided comfort or fear (alternately) to audience members struggling with some of the questions that the times posed about sexual identity. Because law is more inclined to focus on sexual acts than on sexual identity (although the latter is often inferred), lines can be more clearly drawn between what is heterosexual, and thus acceptable, and what is transgressive and therefore illegal. The erotic relationship between Brick and Skipper, which remains unconsummated, is thus less important to my reading, and the shift of focus away from their relationship parallels Williams's own resistance to name what was between them and how it determined their respective masculinities. In their reading of play and film versions of *Cat* in *Hollywood's Tennessee: The Williams Films and Postwar America*, R. Barton Palmer and William Robert Bray wisely emphasize the "homosocial" nature of the relationship between Brick and Skipper, a distinction that may privilege the emotional attraction above the sexual.[21]

As Claire Nicolay suggests, Williams planted many clues in the text of *Cat* to create and maintain a complex, subversive agenda, using "various strategies, most remarkably the oblique 'Notes for the Designer,' the characters Straw and Ochello, and Big Daddy's Depression survivor's backstory, to convey this controversial narrative, one that had been pushed underground by the McCarthyite forces at work when *Cat* was first written and under production."[22] What follows is an explication of these narratives within the specific framework of law, in order to explore the legal elements that frame the "McCarthyite forces at work" and underscore the complexity of what Williams is able to accomplish within the narrow confines of a mainstream Broadway play. Nicolay goes on describe the "hobohemia" in which Big Daddy came of age, when men and boys spent months on the road without women, many of them engaging in homosexual activities. However, as she then suggests, the "new Cold War order, with its affluence and increasing control of sexuality and other social behavior, contrasts markedly with the vanished world of hobohemia that Big Daddy evokes." Her emphasis is on the marked growth of materialism in midcentury, as what she calls the "harsh freedom of [Big Daddy's] workingman's culture has been replaced with the staid and mendacious atmosphere of bourgeois aspirations: the individual struggle to survive and win material success is replaced by the capitalist imperative to consolidate wealth and maintain social control."[23] This explication of Big Daddy's early life provides useful evidence for Nicolay's uncovering of what she calls a "subtle yet persistent historical narrative" that "traces the legacy of homosociality and misogyny as well as the cultural transition from frontier ideals of freedom, self-reliance, and individualism to Cold War imperatives of consumption and conformity."[24] It also provides the framework for another strain of interpretation, one that considers the legal history intertwined with this historical narrative.

Although much of the legal history focus herein is on the period during which Williams wrote, Big Daddy's narrative, as well as the Straw/Ochello partnership, concerns an earlier period, one that the character, and thus Williams, date very specifically; there is also a shift away from character or identity and onto behavior that may be circumstantial and environmental. The details of Big Daddy's transience before he settled into his job as plantation manager suggest the possibility that Williams was quite informed about how laws governing sexuality became more stringent and more systematically enforced as the twentieth century proceeded. Big Daddy's narrative is at once detailed and evasive, for his sentences trail off just as he seems likely to admit to doing something scandalous. He tells his son that "I bummed, I bummed this country till I was—" and "slept in hobo jungles and railroad Y's and flophouses in all cities before I—." Brick's response is what seems to be an odd displacement of accusation onto himself: "Oh, *you* think so, too, you call me your son and a queer. Oh! Maybe that's why you put Maggie and me in this room ... in which that pair of old sisters slept in a double bed where both of them died!" Big Daddy's response, *"Now just don't go throwing rocks at—"* might seem a non sequitur, for it is not here but elsewhere that Brick condemns the pair, but since Big Daddy has actually been hinting about his own activities, this defensive answer, italicized by Williams to show its emphasis, is fitting.

After the Reverend's interruption, Big Daddy continues his story, with the stage directions noting that he is "[*leaving a lot unspoken*]: I seen all things and understood a lot of them, till 1910. Christ, the year that—I had worn my shoes through, hocked my—I hopped off a yellow dog freight car half a mile down the road, slept in a wagon of cotton outside the gin—Jack Straw and Peter Ochello took me in."[25] By the time that Big Daddy had landed, with worn-out shoes and no money, at the former plantation, he had "seen all things." His chronology, moreover, coincides with the date that Eskridge marks as a moment when prosecution of same-sex activity began to increase. Although Eskridge's scholarship on midcentury laws regulating sexual transgression between the two world wars and after is most pertinent to this study of Williams and his era of production, the criminal law data of the entire twentieth century documents a consistent upswing in the prosecution of men for a variety of sex crimes. With a focus on protecting children that stemmed at least in part from Freudian theories about the sexual development of minors, many states and local jurisdictions created and enforced laws designed to protect women and children from sexual deviants, and, after 1900, Eskridge explains, "arrests for aggressive sex crimes against women and minors increased substantially." Because such laws often cast a wide net, prosecution of various kinds of sexual crimes increased. Between 1900 and 1915, in St. Louis, Chicago, and San Francisco, to name a few, arrests for sodomy and for other acts covered under "crime against nature" statutes, many of them involving minors, began to attract public attention and shine a spotlight on sex crimes committed by men.[26] Thus does Big Daddy take refuge with his surrogate fathers just as it began to be more dangerous for a man, especially a man with Big Daddy's self-professed powerful libido, to "knock around" without permanent shelter or adequate financial means.

His earlier remarks to Brick about his sexual prowess take on new shades of meaning if we consider the possibility of Big Daddy as a sexual criminal— his pledge to spend the few sexual adventures left in him includes hints of prostitution and sexual violence: "I'm going to pick me a choice one, I don't care how much she costs, I'll *smother* her in—minks! Ha ha! I'll *strip* her naked and *smother* her in minks and *choke* her with diamonds . . . and hump her from hell to breakfast [emphasis mine]."[27] However, whatever illegal behavior he has yet to engage in, he can do so from a place of protection as a wealthy man with vast resources. That is why, in the speech describing his adventures, his last few words are particularly significant to our understanding of how sexually transgressive activity is represented in *Cat*, particularly in contrast with its representation elsewhere in Williams. When Big Daddy tells Brick, "Jack Straw and Peter Ochello took me in," in an act of what he suggests is generosity and even salvation for a young man without anywhere else to go, they provide, permanently, the safety of a large tract of private property and the resources necessary to keep it so. The legal dangers of homosexual activity are heightened when such behavior is visible and therefore vulnerable to police arrest and judicial prosecution, when private intimacies are publicly visible. But Straw and Ochello, and then Big Daddy, are protected from the law by their ownership of "twenty-eight thousand acres of the richest land this side of the valley Nile."[28] As landowners, and particularly as landowners of an enormous property, their private lives remained so.

In his study of the same-sex intimacy in Southern plantation literature, Michael P. Bibler defines *Cat*, one of the texts he explicates, as a work that depicts "the relationships between elite white men as a licit possibility in which they can express their homosexuality openly and safely and enjoy a private, strangely more liberated space within the plantation household." However, Bibler also points to the fact that such a relationship depends upon the "social superiority of the white planter as guaranteed by the plantation's hierarchies of racial, class, and gender identities." For only as long as such hierarchies "continue to assure his superiority, the possibility that the planter might enter into a homosexual relationship with another white man from the same class—a second patriarch, as it were—does nothing to undermine or threaten his masculine identity." It is the "tragic perpetuation of racial, class, and gender inequalities within the meta-plantation" that becomes "the unfortunate condition necessary for enabling these white men to enjoy the release of homo-ness in the first place."[29] Girding this theory is, of course, the plantation itself as a space separate from the world even though it depends upon the world's patriarchal structure for its power.

This separation exists in *Cat*, quite physically in the construction of stage space, and the power the landowner holds is apparent in our knowledge of Straw and Ochello, and in our extensive view of Big Daddy. From his position as owner and controller of the money and, therefore of everything and everyone on the estate, from Big Mama to his children, from their children to the servants and the visitors, he is protected even to the extent that he is comfortable revealing some details of his "knock around" past. He is powerful in his place of residence, and outsiders and family members alike look to him for direction. Tellingly, he attributes his own lack of a judgmental attitude to the space he inhabits, for he tells Brick that he always "lived with too much space around me to be infected by ideas of other people. One thing you can grow on a big place more important than cotton!—is tolerance!—I grown it."[30] The space gives him freedom, but because of the nature of the space (fertile, productive) it also affords him capital income and thus, power. There is, of course, a plantation known for its "epic fornications" that lurks in the background of *Streetcar*, the "place with the columns" that Stanley pulled Stella down from; it is a place that could not be saved by the last woman on the place, Blanche, who rebukes her sister Stella for abandoning Belle Reve," while she herself "stayed and fought for it, bled for it, almost died for it!"[31] It becomes, finally, the scene of Blanche's own "epic fornications," when the young soldiers from the nearby camp, drunk and on their way home from town would, she says, "stagger onto my lawn and call—Blanche! Blanche!" and sometimes she "slipped outside to answer their calls."[32] In both of the plays, then, we see that the plantation is alternately a place of safety even as it represents a site of sexually transgressive acts.

When Blanche outs Allan on the dance floor, he ends his life; however, there is not one life but two at stake, and her own is tragically derailed by the marriage, her discovery, and the aftermath of the suicide. What remains for Blanche is darkness, as the "searchlight which had been turned on the world was turned off again and never for one moment since then has there been any light that's stronger than this—kitchen—candle."[33] Without the protection she might have received in her marriage to a Southern man, even one who pursues homo-ness, not to mention the protection she failed to provide to him in return, this Southern belle is exposed to the shift in norms that comes with the modern age. While modernity has fostered the creation of a generation of new wives like Stella, *Streetcar* makes clear that the New South has left to destruction a number of women born into one model of femininity who now face their failure to conform to a different model of sexual identity and a new kind of role in companionate marriage. Sex crimes, of which Blanche is guilty both because she sought out a minor but also because she is unmarried (a widow who calls herself an "old maid schoolteacher"), make visible a norm that is shifting toward choice and individual liberty but that also continues to punish and contain bodies deemed as criminal. Blanche finds herself punished and contained because of her lack of attachment to either the old system of plantation security or to the new system of nuclear marriage that Stella has chosen and must re-choose in light of the threat that her sister's stay in New Orleans has presented.

For Blanche and Stanley, however, it is the possibility of a cultural revision of sexual norms that puts their characters in focus, and the Southern backdrops, both New Orleans and the plantation that Blanche has left behind, are likewise indicative of tension and change in the region and the nation that would allow these events to occur. Bibler includes Williams in his study of midcentury American writers as one of the handful of Southern authors whose work he examines, all of whom, he argues, "looked to the plantation in an attempt to reconcile their vision of its influence on the region with their openness to the possibility of social change across the region." More importantly, writers such as Williams participated in the "'democratic revival" in which a "crisis and revival of democratic ideology" prompted Southern writers to locate an "egalitarian homo-ness within the regionalist discourse of the plantation myth" and to entertain the possibility that social equality on some scale is not altogether alien or antithetical to southern culture."[34] Arguably, this regionalist discourse of the plantation myth and its "homo-ness" is nowhere as evident in Williams as it is in *Cat*, and for this reason and others the play has best served critical discussions of Williams's attitudes about homosexuality.

Although not landowners, and although they are dependent on others for financial support, Brick and his friend Skipper enjoy an assumed patriarchal maleness as well as other circumstances that protect them from suspicion about their friendship. They had witnessed firsthand what might have come if they had "attempted" any kind of physical relationship while in college, for when he worries that Big Daddy is interrogating him about the nature of his friendship with Skipper, Brick panics, breaking out in a sweat before he asks his father: "Don't you know how people *feel* about things like that? How, how *disgusted* they are by things like that? Why, at Ole Miss when it was discovered a pledge to our fraternity, Skipper's and mine, did a, *attempted* to do a, unnatural thing with—We not only dropped him like a hot rock!—We told him to git off the campus and he did, he got!" [emphasis in the original].[35] Money is one of Brick's shields against public scrutiny, an example of which appears in the play's opening, with Maggie's revelation that Brother Man Gooper has used his influence to keep the story of Brick breaking his ankle while attempting the hurdles at the high school field, drunk and in the middle of the night, from "goin' out over AP or UP or every goddam 'P.'"[36] The family name must be protected, but it is possible to protect the clan's standing precisely because the clan has a standing in the community through Gooper. This incident also makes clear the risks of misbehavior beyond the plantation gates and the need for family intervention when it does occur.

College and professional sports provided some protection, however, at least in their creation of a viable atmosphere for his friendship with Skipper; the safety extended to close physical proximity, for the veneer of masculinity associated with organized sports allayed any suspicion when they checked into a room together while traveling. Although Brick stands by his friendship as "clean and decent," and therefore diametrically opposed to the "dirty" and the "unnatural" relations he has attributed first to the plantation's forebears and then to his classmate and potential fraternity brother, he reveals cases of physical contact in a confessional style: "Oh, once in a while he put his hand on my shoulder or I'd put mine on his, oh, maybe even, when we were touring the country in pro-football an' shared hotel-rooms we'd reach across the space between the two beds and shake hands to say goodnight, yeah, one or two times we—."[37] Bak suggests that it is "when the primacy of his and Skipper's communion endured long after their college days and up to the point where they began sharing hotel rooms during away matches and refused to be apart" that society "began to have its doubts."[38] What Brick is guilty of, according to Bak, is "only of having failed to discern that modern social mores of intimate male companionship come with an expiration date."[39] I would argue that the policing that Brick himself describes at the fraternity, within the identity flux of university life, "when it was discovered a pledge to our fraternity, Skipper's and mine, did a, *attempted* to do a, unnatural thing," is no longer possible when the men leave the relative public nature of life in a fraternity house, analogous to a boarding house in its mix of private and public. The intimate friendship becomes dangerous in the privacy of a hotel room, a setting that, ironically, would have shielded from view the illegal physical expression of affection.

What is notable about Brick's confession, beyond its acknowledgment of the opportunities for intimacy that the two men had because they played a sport together and the shift that took place when they became adults, is the revelatory nature of Brick's speech: one detail leading to another, each more potentially revealing, until the speech stops in midsentence. It mimics, exactly, the manner in which Big Daddy had earlier revealed his shadowy sexual past. Brick's insistence that his and Skipper's physical relationship never went beyond reaching across the "space between the two beds" to "shake hands to say goodnight" also recalls, of course, representations of married couples in the 1950s and early 1960s in television and advertisements, safely separated by a night stand and therefore sparing audiences and viewers the association of even licit sexual coupling culturally sanctioned by marriage. The contrast of Brick's description to the illicit double bed once shared by the former owners of the plantation, who are nonetheless protected by the white male patriarchy of land ownership, is also evident. The bed we see onstage has been repurposed as Brick and Maggie's bed, and although their relationship is sanctioned by marriage, they do not share it.

The privacy of this bedroom (or lack of it) is mentioned several times in the script, when Maggie challenges Big Mama, who complains of the locked door, that "people have got to have *some* moments of privacy, don't they?," to which her mother-in-law replies, "No, ma'am, not in *my* house."[40] The more damaging intrusion and accusation are made by Mae, however, in act 3 of the Broadway version of the play, when she denounces Maggie's claim of pregnancy by asking insistently, "How can you conceive a child by a man that won't sleep with you?," a circumstance she claims to know because she occupies "the next room an' th' wall between us isn't soundproof."[41] Mae's admission of eavesdropping is in keeping with Maggie's comment to Mae earlier in the play: "Sister Woman! Your talents are wasted as a housewife and mother, you really ought to be with the FBI or—."[42] The privacy and protection from law that Straw and Ochello enjoyed is no longer available, even, in this case, to a married couple in the Cold War age, for there are ears pressed to the bedroom wall.

The historical moment for this kind of spying is quite specific, and quite specifically noted in this play by way of the show's most notorious prop: what the notes for the designer describe as the "monumental monstrosity peculiar to our times, a *huge* console combination of radio-phonograph (hi-fi with three speakers) TV set *and* liquor cabinet."[43] John Bak argues that while the "uncertainties and inconsistences surrounding the 'conventional mores' of heterosexuality are undeniably at the heart of *Cat*, it is Williams's distaste for a society that first determines someone's private identity and then systematically marginalizes those who do not fit its model of normalized sociosexual behavior that mostly drives the play's sociocritical engines."[44] Mae's spying on Maggie supports Bak's case, for Sister Woman and Brother Man are less concerned about Brick's sexuality than they are about the nature of his relations with his wife. Not only is Mae sure that Maggie could not possible conceive a child with a husband who refuses to sleep with her, but she goes beyond that revelation to insist that Brick sleeps on the sofa to keep out of contact with his wife. It is, in this case, the lack of physical union that calls into question the legitimacy of the partnership, and although Brick's sexual identity appears ambiguous primarily because of his friendship with Skipper, the celibate relationship with Maggie and her attempt at sexual transgression with Skipper suggest that both members of this married couple are sexual outliers if not outlaws. In the era of Cold War suspicions signified here primarily by Mae and by her husband and lawyer Gooper, all deviance from "normalized sociosexual behavior" may be critiqued or policed, if not formally prosecuted.

Another Williams play further expands upon the varieties of transgressive sexuality and thus expands the range of sympathetic emotional response; and moves his readers and viewers to more complex conceptions of acceptable sexual responses and behaviors. Williams drafted and revised this play over two decades, from the late 1930s to the late 1950s, and it has been published and produced in several versions and with multiple titles. It has some striking similarities to *Cat* while focusing quite explicitly on the connections of sex and law and how these issues infuse cultural debates about class, race, and patriarchal power. The work has not received as much critical attention as *Cat* or *Streetcar*, was not received and has not endured with as much acclaim, and is not revived as often. However, its premiere production in 1940 was the first professional staging of a Williams play. The play is *Battle of Angels,* later extensively revised and renamed *Orpheus Descending,* and then adapted and renamed *The Fugitive Kind* for the screen. To simplify the discussion of a complicated web of the variably titled play drafts and published texts, I will refer to the dramatic text as *Battle/Orpheus* when analyzing it as a single narrative developed over time, but separate out the two titles as needed to differentiate between them, particularly as they exist in two separate published versions in different volumes of *The Theatre of Tennessee Williams*.

Battle/Orpheus contains all of the best-known features of Williams's dramaturgy: a Southern setting with its rich, metaphor-laden speech; several outsider characters with troubled pasts; the quest for physical and spiritual connection that culminates in violence. David C. C. Matthew calls the play "an elaborate structure of symbols and characterizations upon which to reenact a modern version of the self-immolation of a divine artist," and Claudia Wilsch Case states the predominant themes concisely while alluding to the mix of mortal and transcendent topics: "In addition to the outsider's struggle with an intolerant community, themes that persist through all versions of *Battle of Angels* include the tension between sexuality and spirituality, the economics of marriage, and the revolt of life against death."[45] In a 1944 essay, Williams called attention to what he considered the work's conflicted atmosphere: "The stage or setting of this drama was the country of my childhood. Onto it I projected the violent symbols of my adolescence." The history of the play, he claimed, begins as far back as he can remember, in the "mysterious landscape of the Delta country" and its "smoky quality of light in the late afternoons." But he went on to assert that the work was a "synthesis of two parts of my life already passed through": his coming of age, thus described, with its "sulphurous" and "dustily golden" qualities, but with a very different set of memories added, the "turbulent stuff of later experience" after he had "knocked about the states for five years" (just as Big Daddy had done).[46] S. Alan Chesler calls *Orpheus Descending* a representation of seventeen years of periodic revision that contains examples of Williams's "unique playwriting talent, especially dialogue of poetic intensity," while on the other hand "it illustrated to an even greater extent the playwright's characteristic weaknesses: heavy-handed symbolism, obtrusive theatricality and violence, and excessive and incongruous moralizing."[47]

Robert Bray suggests that the "preponderance of violence in *Battle/Orpheus* most likely resulted from racial injustices that would have been disturbing to the impressionable Tom," noting that Williams had claimed as much himself in a 1966 interview.[48] In that interview, when asked about the violence of the civil rights movement, the playwright remarked that *Orpheus* was "the closest I came to writing directly" on "feelings about what goes on in certain parts of the country," even while insisting on being "always an oblique writer" who uses an allusive method for getting at issues.[49] After summarizing studies that have sought to politicize Williams, Bray concludes that the playwright's political perspectives "surface strongly in *Battle/Orpheus*, both versions problematizing "a sleepy southern landscape with a political climate typical of the pre-civil rights era." The climate of "violence and oppression doubtless assumes great importance from the perspective of New Historicism."[50] These critical perspectives run parallel to and occasionally intersect with the thrust of this study, for I am interested in representations of race in the play, specifically as connected to sexual behavior, law, and the dangers that African Americans or other racial or ethnic groups faced when perceived, as was frequently the case, as sexually other and therefore dangerous.

The memories Williams later recalls as his "feelings about what goes on in certain parts of the country" are connected in this play to the racist South of his childhood; however, the play in many ways reflects more explicitly his experiences as a young man who "knocked about the states for five years." These were the very years that the first of the sex crime panics occurred in the United States, what in 1937 J. Edgar Hoover declared was a "War on the Sex Criminal" and a call on law enforcement to halt "the sinister threat" of the "degenerate sex offenders"; this "war" had multiple and conflicting effects on public attitudes about the link between sex and law.[51] In an early unpublished version of *Battle*, in a speech that was later cut, a discussion of local extra-legal efforts (elsewhere in play drafts identified specifically as the Ku Klux Klan) are tied specifically to fear about sex crimes. Here Williams demonstrates his recognition that there were various ways of policing behavior in the South and in the 1930s, and therefore the dangers of the transgressive identity or action originated with either legal or extra-legal enforcement groups. In this version, Ida Mae Whiteside, an early version of Cassandra/Carol, warns Val when he makes a pass at her: "Let me warn you, my friend, they have an organization in this county that protects women from sex-maniacs. They have a special treatment that's guaranteed to give you hot pants for the last time. So you better start moving, Mr. Pocahontas or whatever it is you think you are, because you're not safe here. Not unless you stop fooling with women."[52] Val's transient status and Ida Mae's perception of his racial otherness ("Mr. Pocahontas") render him dangerous and in danger at once; while the organization that would protect her from Val, if she needs it, may not be legally sanctioned, the mention of it indicates Williams's awareness of the prevailing belief that sex crimes were on the rise.

As Ida's speech continues, she insinuates a common assumption about sex maniacs— that they cannot stop themselves: "But you won't stop, you can't stop. You don't have any brakes in that big machine of yours, you don't even have any steering apparatus. The rational part of your brain, the part that ought to control your actions, my friend, is non-existent." And although she acknowledges that Val is "very attractive in a wild, incredible sort of way," she warns him to "get clean away before something terrible happens!" Later in this draft, when Val is speaking to Myra, he tells her that Ida said "there was a gang of some kind, she said—that would fix me! For fooling with women." Although the KKK action exists outside the law, mob justice as dramatized in multiple versions of this play is executed with the endorsement of, and even at times provocation from, the Sheriff. The cooperation of the legal and the extra-legal thus serves Williams's exposure of "what goes in certain parts of the country" when it comes to the legislation of sexual behavior. This early draft, furthermore, demonstrates that the morphing of Ida into Cassandra/Carol will be a significant reconception, from a female figure who warns Val about his behavior to one who encourages him in it and participates herself in deviant sexual activity. Indeed, the Cassandra character is killed by the mob in a later version of the play, a change that underscores this female figure's "degeneration" from legal to illegal body.

In response to the panic of the late 1930s, Freedman reports that police roundups of "'perverts'" became common, and although it was highly publicized assaults on children that first gained the public's attention, the "targets of the crackdowns were often minor offenders, such as male homosexuals." And while "some politicians supported the call for law and order, others turned to psychiatrists for solutions to the sex crime problem." In New York City, for example, a Mayor's Committee for the Study of Sex Offenders included appointments of psychiatrists, lawyers, and criminologists.[53] Despite the psychiatric community's skepticism about the sex crime panic, and its ambivalence about having psychological diagnoses incorporated into law, five states passed "sexual psychopath" laws between 1935 and 1939. It is also significant that these laws "did not necessarily name specific criminal acts, nor did they differentiate between violent and nonviolent, or consensual and nonconsensual, behaviors. Rather, they targeted a kind of personality, or an identity," resting "on the premise that even minor offenders (such as exhibitionists), if psychopaths, posed the threat of potential sexual violence."[54] By considering the influence of such fears about sex, deviance, and law during the time that Williams had knocked around and had also begun drafting this play, we can look anew at *Battle/Orpheus* for ways that the work reflects and challenges this cultural shift, further contextualizing Williams's confluence of sexuality and mental instability that helps us to understand the representation of Cassandra/Carol of *Battle/Orpheus*.

There are two other conclusions Freedman draws that render analysis of *Battle/Orpheus* a fitting one for interrogating Williams's exploration of the sex panics: she claims that, contrary to what we might assume, the response to the sexual psychopath was not primarily a movement to protect female purity. Adult women were now "suitable objects for 'normal' male sexual desire, even normal male aggression," and so the "discourse on the psychopath mapped out two new forbidden boundaries for men: sex with children or with other men." As we have seen, social and legal historians chart the formation of a public homosexual world in the first half of the twentieth century, even as the larger society remained homophobic; the psychopathic literature, according to Freedman, reinforced the fear of male homosexuality, and at times "it appeared that a major motive of the psychopath laws was to prevent the contagion of homosexuality from spreading from adults to youth."[55] At the same time, the public nature of the panics that Freedman outlines and even the "seemingly repressive aspects of the campaign" had the effect, she argues, of promoting "a new, more open, public discourse on nonmarital, nonprocreative sexuality." But she pushes this point even further, and in doing so helps us to see the significance of Williams's drama in this age: "The literature of the sexual psychopath helped break down older taboos simply by discussing sexual deviance. At the same time, the literature encouraged a reevaluation of heterosexual behavior during a time of rapid flux in sexual standards. At a basic level, the psychopath literature helped disseminate information about sexual practices that had previously been outside the bounds of proper discourse."[56] In her conclusion, Freedman suggests that even as the state "played an increasingly important role in defining sexual deviance" as a result of the panics, the laws' critics "ultimately helped to legitimize nonprocreative heterosexual acts;" the "media and national commissions helped educate the public about both 'natural' and 'perverse' sexual behaviors" but then tended to "draw a firm sexual boundary proscribing all homosexual activity and linking it with extreme violence."[57] Her overall discussion thus points to the complexity of sexual representation in the period. Fear paradoxically led to increased discussion and education, thereby helping to normalize some, but not all, of the behaviors that fell under such cultural and legal investigation.

Williams's representations of sex and law were equally complex. Informed by the social history that Freedman outlines, we come to understand the pre- and postwar years as a time when boundaries of acceptable sexual behavior were being marked and remarked, reinforced and challenged. Dialogues about sexual deviance became more common during an age when social anxieties had come to be considered crucial in the process of identity formation; public attention on transgressions provided a rich source of subject matter for a writer who had been raised with both the strictures of Christian piety and the specter of mental illness weighing heavily on him, further complicated by his experience of "knocking about" for five years; like Big Daddy, Williams had "seen all things" and "understood a lot of them," thereby, like his character, growing "tolerance." As we shall see, there is perhaps no better text (collection of texts) than *Battle/Orpheus* for considering his complex viewpoint on sexual transgression and the law. It is, most significantly for my purposes, one that features treatment of and discussions of the law quite prominently, and doing so primarily through representations of heterosexual but nonetheless transgressive sex. Its drafts exist in such volume and over such a long span of time, not to mention that it was a span of great flux in the formation of American sexual identities. An in-depth examination of this narrative with the focus on law contributes to a more comprehensive understanding of the play while demonstrating the impossibility of settling on a single definitive interpretation. Its structural status in multiple versions is not a unique one for Williams, but the number of years he spent working on this play produced a multiplication of variations almost unmatched in his canon, and these many versions reveal the accumulated textual power of a text that a writer keeps turning back to in order to further explore its issues. Like "One Arm," the existence of multiple versions and the ways each negotiates legal issues provide substantial documentation of Williams's emphasis on the relationship between sex and law.

At the same time, it is not surprising that the play's legal issues have been overlooked, obscured as they have been beneath the tangle of mythic elements in the work that have driven the critical commentary. Because of its long and complicated history, the work captures the tension of Williams's reception over a period of several decades. It is indicative of a time and place, a small Southern town largely untouched by the progress of the postwar period, and to some extent this consistency is protected by the infusion of mythic significance as the playwright revises (reflected also in the change of title). As Judith Thompson suggests, there are not one but several stories that structure the events of this play: the Orpheus of the later title is, of course, Val Xavier, the wandering minstrel, with Lady Torrance as his Eurydice; but Lady in this case serves in another capacity and enacts a second narrative, according to Thompson, engaging Val in "her equally transcendent efforts to *recapture* an idyllic memory" of her young, lost love [emphasis in the original].[58] What may have further preempted considerations of the primacy of law and order topics is the very early critical assessment of the play as a repository of the images, themes, and even place names that Williams would draw on throughout his career, thus perhaps presupposing that worldly concerns were and would remain secondary to the poetic and the symbolic thrusts of the work.

The main setting and situation of *Battle/Orpheus*, however, which do not change over the course of years that he worked on the play, allow for a variety of moral and criminal representations and judgments: a mercantile store in a small Mississippi Delta town, peopled by a large cast of characters. The store attracts everyone to it, as a place of business and as an exchange of community information, and yet it also has a private family dwelling above it. Like the boarding houses common to many of Williams's stories and short plays, the dramatic location allows the playwright to bring together a diverse cast of characters that cross gender, race, and class lines, while also constructing a framework for private and public exchanges. With the exception of the prologue in early versions of *Battle*, which is set a year after the main story in what is no longer the store but has become a *"museum exhibiting souvenirs of the sensational events which had taken place there,"* the setting of the working store is consistent.[59] Even in the published draft of that early version, the bulk of the play has the store in operation and "stocked with merchandise," according to the stage directions, and *"racks of dresses, marked 'Spring Styles,' line the right wall."*[60] By the time the play has become *Orpheus*, the mercantile set has been stripped of its realism: *"Merchandise is represented very sparsely and it is not realistic"* and the confectionary *"is shadowy and poetic as some inner dimension of the play."*[61] While the set shifts from the realistic to the nonrealistic, however, the horrifying punishments meted out to each of the sexual transgressors are of this world.

What is also stripped away over the years of revisions to the play are many of the explicit references to law; but just as the setting remains, so does the topic of law, albeit in increasingly abstract ways. We might wonder if, as the sex panics abated, so did the overt emphasis on crime and punishment for diverse sexual behaviors, or that, as Williams himself was less exposed to arrest and prosecution, his compulsion for representing those dangers in his work diminished. But just as he continues through the 1950s to play with a mix of realistic and non-realistic set pieces, language, and situations, he experimented, throughout the whole of *Battle/Orpheus* and in the film adaptation, with legal tropes, language, and conditions. The consistency of treatment, paradoxically, is best revealed by tracking the changes over time, so that the early explicit focus on legality, shaded by the later veneer of abstraction and mythology, can be brought to the surface.

The published version of *Battle* included in *The Theatre of Tennessee Williams* demonstrates the extent to which Williams initially sets out to include in this play all the major issues that he found pressing. While such a catch-all approach may not have been wise dramatically, the complicated textual and stage histories of *Battle of Angels* and its successor *Orpheus Descending* reveal the challenge he faced in attempting to represent sexuality, privacy, identity, and liberty during the years just prior to and in the decade following World War II. Not only did those years feature the two "sex panics" as described by Freedman, they were witness to ongoing judicial confrontations about sexual freedom. When describing the years that led up to the Supreme Court's first opinion to articulate and defend a "free-standing constitutional right to privacy applicable to sexual conduct," *Griswold v. Connecticut* in 1965, Richards notes that as recently as 1961 the Court had "unanimously affirmed in *Holt v. Florida* the measure of women's rights and responsibilities in their ascribed status 'as the center of home and family life.'"[62] The twenty-five years between *Battle*'s first production and *Griswold*'s articulation of a constitutional right to sexual privacy was the site of many debates, legal and otherwise, about sexual norms, freedom of expression, and the public good.

Williams was haunted by the failure of the initial staging of *Battle*, a production by the Theatre Guild in December of 1940 that closed after a two-week tryout in Boston; audience members found the play offensive, and the guild subsequently issued an apology to its subscribers. Indeed, the management at the Wilbur Theatre where the show appeared had a brush with the law because of *Battle*'s "putrid" content. An anonymous article published in the *Boston Post* during the two-week run reported that City Councilman Michael J. Ward had demanded it be shut down.

Although he had not himself seen the show, he had received six complaints about it, causing him to remark that "the police should arrest the persons responsible for bringing shows of that type to Boston." The council passed an order that the city censor investigate the play, and it was decided that the show could continue if some objectionable lines were removed. The theatre management agreed to the terms, but low ticket sales led to a decision to close the show within days of that negotiation.

In response to the controversy, Miriam Hopkins, who played Myra Torrance, was quoted in the *Post* piece defending the play, saying that it is not "dirty," and that the "dirt is something in the minds of some of the people who have seen it. They read meanings into it according to their own suppressed feelings."[63] Although his first public tussling with American morality went on with Williams himself in the background, the "sedate Theatre Guild subscribers," as Lyle Leverich refers to them, had, because of the play's content, been "witness to the melodramatic violence, as one reviewer put it, of 'seduction, adultery, nymphomania, shooting, lynching, flood and fire.'"[64] The "dirty" and "putrid" characters in this play are so, according to the *Post* article, not because they are, as Williams named them, the "fugitive kind," but because they are the "less than spotless kind." Val Xavier is one of these "less than spotless kind," as we shall see, but the "adultery" and the "nymphomania" are women's offenses and it is Myra/Lady and Cassandra/Carol who provide striking examples of Williams's female "illegal bodies," demonstrating that his conceptions of transgressive sexuality were not limited to homosexuality but included married and unmarried women as well as prostitutes of both sexes.

Hooper notes that Savran's argument for Williams's "politics of masculinity" is limited, for Savran is compelled to admit that in the writer's attempts to subvert a homophobic society, what is lacking is Williams's championing of a "feminine eroticism." The playwright's claims to being a revolutionary, Hooper continues, "are, ironically, blunted by the exclusiveness of his homoerotic politics, the axis of greatest resistance."[65] However, while the politics of sexual transgression in Williams are framed by homosexual desire, they are not limited to that narrow perspective on transgression. Indeed, like the sodomy laws themselves, which were constructed primarily as a legal force containing the "crime against nature" but then used to control and punish other types of sexual activities that were deemed unnatural, Williams's construction of the transgressive body is not limited to the homosexual corpus or act. The law's inclusion, when it came to what it deemed deviant practices, was noted by and mimicked by the writer; his attention to a variety of illegal activities, and his complex representation of them, extended his influence on how sexual mores were received and challenged by both homo- and heterosexual subjects.

Williams's denial that he purposefully or consciously chose controversial and immoral topics for his work is, perhaps, analogous to his vagueness about his political leanings. That is, the denial served to acknowledge the fact of the controversy while diminishing it in specificity, which allowed him to assume a position of bemused impartiality. When writing in years hence about the Boston production of *Battle*, he accomplished the latter by calling into question his own naiveté about the subject matter while affirming that he understood the play's message:

> If it was in the minds of others [that the play would fail], certainly this suspicion was never communicated to me. Was I totally amoral? Was I too innocent or too evil—that I remained unprepared for what the audiences, censors, and magistracy of Boston were going to find in my plays? I knew, of course, that I had written a play that touched upon human longings, about the sometimes conflicting desires of the flesh and the spirit. This struggle was thematic; implicit in the title of the play. Why had I never dreamed that such struggles could strike many as filthy and seem to them unfit for articulation? The very experience of writing it was like taking a bath in snow. Its purity seemed beyond question.[66]

What seems disingenuous in this questioning is the idea that he did not consider how and why his audiences might find the subject "filthy," for, based on the fears he expressed about his fiction of the same period, he knew very well what types of sexual desire and activity are branded as not only dirty but "degenerate." And the earliest versions of *Battle* contain examples of the play's use of the language of disgust; indeed, his persistent acknowledgment of the "conflicting desires of the flesh and the spirit" that struck many as "filthy" seems to have compelled him to use the language of condemnation as part of the complex self-commentary that contributes to the tension throughout his work. While what he sees as the "purity" of the creative form directs his attention, or so he claims, away from the messiness, his readers, viewers, and reviewers are left to grapple with the conflicts: between innocence and evil, between flesh and spirit, between moral and filthy.

Evidence exists, too, that Williams's portrait of himself as naïve or otherwise unaware that the struggles he dramatized in *Battle* would be "unfit for articulation" is not accurate: he wrote to agent Molly Day Thatcher in November of 1939, one year prior to the premiere in Boston, that creating a new draft of the play meant that he needed to "write everything over to tone it down, to eliminate the lunatic note," and, because of the "violent, melodramatic nature of the material," to do a "great deal of smoothing out and toning down."[67] Rather than assume that he is being deceptive in denying his awareness of how the play's subject might offend, however, it is possible to see the choice of self-assessment he offers in the above passage between innocence and evil as telling and true in another way. For in its opposition of extremes, his determination to revise reflects the duality that defined and drove him: the tension between what he called the puritan and the cavalier sides of his nature. It also calls to mind his summation of the play as a "synthesis of two parts of my life already passed through:" his innocent adolescence as it comes up against the "turbulent stuff of later experience."[68] A Christian upbringing in the South solidified the influence of one dominant cultural force with which he would need to reckon, in himself and in others: the emphasis on morality as a guiding principle. How to construct that morality is another issue, however, and the evidence we see Williams putting forth in his creative work is of a morality that incorporates a liberal dose of compassion, the latter a quality widely associated with Christ but not always with "Christian." The idea of writing as a purifying experience is related to the notion of confession, for in reporting sin the supplicant may be forgiven. Thus it is, perhaps, that he claims the purity in the very experience of writing the play.

The cavalier part of his nature insured that the sins he dramatized were of great variety and extremity, and the side of himself he claims to have inherited from his father's lineage made necessary the exploration and embrace of diverse lifestyles; this exploration was fostered by a love of travel, which guaranteed a host of wide-ranging experiences, and allowed that some discussion of those lifestyles and experiences, particularly as they convey "conflicting desires of the flesh and the spirit," would be essential to his presentation of the world. His sexual orientation had made him sensitive to the ways that his society constructed "queerness," defined generally, and on this topic he depicted benign cases of social awkwardness that he recognized in himself, but he did not hesitate to push past such examples and over the very edge of normal, and, as we have seen, legal behavior. Because of his persistent interrogation of desire and his creation of characters who resided beyond the boundaries of behavioral norms, the transgressive acts he featured were usually focused on sexual activities that were illegal and the source of disgust or moral judgment.

Several months before the first production of *Battle*, Williams retreated to Acapulco, Mexico, to work on the play. In an essay written after he returned to the States, he described sitting on a Mexican veranda and recollecting the diverse persons he had already encountered in "twenty-six years of living": the prostitutes, the jobless, the ex-cons. He considered himself one of the "Quarter Rats, as we were called. The prostitute Irene who painted the marvelous pictures and disappeared, Helen who entered my life through a search for a lost black cat, the jobless merchant seaman, Joe, who wrote sea-stories more exciting than Conrad's which were destroyed when the house he lived in burned." Some behaviors were public and illegal, as "the big fight" or the "riot call" meant time in night court and the house of detention, with its "big bare room and the filthy, desperate prisoners. Words scrawled on the dirty white walls" and "life getting bigger and plainer and uglier and more beautiful all the time."[69] While his preoccupation with the marginalized has been discussed extensively from the beginning of his career to the present, this passage contains specific and very tactile descriptions about the law-breaking outsiders he observed and socialized with during his vagabond years.

Case argues that the outsiders in *Battle of Angels* who are most prominently pitted against the community are Val, Cassandra, Sandra, and Myra and suggests that Cassandra, "who is not accepted in the town because of her eccentric behavior, public drinking, and sexual promiscuity, recognizes in the roving Val the same passionate nature and disregard for convention that have attracted the townspeople's negative attention towards her."[70] But Williams also makes explicit, in several of the play's speeches, that outsider status and "eccentric behavior" are bound to law and legal sanctions, and he uses the cross-gender connection between Val and Cassandra to parallel female and heterosexual male sexuality. For instance, Cassandra points out to Val that they are alike by first noting their class and even perhaps their essential difference: "You— savage. And me—aristocrat." But then she delineates their sameness: "Both of us things whose license has been revoked in the civilized world. Both of us equally damned and for the same good reason. Because we both want freedom."[71] That their "license has been revoked" is, in this case, not literal, but the phrase depends upon regulatory language to make its point about their sharing of a similarly "uncivilized" status. As we shall see in *Battle/Orpheus*, it is Cassandra/Carol's expulsion from her family's estate that makes her actions more vulnerable to the law. Although the familial connections she has could protect her and have protected her in the past, once she becomes alienated from her relatives' good graces, she becomes as vulnerable to prosecution as Val, who comes into the town with nothing but his guitar and a desire to make some money.

Battle makes for a very complex study of law, morality, and justice, as we see when we consider some details discussed by the less central female characters. After Sandra and Val depart together midway through act 1, the sheriff's wife, Vee, is left in the store with local women Dolly and Beulah, who serve the play as choral figures and community representatives. The exchange that follows paints a complex portrait of the way that Southern society seeks but fails to regulate itself. Dolly and Beulah's attitudes about the sexual attraction they witnessed between Sandra and Val are judgmental; Williams includes these voices of conventional morality throughout his early work and they are analogous, linguistically and significantly, to the legal condemnation of transgressive sexual behavior during this period. Beulah demonstrates that no explicit illegal act on Sandra's part has occurred, but Beulah does no more than "see how she looked at the boy" and register "the tone of huh voice" before calling Sandra and her behavior "corrupt" and "absolutely—*degraded*!"[72] Vee's protective attitude toward Val begins with the hope that Sandra "doesn't get him to drink," a habit she claims he has given up and which is regulated against in this dry county by law, but then she turns her own judgment toward the other two women: "If some of the older women in Two River County would set a better example there'd be more justice in their talk about girls," going on to blame "people who give drinkin' pahties an' get so drunk they don't know which is their husband an' which is somebody else's." Dolly replies, "Now I've discovered the source of that dirty gossip!" Vee's suggestion of drunken wife-swapping implicate Dolly and Beulah in the illegality of sexual transgression, and thus the drama's pattern of indictment includes both the fugitive kind and those who propose themselves as upstanding citizens. [73]

John Clum has suggested that the Val of *Orpheus* "is mutilated and sanctified for his sexual potency," which is a threat to other men because he is a "sexual free agent" who draws women "outside the boundaries of patriarchal authority and marriage" to him like a magnet. Val, the "reluctant stud," according to Clum, is the object of female attention even though the character, a "heterosexual redeemer," has some of the qualities of Williams's earlier homosexual martyrs. Indeed, Clum questions whether Val is "necessarily exclusively heterosexual," given that during the time of Williams's early manhood the "secrecy surrounding homosexuality made it possible for men to have sex with other men without fear of being branded homosexual."[74] A consideration of *Battle*'s Val, both in the published text and in some of the draft fragments, will provide an answer of sorts to Clum's question about the nature of Val's sexual activity while complicating Clum's assertion of Val as a "sexual free agent" by moving the analysis into the realm of law.

During the verbal exchange in *Battle* between Cassandra and Val about their sameness, Val hints that he may earn his living as a prostitute: he asks Sandra if she supposed he had a "sign 'Male at Stud'" hung on him, to which she responds, "yes, I think you have." Although he claims she is making an inaccurate assumption, he goes on to describe their evening together as "nothing to you. It was like you had hired me to give you a little amusement."[75] The sexual free agent is thus an agent of criminal activity, at least in conception here, and with the suggestion that either or both of them would consider an exchange of money as a component of their physical relationship renders them increasingly suspect in a culture that has already revoked their license and pushed them to the social and legal margins of the community. A section of an undated draft contains a backstory of the relationship between Cassandra and Val, only part of which appears in print in *Battle*; it provides another dimension of their connection as Williams fleshes out Val's illegal past. Although key elements are eventually omitted, the work that Williams does creating a previous relationship between the two leaves trace meaning through a dimension of Val's character that remains on the edge of representation and contributes to the understanding of Val's sexual identity and its fluidity.

In this draft version, Sandra insists that she had met Val in New Orleans, where he was hustling men in a French Quarter bar:

> SANDRA: Yes, that's where I saw you one rainy night between Christmas and New Years when I was doing the Bourbon Street bars with my cousin Bertie. Oh, yes, I remember perfectly, now, it was the eve of the Sugar Bowl game and I was making the rounds with Bertie and his boyfriend Jack and some dumb cluck of an athlete from Tulane. (Snaps her fingers) The Starlite Lounge, that's where! Jack bought you a drink and Bertie went home in a rage.... How did Jack make out?
> VAL: Cut that crap.
> SANDRA: Oh, oh, oh, I remember!—he was rolled!

Her memory of Val is therefore not of a man who was attracted to her, but a hustler who seduced and robbed them, the specifics of being rolled providing a kind of physical bait and switch. Val fulfills his contract to make physical contact, but the roughness is an act of theft rather than an act of desire. For his part, Val denies the incident by producing an alibi, for he says, "As a matter of fact the night before the Sugar Bowl game I wasn't even in New Orleans, I was driving a Diesel truck between there and Houston, Texas, for a buddy of mine that had a ruptured appendix. Have you got that straight? You might have seen me, lots of people have seen me, but I don't go that route you're talking about." Undeterred, Sandra continues with her accusation by producing additional material evidence, recalling a ring that Val had on that night:

> You said it was given you by an antique dealer you met on Jackson Square and that man was good for ten dollars anytime you were broke and that sometimes you'd wire collect from the other side of the country and get a money order from Western Union for twenty or fifty dollars inside of five hours no matter how far you were or how long it was since he'd seen you. I was touched. But I must say Jackie came home in an awful condition. A serious concussion. What did you hit him with?

Val continues to deny her recollection and to do so with legal language and a veiled threat of his own, even as she continues to insist that she does not care about any of it, telling Val to "cool off, play it cool." He reminds her that "charges like that had better be backed up by witnesses or they can get you into a heap of trouble," insisting that he could, if need be, verify his whereabouts on the road to Houston on the night in question.[76]

In the published version of *Battle*, this exchange does not appear in any form, but it is revived for *Orpheus*; however, significantly, the suggestion of Val's engagement with male/male prostitution and larceny are gone. The timeline of the initial construction of this segment of the narrative belies a straight path toward revelation of transgressive sexuality, for the more sexually fluid Val and the hint of multiple legal offenses are not, as we might expect them to be, developed or expanded in the latter text of *Orpheus*, but exist very early. Their presence in early drafts demonstrates that Williams's negotiation of them was most visible at the time when such actions would likely be criminally prosecuted, during the 1940s. In the later *Orpheus* script, on the other hand, the hint of any form of prostitution, male/male or male/female, is downplayed. The antique dealer mentioned in the draft version has become a "lady osteopath" who *loves* Val (love is not mentioned in the earlier version) and who sends money to him in order that he return to her; Carol is still accompanied by cousin Bertie, but Bertie is not specified as a "he" and has no boyfriend Jack. Val has become an itinerant musician who passes a kitty after he plays.[77] These revisions indicate alterations to Val's history and identity, but they also suggest a move to broaden the depiction of sexual transgressors. In other words, if Val is a male hustler and thief, whose prior connections to sexuality are through homosexual trade, he matches the vagrant criminal model of homosexuality familiar to us from other Williams's texts, including his autobiographical ones. But if his prior sexual history includes the love of a lady osteopath, his relationship with Myra/Lady cannot be easily discounted as driven by desperation to legitimize his sexual life. The illegality of the affair with Myra is not contestable, but its immorality is enhanced if Val's past history includes sexual manipulation for profit, for the possibility exists that his gigolo days are not over.

As Case points out, Cassandra includes Myra in the category of exiles, but because the critical focus in Case's essay is on the "tension between sexuality and spirituality," it is not of primary importance to her argument that the links to legal circumstances are, as they are so often in Williams, both actual and metaphorical. However, Williams's use of law as a site of punishment, not just as one of social condemnation, indicates his awareness of the actual dangers that sexual transgressors faced from prosecution, thus implying that only changes in restrictive laws will bring privacy rights and the freedom for individuals to pursue diverse desires. In act 3 of *Battle*, Cassandra tells Myra that she has come to give her what she calls a warning: "They've passed a law against passion. Our license has been revoked. We have to give it up or else be ostracized by Memphis society. Jackson and Vicksburg, too. Whoever has too much passion, we're going to be burned like witches because we know too much."[78] Sandra suggests that in such a restrictive environment, either social expulsion or physical destruction is imminent. The means of destruction that she specifies emphasize social class and gender, neither of which would seem to implicate Val, although she has issued him a very similar warning that also evokes sexual illegality.

"Society" is more likely to ostracize the two women, one of whom was born into old money and property but who is now vulnerable because of her behavior; the stage directions on Cassandra's first entrance describe her family as *"the oldest in this part of the Delta"* and *"once the richest, but their plantation has dwindled with each successive generation."* The downslide of her family's prominence is based on economics, but Sandra's personal social demise is due to her transgressive behavior" for she has been *"'going out' for ten years and is still unmarried."*[79] Myra comes from a less privileged background but she has sought acceptance and social standing in a loveless marriage that provides her with a home and an income. Her situation is not ideal, and in fact she married into the mercantile class after being prevented from fulfilling her social aspirations when her youthful beau, a "prominent planter's son," quit her and married instead "some aristocratic girl, a girl like Cassandra Whiteside."[80] This description of their respective histories and circumstances makes clear that they were vulnerable to being ostracized even before they made choices to pursue their desires.

Val's family worked the land but did not own it; even sharecropping was out of reach, for he says that they did not farm on shares but on "leavings, scraps, tidbits! They never owned a single inch of the earth, but all their lives they gave to working on it."[81] As a sexual outlaw he is not vulnerable to the threat of social ostracizing, for he has no standing, past or present. As for the physical threat, however, all three are equally endangered by the "law against passion," their fate prophesized by Cassandra as one that will be enacted by public execution ("burned like witches"). The particular style of stake burning has both law and lawlessness about it, for its association with Puritan witch hunts reminds us of judgment based in extreme fanaticism. It will be Val alone who is literally burned, and, as we shall see, the law (Sheriff) and the extra-legal forces (Ku Klux Klan/mob) are both involved in pursuing the fugitive kind, but particularly Val.

Clum argues in his analysis of *Orpheus* that in essence, "Val is killed for bringing life to the town. He literally brings life to the imprisoned, embittered Lady" and he is "killed by men who can only bring death and destruction." In *Battle*, death comes to all three of them, and their deaths involve law, passion, and fire just as Sandra has predicted. In *Orpheus*, however, Carol survives, taking possession of the snakeskin jacket and thus, according to Clum, the conclusion ultimately suggests that the men of law are not victors or that the "victory of the white patriarchy is temporary at best." If Val "still exists and prevails," however, according to Clum, it is "through the body and voice of a transgressive, isolated woman." Clum designates Carol as "transgressive" and "isolated," and he claims that it is the sexual energy of multiple rebels that "prevails," as symbolized by the jacket of the man who "will not conform to patriarchal order" and "threatens the social order by bringing life and a measure of autonomy to the women."[82] With the survival of Carol in late versions of the work, Williams provides evidence that neither the law nor the mob can maintain a system that seeks to regulate and punish the passion of the most marginalized individuals.

Furthering what began in *Battle* as an extended study of sexual transgression and law is another piece of Val's history, a piece that unfolds as a result of the Sheriff's appearance in act 2, scene 3 but that begins with the Sheriff's attempted arrest of a young black musician, Loon, who has appeared outside the store in the scene immediately prior to play his guitar in the *"fading warmth of the afternoon sun."* The brief exchange, nonessential to the storyline and cut from later versions, nonetheless has significance for its demonstration of Williams's knowledge of minor criminal offenses and their circumstances, as well as his acknowledgment that the fugitive kind and the legally confined are often economically and/or racially vulnerable citizens. As scene 3 begins, the Sheriff attempts to either run Loon out of town or arrest him for vagrancy, declaring that "we don't allow no unemployed white transients in this town an' I'll be dogged if I'm gonna put up with colored ones." Loon's defense of being "dispossessed" from his job as a farm hand despite his hard work does little to protect him; rather, it convinces the Sheriff that, once arrested, he "oughta make the state a good road hand." Val interrupts the exchange, paying Loon ten dollars for the guitar and then saying, "You can't fine a man for vagrancy when he's got ten dollars, can you, Sheriff? Not if I'm acquainted with the law." He then extracts a promise that Loon will return to give him guitar lessons, hoping to further undermine the threat of a vagrancy charge.[83] Legal safety is thus defined, here and elsewhere in Williams's canon, as a capacity for possession, an ideal much in favor throughout the era of increased home ownership and the beginning of the decline of American transience and communal living that marked the Depression years and earlier. But a consistent theme in his work focuses on a troubling side of domesticity, which is its similarity to imprisonment. Indeed, in several versions of *Battle*, the jail is adjacent to or even part of the sheriff's home, and Vee's offer of shelter for Val consists of a bed in the jail house. It is not surprising that such an offer unsettles him, and in the published version of *Battle* Vee tells Dolly and Beulah that she met Val when he "come to the lockup las' night an' ast for a bed, but he couldn't stay in it, though, the bars made him nervous." She gave him a blanket and "he went out to sleep in his car," a safer place as far as he is concerned but one that could make him subject to vagrancy prosecution.[84]

Among the drafts of *Battle*, an undated folder containing notes and fragments explore several directions of law's representation that

Williams tried out over the early years of the work's composition. These pieces help to strengthen the argument that Williams's awareness of law was connected but not limited to homosexual offenses, and that in *Battle/Orpheus* he focuses primarily on heterosexual crime and statutes that target transients and people of color. Loon's role is expanded, as are the themes of vagrancy and imprisonment, in a typescript outline and a draft version. The timeline differs from the published versions of the text, for in this treatment of the material both Myra and Jabe are dead by the end of act 2. The outline for act 3 sets its opening in the Sheriff's house, while a "posse is combing the country" and, since Jabe died the night of the killing, "Val's guilt seems unquestionable" and "public feeling is savage." With a "posse" looking for Val, we see Williams's linguistic attempt to represent group punishment sanctioned by law, for such a group draws from the community of men in a town or region, but does so in cooperation with law enforcement. As we know from popular representations of the posse, however, emotions run high and the search for a criminal can become a quest for revenge rather than for justice.

The outline reveals the extent to which Williams's reflections on law, religion, marriage, and sex come together in his early work on the play. The passage that follows is particularly noteworthy to the character construction of Vee Talbot, the Sheriff's wife and the third of the three women who orbit Val, attracted to him because of his sexual power. Vee is returning from Easter services, an apt amplifier for Val's sacrificial identity, and she "has had a religious revelation on the road, a vision of Christ under the cottonwood trees where the road turns off toward the levee." In a trance-like state, she returns to her house, which is also the site of the local jail, and as the Sheriff and two others who have captured Val bring him in, "Vee is struck speechless" when she realizes that it was not Jesus, but Val in her vision. As the outline description continues: "The two of them had become confused in her mind, her religious preoccupation being artificially imposed over her sexual nature." Then Williams indicates his interest in exploring how mob violence might be a fit dramatic punishment for Val; after the latter is put in lock-up, "the Sheriff hastens off to get state troopers from Jackson to convoy Val out of the county as there is imminent danger of mob violence by the K's (KKK) if his presence in the jail is discovered." The curtain falls with Vee standing motionless.

The next scene is set in the lock-up, reminding us of Williams's persistent interest in places of confinement, legal or otherwise. If the critical perspective on this play is correct in suggesting that it contains most or all of Williams's tool kit of themes and dramatic devices, Val may represent the ultimate example of a Williams figure: artist and outcast, sexual and adverse to capture. As Leverich notes, Val is "virile and handsome and seeks simply the itinerant existence;" however, as a loner, "he is also a 'fox in the chicken coop,' attractive to women of the town and the hunter's quarry to its men. He represents something wild, free, and alien that both women and men resent and try in various ways to capture and imprison."[85] Williams's incorporation of legal topics, especially as the legislation of human activity includes sexuality, allows him the representational range to explore all aspects of desire and their relationships to possessiveness and freedom.

Indeed, Val riles all members of the community, inviting conflict as he presents an example of a life that is both enviable and repulsive. He is that part of a society that is not only prone to lawlessness but will engender it in others. Val's companions in this outline of the jail cell scene are also dangerous and marginalized figures whose interactions with Val provide further commentary: they are Loon and a "brutal white vagrant," the first attempting to "comfort him in his hysteria" while the second "heightens it with sadistic hints at torture he will receive from the mob." They are also examples of the kind of attention Val receives from the other townspeople, female and male: comfort from Loon that reflects the way that women react to Val, and threats from the white vagrant, similar to what he experiences in the presence of the Sheriff and the other men. Even though this scene does not end up in the play as produced and published, it provides a glimpse into Williams's vision of legality and violence, of the play's doubling of characters that exist inside the law and outside of it. The draft is indicative of Williams's greater project of conveying to midcentury American audiences the blurry line between moral and immoral, legal and illegal, natural and unnatural.

The action, as described by Williams in his outline, next involves Val and Vee, with the former's attempt to seduce the Sheriff's wife with talk of love and freedom; he asks her to release him and promises that they will escape together to bayou country. As she unlocks the cell door, however, "the Klan arrives, the flickering light of their pine-torches is thrown on the jail walls and Val's mind cracks with hysteria. He cowers against the wall of the cell" as "the mob rushes in, like dream phantoms in their white hoods, and seize him." He is taken away as he screams "fire!" in anticipation of his fate, and rightly so, for when the Sheriff returns he is told that the men who took Val away had blowtorches. In another folder of unsorted pages of incomplete drafts, Val is in a jail cell with Loon and a Mexican, with Loon speaking to Val: "All I hope is they recognize which one of us is you."[86] Because Loon is African American, his anxiety about being mistaken for a man who has committed a sexual crime is quite understandable, and the line makes an allusion to lynchings that were often perpetrated with no more than a vague or completely unfounded suspicion of guilt. This snatch of dialogue also raises an issue of the tension between what could be two very different fates: being punished by the legal system, and being punished by the KKK.

Robyn Wiegman argues that "above all, lynching is about the law," for in the "circuit of relations that governs lynching in the United States, the law as legal discourse and disciplinary practice subtends the symbolic arena, marking out a topos of bodies and identities that gives order to generation, defines and circumscribes social and political behavior, and punishes transgression, from its wildest possibility to its most benign threat."[87] Val is the kind of criminal, a sexual criminal, who is threatened by the possibility of punishment by either the mob or the judiciary. Although Wiegman's essay on lynching focuses on African American men and on nineteenth-century literature, her ideas can be extrapolated for Williams's representations of Val and his punishment in the twentieth century because of her attention to the "sexual economy that underlies lynching's emergence as a disciplinary practice for racial control" and its "means for (re)articulating white masculine supremacy." Her description of lynching and its operation "according to a logic of borders—racial, sexual, national, psychological, biological, as well as gendered"—suggests, she argues, the extent to which it "figures its victims as the culturally abject, monstrosities of excess whose limp and hanging bodies function as the specular assurance that the threat has not simply been averted, but thoroughly negated, dehumanized, and rendered incapable of return."[88] Although Val is not lynched, his connections to the racial other are multiple, and these connections help to develop and extend Val's sexual illegality and its dangers, to him and to others, to those who desire him and to those repulsed by him. In him we see perhaps the full extent of the illegal body as expressed in Tennessee Williams: Clum's "sacrificial stud," object of both homo- and heterosexual desire; the transient figure with a shadowy sexual past; the character who in reaching for freedom challenges the restricted legal lives of those around him.

Val's link to the racial other bears further explication, as it refers back to his origins in the Bayou and his connections to other characters in the play, but also because it recalls Williams's suggestion that *Battle/Orpheus* was an attempt to come to terms with his own childhood and his years of knocking around, both of which were done in Southern states and charged his work with a fusion of racial and sexual politics. We can begin with his self-proclaimed brotherhood with Loon as mutually part of the "dispossessed" "kind of people," but that becomes little more than an offhand remark when compared to the other connections that exist in multiple drafts and in the printed texts. Most, if not all, of these textual and thematic developments further elucidate Williams's emphasis on law. We have already seen that Williams worked through several different comparisons of Val and Loon, including the unpublished segment described above with the two of them in a jail cell together and Loon worried that he will be mistaken as the man the Klan is looking for, adulterer and murderer. Hooper argues that in Williams's "plays where racial hatred is at its most intense, he is not so much seeking to define blackness as the anger stirred in whites. This is then transposed to dealings with other whites, with the result that 'race crimes' indirectly serve to spotlight a sadistic, riven and diseased society."[89] We see this transposition acted out in this draft sequence, somewhat ironically, as Loon's fear of being identified as Val links the two men but also serves to transfer Loon's race-based fear of false accusation to his white cellmate.

Judith Thompson notes Val's connections to black Americans but stops short of fully exploring the link she identifies. In her discussion of the *Orpheus* version of the text, she notes that the guitar is "inscribed with the autographs of immortalized black musicians and singers." Since her goal is to connect Val directly to mythic Orpheus and therefore to an "ideal of harmony," she concludes that Val's association to blues and jazz is ironic because the latter musical forms "reflect the essential discord in the history of black people in a predominantly white America." She does go on, however, to acknowledge the multiple connections Williams makes between Val and other racially charged characters: even as he himself is "stigmatized as an undesirable outcast and alien in this oppressive Southern town," she explains, he is further marginalized in his links to Carol Cutrere in her role as "disillusioned civil rights reformer," to Lady's murdered father, Papa Romano, a foreigner, with the "feared Negro Conjure man exiled to Blue Mountain," and to the black "runaway convict" "torn to pieces by the sheriff's dogs."[90]

The latter may be a later version of Loon, who does not appear in *Orpheus* by name; although Val does not have direct interaction with this convict, he serves the same function as Loon did, for Val establishes a familial connection with the convict: when he hears the baying of the dogs in pursuit, he urges the convict to *"Run boy! Run fast, brother!"* Thompson's list of other outcasts does hold up under careful scrutiny of the mutual connections to law, of course, not only with the convict but with the other characters she mentions. Carol's speech in *Orpheus* tying her former activities to civil rights, for example, connects her not only to African American causes but to illegal sexual behavior: as "Christ-bitten reformer" and "benign exhibitionist," she tells Val, she delivered speeches and wrote letters protesting the "gradual massacre of the colored majority in the county." But it was when that "Willie McGee thing came along—he was sent to the chair for having improper relations with a white whore," she put on a potato sack and set out for the capital to "deliver a personal protest to the governor." Although she admits to a strain of exhibitionism in the act, "there was something else in it, too." Tellingly, however, she was charged with "'lewd vagrancy'" because the sack was not a "respectable garment." At present, however, as she goes on, "I'm not a reformer any more, I'm just a 'lewd vagrant.' And I'm showing the 'S.O.B.S.' how lewd a 'lewd vagrant' can be if she puts her whole heart in it like I do mine!"[91] Hooper may be correct in suggesting that the "importance of racial intolerance can be lost in dramas that do not foreground it, which forge links between white protagonists and African American victims but that valorize white suffering in the main plots"; it seems to be the case here with Carol, as her attempts to fight injustice underscore her efforts rather than the racism she protests. But the more significant element of this speech is the weaving together of sex and law: Willie McGee's execution for a sex crime, and the lewd vagrancy charge against Carol for being improperly clothed during her march to the capital. For in it we recognize Williams's ongoing process of representing transgressive sex in its many forms and through multiple characters and situations.

One other figure featured in several draft versions also demonstrates Williams's attention to law. In his bibliographic survey of *Battle/Orpheus*, Robert Bray refers to the "'Jonathan West' version" of the text, its character and subplot ones that Williams worked on in between the print versions of *Battle* and then *Orpheus* in *The Theatre of Tennessee Williams*. The West scenario is connected to Val's early artistic identity as aspiring writer; in *Battle*, Val is a precursor to Tom Wingfield, "writing poems on shoeboxes."[92] In unpublished notes and drafts exploring the Jonathan West scenarios, Val's purpose in coming to the area is connected to his ambition as a writer and an activist: he tells Myra that his goal is "to reproduce the sermons of Jonathan West," the former black preacher who has been driven away by whites. What remains to be done, he tells her, is for him to "learn it all by heart so I can become the new preacher." In order to evolve, he plans to spend time in the desert, and he cannot take her along as she would make the desert more crowded.[93] The collection of notes and fragments from this period also contains an exchange between the Sheriff and Val that introduces the latter to a possible fate by baying hounds, the Sheriff warning him that he better "watch out you don't get better acquainted with 'em" for "they're the same breed of dogs that got rid of Jonathan West, the famous Yankee preacher." In an unusual instance of hand-written correction, Williams crosses out "Yankee preacher" and replaces it with "nigger preacher."

In an outline from the same period, the connection is made between West and the Conjure Man. Although the former is eliminated from the text in subsequent revisions, the Conjure Man is not, and therefore the shadow of murdered black men that Val relates to continues to hover over the work. After Val learns of the blind Conjure Man who was West's most faithful disciple, Williams conceives of a long monologue that would replace the bayou speech, about Val's search for meaning. The outline summarizes the speech as follows: "Bound up in the snakeskin jacket—Sex experience and a rootless wandering from place to place have both failed to satisfy his deep spiritual hunger."[94] Although further revisions eliminate this draft tangent, the outline fragment is significant in its consideration of the link between sex and wandering, lust and vagrancy. Furthermore, the binding of the snakeskin jacket indicates the imprisonment that comes, ironically, with both sex and with rootlessness, and implies that their combination is significant and perhaps even intrinsic. For if Val represents just one important truism about the law, it is that a variety of sexual experience leads, almost necessarily, to the fugitive life. Lust and vagrancy are tied to each other, and their connection reminds us that the tension between freedom and confinement is one of Williams's richest and most complex creative sources.

Another example of Williams's persistent attention to legal issues, particularly as they pertain to sexuality, is contained in a fragment of dialogue, presumably between Val and Myra even though it does not name the speakers: "Look! What? This note was in the pocket of the pants I sent to the cleaners. Quit foolin' with married woman. K.K.K. Yeah. Nice, huh?" No more than a few lines on a draft page, it conveys much that is at work in this play. The inability to keep a relationship private, and the dangers of revelation to a sexual coupling that exceeds the boundaries of propriety if not the boundaries of law; the threat of violence posed by a group that is not legally sanctioned but that nonetheless consists of citizens who would be considered upstanding and law-abiding.

In the published version of *Battle*, the suggestion that Val poses not only a danger to himself but to the women around him is hinted at in several early scenes between him and Myra. Just before Myra's first entrance, Sandra has fired her pistol into the air just outside the door to the mercantile; Val grabs it from Sandra as she comes "*unsteadily back into the store*," but when Myra enters and "*sees Val with the revolver in his hand, she gasps and starts toward the door.*" This moment is a critical one not only for its foreshadowing of Myra's death, an act that Jabe executes but that Val is held responsible for, especially since in that later scene he also grabs the gun from the guilty party, but also for what it suggests about Myra's perception of Val as someone dangerous to her.[95] Later in the scene, when Myra thinks that she is alone, her sudden recognition of Val's presence makes her gasp once more as she "*clutches her wrapper around her throat.*" His apology for scaring her has little effect, and, after asking who he is but not waiting for his answer she commands him: "Get out or I'll call the Sheriff!" His response to her echoes what Vee has told the other women earlier, that she had taken him into the lockup and offered him a "night's flop" there but he didn't stay because, he tells Myra, "It made me uneasy being locked up. I got to have space around me."[96] While Myra's initial uneasiness around him may be a harbinger of sexual tension, her threat of calling the law is complicated by what we come to know of his past and, ultimately, by the illicit and illegal relationship that she is about to embark upon with him.

There are multiple examples in the play of the dangers involved with trying to trap Val, but Williams also creates and revises scenarios that reveal the threats as dual-sided: they affect the women and Val, and it is difficult to determine who gets the worse end of the deal. When Sandra claims to have returned from New Orleans because she can't stop thinking about him, he suggests that she ought to return to Mardi Gras because he wants to keep his job and he has come to know that "every place

I've gone to it's been some woman I finally had to leave on account of."[97] But there is one particular case of a woman who, according to Val, could not bear to let him go that has had serious legal implications for him. Although Val's illegal sexual past receives extensive revision over the years of work that Williams devotes to the play, his backstory is significant with regards to the charge he faced of having committed a violent sexual crime: rape. In *Battle*, Myra's relationship with Val develops over the course of several scenes together, and she is initially suspicious of him, accusing him of sexually suggestive behavior in a way that has mixed connotations: "slew-footing this way and that way like one of those awful, disgustin,' carnival dancers," her description provided as a huckster is heard out in the street.[98] He shares with her details of his early life, his family's poverty and his illicit love affair with a bayou girl who enticed him by standing naked outside a dogtrot and who had lonesomeness "carved on her body," and he suggests that he might have settled down and "got connected with something" but things went wrong. He continues in the same vague vein: "Something happened" and "everything was different after that. I wasn't free anymore. I was followed by something I couldn't get off my mind."[99] At this point, he keeps further details to himself, for sexual crimes in Williams's texts are usually revealed a bit at a time, in order that the audience becomes part of the investigation. This strategy of revelation also creates a dramatic arc of illegality and dramatic interrogation that infuses the play with tension.

However, the theme of captivity is continued, and is tied to sexual illegality. It is with Val's attempt to defend Loon and keep him from being locked up that the revelation of what "happened" is revealed to Myra, and only after Val has come dangerously close to arrest himself. The Sheriff clears out the men who protest Val's argument for Loon's rights, but then begins his own interrogation of Val, throughout which the latter is defended and protected by Myra. When the Sheriff suggests that she let Val answer the questions himself, she says, "Well, don't snap questions at him like he was up on trial." The Sheriff drops the matter, clearly out of respect for Myra, but not before warning her to "do yourself a favor an' get a new clerk" for this one will, he predicts correctly, "bring yuh nothing but trouble." Now that he is "under suspicion," Val tells Myra after the Sheriff leaves, it "wouldn't be safe to stay": he is wanted for rape in Texas. Drawing further on the connection between Val and Loon, Myra responds by saying that it's "something *nigguhs* are lynched for—not you, Val." But Val has only a moment ago pointed out to her that Loon is "his own kind of people," that is, "dispossessed."[100] It is not the first time we have seen this particular past attached to a young vagabond male, and the story here is similar to the one told of Ollie in "One Arm," for both he and Val claim to have had consensual physical relationships with married women that, in the aftermath, became problematized by female attachment and prompted the men to flee the scene. The criminal charge filed against Val makes his escape more pressing and his fugitive status more lasting.

To a greater extent, such narratives, as they recur throughout Williams's representations of law, help to signify and complicate a larger issue about sexual intimacy and power and, even more specifically, about the ambiguity that often surrounds legal notions of consent, particularly when an age gap exists between the two parties. Such examinations on Williams's part demonstrate his interest in how laws and judicial decisions made sense of sexual "crimes" that were often committed in private and whose details could be contested. The narrative about Val's alleged sexual crime moves through many variations as Williams revises this text and confirms his interest in the danger that Val faces because of his sexual attractiveness and activity.

By the time of *Orpheus Descending*, Myra has evolved into Lady but, given the name change, it is ironic that she has become more developed as an illegal body. These shades in her character are evident as early as the Prologue, while Dolly and Beulah, who have been consistently represented as the "wives of small planters" lay out a buffet as they wait for Lady and Jabe to return from the hospital in Memphis. As in the earlier version, they gossip about the couple, about Jabe's condition, and about the separate bedrooms upstairs. In *Battle* the bedroom situation is speculated about as the outcome of Jabe's illness, a theory that Dolly discounts, calling it "permanent," even though she allows that Myra was not "cold-blooded" as a girl and would regularly go to the orchard with boyfriend David before he was forced to marry into money and thus save his family's plantation. But in *Orpheus*, the upstairs of the store, both its accommodations and its atmosphere are elaborated on, as are the premarital circumstances of Lady. These elaborations seek to highlight various images and circumstances that emphasize the play's depictions of law.

The mystery of the upstairs and the invasion of the apartment are both featured elements that Williams revised significantly, calling attention to the space for a family and the ways that community tensions, particularly as they are connected to sexuality and to the regulation of mores, affect the privacy of a marriage. Explaining the upstairs layout to Beulah, which is unnecessary since Beulah has also trespassed above, Dolly describes the two bedrooms "which are not even connectin'" but at "opposite ends of the hall," with everything "so dingy and dark." Moreover, she tells her friend, "Y'know what it seemed like to me? A county jail! I swear to goodness it didn't seem to me like a place for white people to live in!"[101] While jail is an appropriate way to describe the marriage, particularly as far as Lady is concerned, the legal references continue and, as they do, they draw attention to Lady's ethnic otherness, another avenue through which Williams can pursue his interest in transgressive sexuality.

Beulah tells the story of Lady's family history, an illegal one, to Dolly, who moved recently to the county. But the stage directions also stipulate that Beulah come *"straight out to the proscenium, like a pitchman,"* and direct her speech to the audience. She describes Lady's father, "The Wop," who came from the old country with a "mandolin and a monkey" and who, when Prohibition came, "took to bootleggin' like a duck to water!" On cheap land he planted an orchard with grape vines and fruit trees and made "Dago red wine," and one Sunday, Beulah recalled, "old Doctor Tooker, Methodist minister then, he bust a blood vessel denouncing The Wop in the pulpit!"[102] So Lady's genetic legacy is not only suspect in its ethnic strangeness: she is born of a bootlegging criminal. That is not the end of it, however, for her father's vineyard was populated at night by young couples who would go out there to "court up a storm" in the orchard, with its "little white wooden arbors with tables and benches to drink in and carry on in, ha ha!" For, as Beulah explains, "each of the arbors had a lamp in it, and one by one, here and there, the lamps would go out as the couples begun to make love." The setting she describes as the site of Lady's upbringing was not only a place to drink alcohol illegally, but to engage in illicit sex, a place of "calls, cries, whispers, moans—giggles." Hooper notes that the permissive atmosphere of Papa Romano's garden was one of his crimes, for he created a "garden of pleasure in which the young could liaise freely and secretly."[103]

Lady herself participated in the business and the pleasure of the wine garden, initially by helping her father to entertain the youth, after their sexual encounters, as "one by one, the lamps would be lighted again," and Lady would sing and play "Dago songs." But there came a time when she snuck off herself, with David, not heeding the calls from her father "no matter how long he called and no matter how loud." To which Dolly responds, "Well, I guess it's hard to shout back, 'Here I am, Papa,' when where you are is in the arms of your lover!"[104] Lady's illicit premarital relationship with David, whom she does not marry, marks her as an illegal body and one of Williams's women who values desire over respectability. Her loveless marriage to Jabe is the price she pays for this choice, the years spent above the store with him a punishing incarceration. Her ethnic otherness and the illegal activities of her father contribute to her downfall and to her questionable social status; the vulnerability that originates in nature and family connections and is fed by her own impulses imprisons her in a stultifying emotional life and thus does she pay for her sexually criminal activity with David. Using the physical and psychological framework of a loveless marriage, Williams expands our conceptions of crime and punishment to include nonlegal and self-inflicted means of atonement, and in doing so his work conveys the deep loss suffered by those who cannot live and love as they please.

The next part of Beulah's speech foreshadows Val's fate, as the man with whom Lady now hopes to find one last possibility of happiness:

"Papa Romano made a bad mistake," she tells Val, selling "liquor to niggers," and the "Mystic Crew took action," riding out to the orchard one night and setting fire to the place, burning it to the ground and its owner with it. The mob that we have seen in various forms throughout versions of this play now serves Williams in yet another way. The mob's connection to Lady is drawn: having been sexually intimate with David prior to marriage, having a father who was also a known bootlegger and transgressed the communal norms by doing business with African Americans, meant that she could be "bought," indeed, "bought cheap," by Jabe Torrance, the very man, Beulah claims, who "was the leader of the Mystic Crew the night they burned up her father in his wine garden on Moon Lake."[105] The family, sexual, and marital histories provided by Beulah in this prologue scene of *Orpheus* indicate that Lady may be a sexual criminal complicit in the murder of her own father, although Dolly exclaims that Lady could not possibly have known that Jabe was behind it and still married him. Beulah retorts that Lady might "live with him in hate" and with her eye on spending and inheriting his money as an act of revenge. The union of Lady and Val is one that puts both parties in danger, and because they have transgressed and been punished for their actions in the past, they are both aware of desire's consequences. To be identified as lawless in Williams's work has the effect of increased vulnerability.

The types of details that Williams develops as he drafts and revises this complex text indicate his investment in the historical and cultural milieu of the play and its period. Prohibition and its upheaval of the legal structure provide both a realistic and dramatic backdrop for this narrative, and the financial and social ramifications for a Southern bootlegger and his family are significant. For Lady, the search for intimacy and for safety, which can only come with escape from her family's illegal and outsider past, helped to determine her choices within a limited structure of the place and time. What these drafts and fragments show, generally, is how many possible resolutions of the action there are, while at the same time much of the revision material is similar and/or shows repetitive patterns of thinking and drafting. The characters of Val and Myra/Lady and the relationship between them, for instance, is fairly constant, while the different versions of the other women attracted to Val, and the inclusion or exclusion of scenes between Val and the other men in the play, suggest some of the many ways that the different drafts are also struggling to come to terms with elements of justice and how to represent the illegal body that has been thrust into this mix of characters.

What we have seen earlier in Cassandra's warnings about the law against passion that makes her, Val, and Myra/Lady "outlaws" is not merely the turn of a poetic phrase, a metaphor for the social exile that Sandra goes on to describe as undesirable. At one time or another throughout the drafting process, Williams marks each of the three with explicit criminal behavior, and connects the behavior to sexuality, demonstrating his persistence for interrogating the legal constraints of the time. Such interrogation includes challenges to these constraints, for the characters marked clearly as deviants in his plays evoke sympathetic audience responses, and these figures often emerge from condemnation with renewed spiritual value. Their bodies perish, but their spirits transcend the violence of their endings; to some extent their crimes are vanquished because their punishments are meted out with cruel vengeance rather than justice. Like other parts of the play that Williams revised, the conclusions vary in detail; they do not, however, differ considerably in significance, for they all point to survival, however qualified, of the fugitive kind. Although Val serves as the centerpiece of the dangers of the transient and illegal life, the play and its many versions demonstrate Williams's interest in multiple examples of lives consumed by, and often destroyed by, what he considers expressions of the human need for contact in conflict with another necessity: to retain one's private identity intact, without condemnation or threat.

The epilogue in the printed version of *Battle* is set, as had been the prologue, a year after the main events in what is now the store turned museum. We learn in these frame scenes that all three of the main characters plus Jabe are dead, and that Vee Talbot has lost her mind, a fate analogous to death for Williams. As Eva and Blanch (the spinster sisters who run the museum) put it in the epilogue, quoting the news account of the events, there are "five lives 'tied together in one fatal knot of passion'" remembered in this museum, which is described in the stage directions as *"sinister with its testimony of past violence."* Nonetheless, the testimony receives ongoing attention not only from the sisters but also from the visitors who come to witness. Although the sensational nature is no doubt a big part of the draw, the preservation of items and the retelling of the events give them both some weight of significance that is religious in nature. But the legal and illegal elements of the fates met by those "tied together in one fatal knot of passion" are also emphasized in the scene, serving to remind us that these passions were secular crimes as well as spiritual ones. In the epilogue, the deaths of Cassandra and Val are described in detail and the items that remain of them examined as part of the tour. Cassandra has left behind her sunglasses and a bright red cape, even though her "body was never recovered from the Sunflower River." Deemed an accident by some, the sisters "know better," that she "deliberately drove her car into the river and drowned because she knew that *decent* people were done with her." Eva concurs: "Absolutely. The Vigilantes had warned her to get out of town."[106] Cassandra is not murdered (and survives in later versions), but her death here is consistent with the hunting down experienced by all those caught up in illegal passion. However, the items of hers that remain in the museum are those of a blind seer, of one who can predict the future but cannot escape its fates.

Myra's legacy is most clearly represented by the confectionary behind the store that she designed as a tribute to her youthful love affair with David. In Clum's discussion of *Orpheus*, the Myra figure, now Lady, "lives for the moment she turns part of the general store into a recreation of her father's wine garden," thus "recreating the sexually free past the men in the town destroyed." Clum's comment reminds us of the variety of punishments that are suffered by the sexually transgressive characters consistently represented in this work, and we must remember that a "sexually free" unmarried woman who fornicates out of doors would have been subject to criminal prosecution under a vagrancy statute. In all versions of the play, Myra/Lady pursues Val sexually and successfully, and Ima Herron wrote in 1969 of Lady entering into a "state of legal prostitution" by way of her loveless marriage to Jabe.[107] The confectionary is featured in the museum tour in *Battle*, but although the sisters Temple call it a place of dreams and of springtime, Eva asks that Blanch remind her "to sprinkle a little roach powder on this floor."[108] Myra/Lady designed the space as one of freedom and fulfillment, but the complex circumstances that have enabled her to exert control over this part of the store have left a sordid residue in the form of insect tenants.

The epilogue is cut from later versions of the play, and Williams focuses his revision efforts on closing the play with the deaths of Myra/Lady and Jabe, as well as the attack on Val. In all cases, however, the latter involves a blend of judicial action (with the sheriff as the representative of law) and a blend of vigilante/Klan "justice." The blowtorch that the mob uses to attack Val evokes the Klan's fondness of fire as well as Val's fear of it. In *Battle*, the museum has a "blow-tawch" among its artifacts, "not the original one but it's one just like it," but in the epilogue, Blanch and Eva report that the group "torn off his clothes an' thrown him into a car," driving him right down the road to the lynching tree." In an outline version of the script, the Marshall returns with the snakeskin jacket, all that was recovered from the hounds that tore Val to pieces, and Sandra takes possession of the jacket.[109] Whatever his disastrous off-stage end, Val's snakeskin jacket survives and is brought back onto the stage by either the sheriff or the Conjure Man. In *Orpheus*, Carol takes it from the latter and listens "*attentively*" to an offstage "*cry of anguish*" before speaking: "Wild things leave skins behind them, they leave clean skins and teeth and white bones behind them, and these are tokens passed from one to another, so that the fugitive kind can always follow their kind."[110] Val has been trapped and killed, but his temperament as one of the fugitive kind will be channeled by similar outlaws, Carol and others. After the cry of anguish is repeated, Carol puts the coat on and heads out the door. As she leaves, the sheriff makes an unsuccessful attempt to stop her, but she ignores him and departs. Law's power seems to have played itself out, at least temporarily, and the tokens of wild things allow a break for freedom by the last of the trio.

In a review of *Sweet Bird of Youth* that appeared in the *Village Voice* in 1959, two years following the Broadway production of *Orpheus*, Sylvia Gassel takes aim at Williams for following "in the familiar tracks of those who whip up forbidding and tempting concoctions of vice in direct proportion to the wages of sin and flames of hell for those who transgress." Calling him a "dyed-in-the-wool Puritan, Southern variety," she lists the women in his plays as follows:

> In any other role she is a whore, a nymphomaniac, a monster, a man-devourer. Any sexual activity outside the bounds of matrimony leads to 1) disease of infection by a male (*Sweet Bird*); 2) illicit pregnancy, which means abortion (*Sweet Bird*), or possible death in childbirth (*Orpheus*); 3) whoredom (*Streetcar, Summer and Smoke*); 4) loss of her only justification for being, the ability to bear children (*Sweet Bird*); 5) corruption and misanthropy (*Sweet Bird*).

Gassel concludes from these examples that they are Williams's way of issuing "time-worn warnings" to females, for any "rash, passionate members of that sex will burn in more ways than one before the end. Marriage with intention to bear children (*Streetcar, Rose Tattoo*) is the only safety zone." Her commentary supports my argument about the frequency of transgressive sexual behavior in women in the plays of this period. But she does not acknowledge that marriage was the only legally sanctioned route to sexual activity for women at this time, or that in many jurisdictions some consensual activities a husband and wife engaged in could lead to their arrests. What she fails to note is that Williams proves quite knowledgeable, as her list indicates, about crime and punishment as it relates to sexuality in the era of late-1950s repression during which he wrote plays and she wrote reviews.

However, she does admit that men other than the seed-bearing married types such as Stanley Kowalski do not fare well either: "Once they have lost their innocence, or their purity, they may become diseased," or they may have a "highly effective instrument removed." If "engaged in an extra-marital affair, they will lose their potency," and if—white or colored—they sleep with anybody's sister . . . well!" The punishments she lists are extra-legal, and she frames the many transgressions she includes as immoral and in keeping with her assessment of Williams as a Southern Puritan. More important is what she does not acknowledge: that whether punished through legal channels or through vigilante acts of violence, these characters, as they were created and presented, were regularly viewed by audiences and readers through a lens of compassion that Williams created and controlled, while those who exacted the punishments were brutal and often underdeveloped characters who displayed little more than ignorance.[111] Moreover, the sexual transgressors and their actions in Williams's work were regularly depicted as figures who sought connection with others as a means of survival, but doing so has made them vulnerable to the judgment and punishment. Seen from this perspective, Williams's insistent inclusion of women among the transgressors may have an outcome opposite to the one Gassel concluded, sending a message of equality and underscoring the fact that laws restricting sexual behavior in mid-twentieth-century America were directed at men and women, the high-born and the low, the young and the old, the hetero- and the homosexual.

Deborah Nelson suggests that the "Supreme Court's shift toward embracing a constitutionally guaranteed right to privacy correlates with the sudden emergence of privacy as an object of intense anxiety, scrutiny, investigation, and exploration in mid-1960s American culture."[112] Nelson's chronological contextualization of the issue indicates that attitudes about privacy were developing exactly during the period when Williams made it such a huge concern in his creative texts, texts disseminated widely in the decades on which Nelson focuses in her study. Although her book is primarily concerned with key moments of the legal privacy debates that occurred in 1965, 1973, and 1986, the timeline she establishes allows for the possibility that Williams's works, both those that predate and those that coincide with her chronology, were a part of the cultural dialogue about privacy. She names three spheres of privacy anxiety, one for each of the dates she sets forth as significant: 1965, "the police state and the sanctity of the home;" 1973, "the woman's body;" and 1986, "the homosexual relationship."[113] These spheres, both physically and ideologically, coincide exactly with three of Williams's major concerns: the family, female sexuality and desire, and the homosexual relationship. All three are narrated or dramatized by Williams as sites of transgressive sexuality. Nelson's argument suggests that the constitutional cases corresponding to the dates she lists—*Griswold v. Connecticut*, *Roe v. Wade*, and *Bowers v. Hardwick*—"provide temporal anchor points where we can see the *belated* expression of cultural changes wrought by the visibility of privacy at a given historical juncture [emphasis mine]."[114]

Although Nelson's concerns are not limited to privacy and sexuality, there are several more points she makes that serve my discussion. One is her acknowledgment of Hannah Arendt's 1951 study of *The Origins of Totalitarianism* to help her readers understand what Nelson calls the "*scripting* of privacy violation in the cold war" [emphasis in the original]. What she suggests is Arendt's most important conclusions is the latter's assertion that like other tyrannies, totalitarian government destroys the "public realm of life" and human beings' "political capacities." But totalitarian domination as a form of government," Arendt continues, "is new in that it is not content with this isolation and destroys private life as well" by basing itself "on loneliness, on the experience of not belonging to the world at all, which is among the most radical and desperate experiences of man."[115] If Arendt's statement supports Nelson's scripting of privacy violation in the cold war, it also describes one of Williams's major and ongoing creative "scriptings" and the source of many of his characters' most pervasive struggles. We need not look further than the epigraph he used for *A Streetcar Named Desire*, several lines from "The Broken Tower" by poet Hart Crane: "And so it was I entered the broken world/To trace the visionary company of love, its voice/An instant in the wind (I know now whither hurled)/But not for long to hold each desperate choice."[116] In his choice of epigraph, Williams conveys his preoccupation with the challenges to private and public identity and relations in a "broken world."

Finally, Nelson points to the contextual significance of the death of privacy in the modern era:

> Privacy was dying because it was vulnerable to penetration from without and exposure from within. As the tabulation of privacy invasions mounted, moreover, it was becoming evident that the cold war had created a rationale for surveillance that was infinitely expandable. Defining the subversive as the "enemy within" and the "invisible threat" had an unanticipated rhetorical flexibility as has been now well documented in cold war histories. This formulation could describe the communist in the State Department or the homosexual on the job . . . extending surveillance deeper into regions that did not then appear to be political, such as gender, sexuality, mental health and personality.[117]

The regions that Nelson lists, as well as the assertion that these regions did not appear to be political at the time, echo precisely the topics to which Williams devoted himself, and help to explain why his work was not considered political in its day but has since come to be understood or at least debated as such.

With *Battle/Orpheus*, we can trace Williams's interest in depicting diverse sexuality and its impact on a single, relatively closed community of a small Southern town. Its large cast of transgressive figures interacted on a set demarcated into public and its private spaces, and although he explored many of the themes that appear elsewhere in his oeuvre, the work's long composition period and multiple published and draft versions provide a unique opportunity to trace his depictions of law and sexuality over two decades immediately preceding the judicial changes that Nelson cites above. The play becomes, in this context, another set of documents interrogating social and sexual norms and the impact of their restriction on a community's citizens.

NOTES

1. Letter from Isabel Williams (Brownlaw) to Tennessee Williams, March 1937, Tennessee Williams Collection, Harry Ransom Center, Austin, TX.
2. Albert J. Devlin, ed, *Conversations with Tennessee Williams* (Jackson, MS: University Press of Mississippi, 1986), 38–39.
3. Tischler, *Tennessee Williams: Rebellious Puritan*, 300.

4. Esther M. Jackson, "Tennessee Williams: Poetic Consciousness in Crisis," and S. Alan Chesler, "Tennessee Williams: Reassessment and Assessment," both in *Tennessee Williams: A Tribute*, ed. Jac Tharpe (Jackson: University of Mississippi, 1977), 53, 878.

5. Williams, *Memoirs*, 37, 95.

6. George Whitmore, "George Whitmore Interviews Tennessee Williams," *Gay Sunshine Interviews*, Vol. 1, ed. Winston Leyland (San Francisco: Gay Sunshine, 1984), 316.

7. Leverich, *Tom*, 136–137.

8. Hooper, *Sexual Politics*, 21.

9. "Tennessee Williams," New Directions Books, accessed October 16, 2012, http://ndbooks.com/author/tennessee-williams.

10. Bigsby, *A Critical Introduction*, 1.

11. Bigsby, *A Critical Introduction*, 4, 5.

12. Bigsby, *A Critical Introduction*, 32–33.

13. Bigsby, *A Critical Introduction*, 123–124.

14. Bigsby, *A Critical Introduction*, 123–124.

15. Savran, *Communists, Cowboys, and Queers*, 80–81.

16. Williams, *Memoirs*, 168.

17. Clum, *Still Acting Gay*, 127.

18. Clum, *Still Acting Gay*, 132.

19. Clum, *Still Acting Gay*, 128.

20. John S. Bak, *Homo americanus: Ernest Hemingway, Tennessee Williams, and Queer Masculinities* (Madison, NJ: Fairleigh Dickinson University Press, 2010), 147–148.

21. R. Barton Palmer and William Robert Bray, *Hollywood's Tennessee: The Williams Films and Postwar America* (Austin: University of Texas Press, 2009), 163 and following.

22. Claire Nicolay, "Hobos, Sissies, and Breeders: Generations of Discontent in Cat on a Hot Tin Roof, *The Tennessee Williams Annual Review*, 12 (2011): 1–46; 6.

23. Nicolay, "Hobos, Sissies, and Breeders," 13–17.

24. Nicolay, "Hobos, Sissies, and Breeders," 1.

25. Williams, *The Theatre of Tennessee Williams*, Vol. III, 115–116.

26. Eskridge, *Gaylaw*, 40–41.

27. Williams, *The Theatre of Tennessee Williams*, Vol. III, 96.

28. Williams, *The Theatre of Tennessee Williams*, Vol. III, 86.

29. Michael P. Bibler, *Cotton's Queer Relations: Same-Sex Intimacy and the Literature of the Southern Plantation, 1936–1968* (Charlottesville: University of Virginia, 2009), 19.

30. Williams, *The Theatre of Tennessee Williams*, Vol. III, 120.

31. Williams, *The Theatre of Tennessee Williams*, Vol. I, 260.

32. Williams, *The Theatre of Tennessee Williams*, Vol. I, 389.

33. Williams, *The Theatre of Tennessee Williams*, Vol. I, 355.

34. Bibler, *Cotton's Queer Relations*, 15.

35. Williams, *The Theatre of Tennessee Williams*, Vol. III, 119.

36. Williams, *The Theatre of Tennessee Williams*, Vol. III, 22.

37. Williams, *The Theatre of Tennessee Williams*, Vol. III, 121.

38. Bak, *Homo americanus*, 149.

39. Bak, *Homo americanus*, 140.

40. Williams, *The Theatre of Tennessee Williams*, Vol. III, 42.

41. Williams, *The Theatre of Tennessee Williams*, Vol. III, 211.

42. Williams, *The Theatre of Tennessee Williams*, Vol. III, 71.

43. Williams, *The Theatre of Tennessee Williams*, Vol. III, 16.

44. Bak, *Homo americanus*, 153.

45. David C. C. Matthew, "'Towards Bethlehem:' *Battle of Angels* and *Orpheus Descending*," *Tennessee Williams: A Tribute*, Jactharpe, ed., Jackson: University Press of Mississippi, 172; Claudia Wilsch Case, "Inventing Tennessee Williams: The Theatre of Tennessee Williams Guild and His First Professional Production," *Tennessee Williams Annual Review* 8 (2006), 51–71, 56.

46. Tennessee Williams, "The History of a Play," *New Selected Essays: Where I Live*, ed. Jon S. Bak, foreword by John Lahr (New York: New Directions, 2009), 16–17.

47. S. Alan Chesler, "Tennessee Williams: Reassessment and Assessment," in *Tennessee Williams: A Tribute*, ed. Jac Tharpe (Jackson: University of Mississippi, 1977), 849.

48. Robert Bray, "*Battle of Angels* and *Orpheus Descending*," *Tennessee William: A Guide to Research and Performance*, ed. Philip C. Kolin (Westport, CT: Greenwood Press, 1998), 22.

49. Devlin, *Conversations with Tennessee Williams*, 128–129.

50. Bray, "*Battle of Angels*," 31.

51. Quoted in Freedman, "'Uncontrolled Desires,'" 94.

52. Tennessee Williams, "The Battle of Angels" [play], n.d., Tennessee Williams Collection, Harry Ransom Research Center, University of Texas at Austin.

53. Freedman, "'Uncontrolled Desires,'" 94.

54. Freedman, "'Uncontrolled Desires,'" 98.

55. Freedman, "'Uncontrolled Desires,'" 103.

56. Freedman, "'Uncontrolled Desires,'" 104.

57. Freedman, "'Uncontrolled Desires,'" 105–106.

58. Judith J. Thompson, *Tennessee Williams' Plays: Memory, Myth, and Symbol*, revised edition (New York: Peter Lang, 2002), 81.

59. Williams, *The Theatre of Tennessee Williams*, Vol. I, 5.

60. Williams, *The Theatre of Tennessee Williams*, Vol. I, 10.

61. Williams, *The Theatre of Tennessee Williams*, Vol. III, 227.

62. Richards, *The Sodomy Cases*, 35.

63. Anonymous, "Play Must Have Lines Taken Out," *Boston Post* 7 January 1941: 1, 8. Reprinted in *The Critical Response to Tennessee Williams*, ed. George W. Crandell (Westport, CT: Greenwood Press, 1996), 2.

64. Leverich, *Tom*, 393.

65. Hooper, *Sexual Politics*, 22.

66. Tennessee Williams, "The History of a Play (with Parentheses)," in *New Selected Essays: Where I Live*, revised and expanded, ed. John S. Bak (New York: New Directions, 2009), 19–20.

67. Williams, *Selected Letters, vol. I*, 214.

68. Williams, *New Selected Essays*, 16.

69. Tennessee Williams, "Amor Perdida, or How It Feels to Become a Professional Playwright," *New Selected Essays*, 5.

70. Case, "Inventing Tennessee Williams," 9.

71. Williams, *The Theatre of Tennessee Williams*, Vol. I, 45.

72. Williams, *The Theatre of Tennessee Williams*, Vol. I, 24.

73. Williams, *The Theatre of Tennessee Williams*, Vol. I, 24.

74. John Clum, "The Sacrificial Stud and the Fugitive Female in *Suddenly Last Summer, Orpheus Descending*, and *Sweet Bird of Youth*, *The Cambridge Companion to Tennessee Williams*, ed. Matthew C. Roudané (Cambridge, UK: Cambridge University Press, 1997), 136, 139.

75. Williams, *The Theatre of Tennessee Williams*, Vol. I, 44–45.

76. "The Battle of Angels" [play], n.d., Tennessee Williams Collection, Harry Ransom Research Center, University of Texas at Austin.

77. Williams, *The Theatre of Tennessee Williams*, Vol. III, 244–245.

78. Williams, *The Theatre of Tennessee Williams*, Vol. I, 99.

79. Williams, *The Theatre of Tennessee Williams*, Vol. I, 99.

80. Williams, *The Theatre of Tennessee Williams*, Vol. I, 65. In *Orpheus*, Myra/Lady's young beau is Sandra/Carol's brother.

81. Williams, *The Theatre of Tennessee Williams*, Vol. I, 51.

82. Clum, "Sacrificial Stud," 138–139.

83. Williams, *The Theatre of Tennessee Williams*, Vol. I, 67–68.

84. Williams, *The Theatre of Tennessee Williams*, Vol. I, 16.

85. Leverich, *Tom*, 381.

86. "The Battle of Angels" [notes and fragments], n.d., Tennessee Williams Collection, Harry Ransom Research Center, University of Texas at Austin.
87. Robyn Wiegman, "The Anatomy of Lynching," *American Sexual Politics: Sex, Gender, and Race since the Civil War*, eds. John C. Fout and Maura Shaw Tantillo (Chicago: University of Chicago Press, 1993), 223.
88. Wiegman, "Anatomy of Lynching," 224.
89. Hooper, *Sexual Politics,* 126.
90. Thompson, *Tennessee Williams' Plays,* 82–83.
91. Williams, *The Theatre of Tennessee Williams*, Vol. III, 251–252.
92. Williams, *The Theatre of Tennessee Williams*, Vol. I, 35.
93. "The Battle of Angels" [play], n.d., Tennessee Williams Collection, Harry Ransom Research Center, University of Texas at Austin.
94. "The Battle of Angels" [play], n.d., Tennessee Williams Collection, Harry Ransom Research Center, University of Texas at Austin.
95. Williams, *The Theatre of Tennessee Williams*, Vol. I, 20.
96. Williams, *The Theatre of Tennessee Williams*, Vol. I, 28.
97. Williams, *The Theatre of Tennessee Williams*, Vol. I, 44.
98. Williams, *The Theatre of Tennessee Williams*, Vol. I, 49.
99. Williams, *The Theatre of Tennessee Williams*, Vol. I, 55.
100. Williams, *The Theatre of Tennessee Williams*, Vol. I, 71–73.
101. Williams, *The Theatre of Tennessee Williams*, Vol. III, 229.
102. Williams, *The Theatre of Tennessee Williams*, Vol. III, 230–231.
103. Hooper, *Sexual Politics,* 127.
104. Williams, *The Theatre of Tennessee Williams*, Vol. III, 231, 232.
105. Williams, *The Theatre of Tennessee Williams*, Vol. III, 232–233.
106. Williams, *The Theatre of Tennessee Williams*, Vol. I, 119–121.
107. Ima Honaker Herron, *The Small Town in American Drama* (Dallas, TX: Southern Methodist University Press, 1969), 352.
108. Williams, *The Theatre of Tennessee Williams*, Vol. I, 9.
109. "The Battle of Angels," new outline, n.d., Tennessee Williams Collection, Harry Ransom Research Center, University of Texas at Austin.
110. Williams, *The Theatre of Tennessee Williams*, Vol. III, 341.
111. Sylvia Gassel, "Sex, Sin, and Brimstone in Tennessee Williams," *Village Voice*, 24 June 1959: 8–9. Reprinted in George W. Crandell, *The Critical Response to Tennessee Williams* (Westport, CT: Greenwood Press, 1996), 168–170.
112. Nelson, *Pursuing Privacy*, 3.
113. Nelson, *Pursuing Privacy*, 3.
114. Nelson, *Pursuing Privacy*, 9.
115. Quoted in Nelson, *Pursuing Privacy*, 9.
116. Quoted in Williams, *The Theatre of Tennessee Williams*, Vol. I, 239.
117. Nelson, *Pursuing Privacy*, 11.

FOUR

The Politics of Recognition

In December 1973 the American Psychiatric Association (APA) approved a proposed change to the *Diagnostic and Statistical Manual of Psychiatric Disorders* (DSM-II), removing homosexuality from its list of mental disorders. The revision was a contested one among the association's members, however, and a compromise was crafted. The new edition of the manual defined "sexual orientation disturbance [Homosexuality]" as a diagnosis "for individuals whose sexual interests are directed primarily toward people of the same sex and who are either disturbed by, in conflict with, or wish to change their sexual orientation." The group clarified its new position by adding that homosexuality "per se is one form of sexual behavior, and with other forms of sexual behavior which are not by themselves psychiatric disorders, are not listed in this nomenclature."[1] Two years later, Bruce Voeller, president of Gay Activists Alliance and later a cofounder of the National Gay Task Force, was one of two plaintiffs in a lawsuit designed to challenge Virginia's state sodomy law. Relying on the privacy argument developed in *Griswold*, which had granted married couples the right to use birth control and was significant to *Roe* by strengthening constitutional rights to sexual freedom, *Doe v. Commonwealth's Attorney* was filed in a federal district court, attacking the constitutionality of the Virginia Code, which made it a crime, even for consenting adults acting in private, to engage in homosexual relations. A three-judge panel split two to one against the litigants, and the Supreme Court held up the lower court's decision by a vote of six to three.[2] It would be almost thirty years before *Lawrence v. Texas* would end with the Supreme Court's ruling, in another six-to-three opinion, that the Texas sodomy law violated the Due Process Clause of the Fourteenth Amendment. Justice Kennedy delivered the majority opinion of the court, arguing for liberty's protection of the person from unwarranted government intrusions: "In our tradition the State is not omnipresent in the home. And there are other spheres of our lives and existence, outside the home, where the State should not be a dominant presence. Freedom extends beyond spatial bounds. Liberty presumes an autonomy of self that includes freedom of thought, belief, expression, and certain intimate conduct."[3] Although legally endorsed sexual activity discrimination did not end nationally until the twenty-first century, court cases that brought civil liberty violations to the public's attention had been increasing in frequency at all levels of government throughout the second half of the twentieth.

A legal challenge more than a decade before the Virginia case was brought by Franklin Edward Kameny, who would go on to co-found a chapter of the Mattachine Society in Washington, D.C., in 1961. Kameny's arrest for lewd conduct with another man in San Francisco in 1956 led to questions about his sexuality from the Civil Service Commission and to his dismissal from a job with the Army Map Service the following year. Kameny's sixty-page petition to the Supreme Court, an early version of the gay-pride statement, sought to appeal the dismissal on the grounds that the federal government had excluded him from employment opportunities and had, therefore, discriminated against him. Although the Supreme Court's denial of his petition ended the case, Kameny's argument was notable, according to Eskridge, for going "beyond the liberal politics of privacy" to assert a Progressive *politics of recognition* that there was "no connection between sodomy and any kind of civil harm" and that "homosexuals were honorable people entitled to full equality [emphasis in the original]."[4] Despite the legal failure of the petition, Kameny's efforts underscored issues of privacy and freedom while asserting a plea for dignity and equality, a personal and political stance that Williams supported in his creative work throughout his career. Revisions and challenges to medical and legal attitudes about homosexuality provide evidence of the slow and complicated progress toward acceptance, decriminalization, and equality; despite the cultural and generational shifts that occurred during the 1960s, the repeal of discriminatory laws would continue to be blocked, legislatively and judicially, for several decades. However, the examples above underscore the increased visibility of homosexuals, on the street and in the courts, demonstrating that debates about diverse sexuality had begun to replace silence.

The politics of recognition also began to inspire gay people to organize themselves in protest against police harassment and government abuse; the formation of such communities and their increased visibility were invaluable to the individuals involved and to the younger generation of homosexuals seeking to exert their sexual identities without fear. What is evident throughout the decade is that the increase in public pride among gay individuals and groups contributed to the development of a new body politic with an increased acceptance of difference and an expanding application of equal rights. For example, many Americans agreed with Kameny that the government had no right to interfere with or regulate private sex acts; the state of Illinois became the first state to deregulate consensual sodomy in 1961. But change came slowly, for many states revised existing sodomy laws by decriminalizing some behaviors previously considered deviant, thereby shifting the criminal focus to homosexual activities that had not been legalized.

In the late 1960s, social pressure resulted in the revision of public mores as members of the younger generation came of age; large numbers of them, particularly those who left home for college or moved to urban areas, supported sexual diversity. The increased freedom they exercised in their personal habits and lifestyles suggested that legal revisions to sex regulation would be forthcoming. Throughout the decade, states worked to revise their penal codes and used the Model Penal Code for guidance; because it promoted the decriminalization of consensual sodomy, the topic arose as various state commissions conducted their reform. Among the range of concerns was the possibility that the complete decriminalization of sodomy would encourage homosexuality, which prompted discussions about the state's rights and responsibilities to regulate sexual misconduct. Such misconduct included the sexual activity of adulterous and homosexual relationships, and resistance to sexual diversity remained a powerful force. A majority of Americans continued to believe that the law represented one of the best ways to insure the morality of its citizenship, with states and municipalities responsible for maintaining decency, locally, and without the need for enforcement whenever possible.

Some states took on the review and reform of their sodomy laws in ways that provided increased freedom for the majority of the voting populace, decriminalizing selected acts of "sexual deviance" while continuing to regulate those behaviors that were seen as most threatening to the moral fabric. This line, between "sexual freedom and community values," Eskridge argues, was "provisionally drawn across the backsides of homosexuals, still the universal scapegoats."[5] The example he provides of such line-drawing in Texas illustrates the mind-set of those at the state level charged with reforming the penal code. Like other state groups engaged in this work, the Texas Bar Association formed a committee to revise the state's penal code, and took the Model Penal Code as its template. Over the course of three years the group drafted its proposal. The draft of proposed sex crime provisions aligned itself with the model code, asserting the individual's rights to privacy and freedom when it came to fornication, adultery, and consensual sodomy. Only the latter was contested during the discussion: the committee's representative from law enforcement favored retaining criminal status for sodomy because "the act itself is so destructive of moral fiber and so insidious—especially regarding the young."[6] Thus do we see that the legal atmosphere at the time was changing, from a postwar climate that allowed the possibility of prosecution for all kinds of perceived sexual transgression, to a more relaxed one that continued to identify certain types of personal actions as too dangerous to legalize. The prohibitions against various types of illegal acts were therefore, and for multiple reasons, not consistently or immediately lifted in the era of increased rights, and the diversity of legislative reform from one state to another reflected a national diversity of opinion about the usefulness of such laws. The heterosexual's relative freedom from prosecution, particularly for illegal acts conducted in private, meant that despite the influence of the Model Penal Code in some jurisdictions, changes to adultery and fornication laws were not considered pressing in all states.

Gay activism in cities discouraged enforcement of existing sodomy laws. In New York City, for example, Eskridge reports, "police beatings or harassment of gay people triggered detailed documentation, press coverage, and often protests, followed by meetings with the mayor's office and the human rights office." When Ed Koch became the city's mayor in 1978, "one of his first acts was a directive prohibiting sexual orientation discrimination by all municipal agencies, including the police department." In San Francisco, on the other hand, police actions against gays had abated after 1965, "but the flourishing of the gay subculture generated one last effort at suppression" under Mayor Joseph Alioto in 1970–1971. Arrests for oral copulation went from eleven men in 1967 to ninety-seven in 1970, and Alioto's administration ignored protests by gay organizations. In Los Angeles, "whose police department was the most aggressive sodomy and solicitation enforcement machine in the nation," the turning point was the 1973 election of City Attorney Burt Pines, "with critical gay support."[7] Although it became less likely that private acts between same-sex consensual adults would result in arrest, even in jurisdictions where those acts remained felonies, the increased divide between activities accepted or decriminalized and those that remained subject to prosecution indicate the legal schizophrenia of the period when it came to individual rights and freedoms.

Such contradictions would, in many cases, actually become more marked over the decade that many consider a watershed time in the advancement of equal rights, and Williams contributed to the debates by communicating his opinions and perceptions through his writing. It was within this increasingly visible polarized public sphere that he created ever more complex representations of gendered desire while providing ever less readily explicable context for their interpretation. Even as the reality and the representation of diverse sexualities became increasingly visible during the early years of the contemporary period in America, it remained illegal to conduct certain activities in private throughout many jurisdictions. The discrepancies found in laws of this period are comparable to the narrative or thematic contradictions that marked Williams's late work. Legal context directs this consideration of him as a person and as a writer, but, more importantly, it frames his work's continued interrogation of inequality, oppression, and public attitudes about sexual deviance.

Cultural expansion of freedom and equality occurred unevenly, with law's texts tracking the push and pull, forward and back—the drag of history in conflict with forward momentum. This unsteady progress is reflected in Williams's work, the illegal bodies in his texts constructed from the residue of the past and the raw material of the present. Prior to the 1960s, the legal system at all levels reinforced the notion of a shared infrastructure of national moral values, whether or not such conformity existed, and other institutions worked in tandem with the law to keep this idea at the forefront of cultural production. Within a framework that supported hegemony, Williams's challenges to it, especially his representations of resistance to the legislation of sexual behavior, had a relatively clear and unambiguous target: the dominant culture and its power to direct individual behavior and attitudes. As a structure within which to create dramatic or narrative conflict, the target served him extremely well. Not all of his plays of the early period were critical and/or popular successes; the ones that were, however, often relied upon a clear dichotomy of values that in his skilled hands exposed a fascinating web of tensions and contradictions. He revealed what had seemed a straightforward ideology as a complex network of competitive values, thus fulfilling a significant artistic mission. In his late period, that mission underwent a series of revisions, as his own relationship with sexuality matured and as he redefined his own sexual history in an era of increased transparency. We can trace Williams's written reflections on his self and on his relationship to the world both in the personal documents meant for self and in first-person narratives that indicated the presence of audience: in letters he wrote to friends and associates, in his *Memoirs*, and in the essays he wrote throughout his life. The personal documents produced in great abundance in the 1930s and 1940s, the journals and letters that chart Williams's construction of identity as a writer and as a homosexual, were later supplemented with other more public kinds of personal statements: essays and the memoir, newspaper and television interviews, biographical spotlights at various award ceremonies. But when it comes to what I have proposed as a new narrative of Williams's place in the public sphere over the course of five decades, the more openly he discussed sexual transgression and its reception in American society, the more complex and ambiguous his representations and statements became.

In the introduction to *New Selected Essays: Where I Live* (2009), the revised and expanded edition of a 1978 collection, John Lahr argues that Williams "evolved styles that spoke for each aspect of his self" and served the writer "as both a mask and a peephole into personality." His epistolary style, Lahr argues, "is direct, unbuttoned, and loosey-goosey, an improvisational display of his sharpness of mind and tongue," while what Lahr called his "public prose style" as exhibited in the volume of essays is a "different kind of discourse with the world."[8] In seeking to understand the changing nature of Williams's work and the changing conditions of his private and public selves in a world that was itself in revision, this assertion by Lahr is informative: "All great stylists have to teach their idiom to the public. Williams's essays, with their polite phrasings, make a shrewd case for what was actually a radical revolt against theatrical naturalism and its shallow, melodramatic rendering of human emotion."[9] Lahr's remarks touch on themes significant to this study: writing as reflection of self, the tension and difference between private and public, the nature of Williams's "radical" self, and his indictment of "shallow" representations of "human emotion." Meanwhile, the legal environment continued to force gay Americans to create their identities according to context and audience, with their lives or their livelihoods depending upon their success in developing a range of private and public personas. The first-person nonfiction of his *Memoirs* (1975) is one of Williams's most personal and most public late-life negotiations with sexuality and law.

As early as 1977, Victor A. Kramer argues that at the core of the confessional autobiographical *Memoirs* is Williams's "awareness of the disjunction between the public person (artist, lover, family member) and the private person."[10] The parenthetical list suggests an additional demarcation to the one that has already been drawn here, for it creates of Williams and his private self an island set apart from his relationships with others and from his many texts, autobiographical or not. One fact that "emerges from this recollection," the *Memoirs*, is that "much of Williams's career has been spent isolated from others" and what "seems memorable," in Kramer's view, is "that what he learned best to do as an artist was accomplished apart from others, and especially in isolation from other artists."[11] That said, Kramer also notes that like most artists Williams "seems to have been driven to his writing partly as an escape from a private world" and his memoir "stresses his realization of how for him both life and art blend."[12] To some extent the late work cannot be understood without at least a positing of the connection between experience and representation as America and Williams moved into a new era.

Identities constructed in parts, subject to regular revision, and sometimes made available for public viewing, or consumption, describe Williams's published selves. In his 2011 essay on what he calls "Williams's many Ur-*Memoirs*," John S. Bak suggests that we can understand the text today by letting go of "our own continued insistence on viewing it as a finished uber-text" in order to focus on the book's gradual composition over the years, thereby freeing *Memoirs* from the "debate surrounding its anecdotal content and its unorthodox structure."[13] Bak's interest is in the elongated gestation period that he traces through the manuscripts, and the evidence he provides that the work is the product of "decades of autobiographical ruminating," or what Williams called his "'scattered idioms,'" demonstrate the volume's connections to gay identities and their constructions, in texts and in society. What can be seen as Williams's significant revision to self-representation was a timely reaction to an age that simultaneously allowed for more exposure of and dialogue about diverse sexualities, while insisting, legally and culturally, that illegal bodies not convey an integrated whole, but continue to be perceived and treated in American society as fragmented, contradictory, and undervalued.

The form and the content that Williams relied upon to convey his experience emerged, as they always did, from the most pressing and repressive elements of the social and political climates he witnessed. *Memoirs* can be read as an act of witness to an age of transition by a man and artist in transition. In the foreword of his book, Williams lamented the sea change that suggested to him that he might not again "receive a persuasively favorable critical response" to his theater, but he went on to say that his own theater was "in a state of revolution." As he wrote: "I am quite through with the kind of play that established my early and popular reputation," even while asserting that he will pursue the same course he always had, which was "to express my world and my experience of it in whatever form seems suitable to the material."[14] While we might assume that Williams believed that the form of *Memoirs* was suitable to the material he presented, Terri Smith Ruckel questions whether "the homosexual attestations in *Memoirs* may have breached the model, canonical standards of social behavior and culture, resulting in a text of scandal."[15] With her focus specifically on the autobiography and its historical development, Ruckel goes on to suggest that "*Memoirs* seemed to violate the canon of acceptable autobiography in significant ways, since autobiographies generally follow a narrative path telling the story of the writer's past and moving toward the present." Williams, however, "took a postmodern approach by looking back and also forward, conflating past and present."[16] By creating a "text of scandal," he violated the social contract of decorum by revealing untoward details of his sexual life; by defying the presumed chronological structure of the autobiography, he rendered his life's narrative incomprehensible.

Ruckel's argument suggests that through *Memoirs*, Williams "hoped to communicate the myriad mysteries of what it meant to be homosexual male. As a kind of *l'écrivain maudit*, or outcast writer, Williams intended for *Memoirs* to address not only personal issues but social and cultural issues that existed outside his own experiences and, yet, were responsible for negotiating his life."[17] His goal was thus similar to what this study maintains about his textual production throughout his career: that his persistent interrogation of the law was achieved by transforming his experiences into the appropriate literary or theatrical formats, and then setting those experiential transformations in an environment of legislative and cultural restrictions and opinions.

A public document that is nonetheless infused with the personal and the sexual, *Memoirs* is a significant contribution to discourses on homosexuality during the 1970s. The examples provided at this chapter's opening convey the tensions between the increased transparency of sexual difference and the determination to maintain the values of homogeneity in psychiatry and law. The compromise documented in the 1973 revision to DSM-II, to change the previous category of "Homosexuality" to "Sexual orientation disturbance," seems to suggest a transformation of professional perceptions about same sex interest to a mental conflict and/or a desire for alteration of that urge. On the surface, then, the revised text reflects the APA's move in what may be an appropriate direction, toward a psychiatric theory of homosexuality. But the background section of the proposal for change reveals the compromise as the result of the ongoing social and political debates. The text outlines the two sides of the argument, describing the elimination of homosexuality in a manual of psychiatric disorders as justified not only because it is scientifically inaccurate, but because it "encourages an adversary relationship between psychiatry and the homosexual community, and is misused by some people outside of our profession who wish to deny civil rights to homosexuals." By including the issue of civil rights in this rationale, the APA acknowledges its role in decisions legislating sexual activity in the public sphere. On the other hand, the opponents of the revision "assert that to remove homosexuality from the nomenclature would be to give official sanction to this form of deviant sexual development," and "would be a cowardly act of succumbing to the pressure of a small but vocal band of activist homosexuals who defensively attempt to prove that they are not sick."[18] The proposal that leads to the change in the manual reflected the contention in society, a contention that had become more visible as states revised their penal codes and individuals began to openly challenge the legislation of their private lives.

Furthermore, the proposal's summary of the two sides raises an issue that contextualizes Williams's confessional and its 1975 appearance, for Roy Cain begins a 1991 essay by reminding readers that the APA's "normalization" of homosexuality represented a significant shift in attitudes about privacy and publicity. When homosexuality was considered pathological, "secretiveness about one's homosexuality was widely viewed as normal and desirable; openness, conversely, was seen as an expression of personal and social pathology and as a political liability to gays in general." With normalization came a preference for openness, while "secretiveness came to be seen as problematic."[19] Cain's argument is focused on the benefits of the shift, personally and politically, limiting his examination of its impact on three specific groups: "mental health professionals, gay political activists, and sociologists."[20] The significance of this research to the reception of *Memoirs* is not the results of the changing perspective, however; what matters is that the shift coincides with the book's publication. In the light of a developing and rather radical revision to the politics of "coming out," we see Williams's memoir as a text that straddled this cultural moment. It is not surprising, then, that the book exemplifies the conflict that gay individuals faced as the transparency that advanced civil rights challenged the long-held necessity of obscuring an identity deemed deviant.

Also significant to this study is the way that the critical reception of *Memoirs* provided a bridge to the legal environment of his late plays and their complications of representation. Ruckel proposes that *Memoirs* was Williams's apologia pro vita sua, a defense of his life, but she insists that the text also had a broader purpose: "Williams's *Memoirs* documents the social and historical attitudes of his lifetime toward homoeroticism to vindicate not only his choices but the homosexual lifestyle in general. *Memoirs* offer an apologia for homosexuality to Williams's gay and straight readers alike. Moreover, as a memoir that breaches the conventions of respectable society," the text resists the "homophobic tide that swept over the world of his lifetime."[21] In her conclusion, Ruckel acknowledges that Williams's defense of life was not successful in lifting "the onus of public disapproval for the 'laureate of the outcast.'"[22] Certainly, the reviews of the book at the time of its publication bear out her assertion; Bak writes of the book's immediate climb on the bestseller list, but claims that in spite of the book's success, "or rather because of it, *Memoirs* also became a lightning rod for the continued harsh, and ostensibly homophobic, attacks levelled against him by many of the nation's leading theatre critics."[23] One of the major strains of criticism stemmed from disappointment that the author failed to explain or theorize his writing process in the book, and Bak concurs, concluding that it offered "readers little in the way of insight into Williams's dramatic theory or his creative process, teetering between a string of disjointed anecdotes, several of which detail his sexual escapades, and his daily struggles over the production of *Small Craft Warnings*."[24] If, however, the book documented the inexplicable path of the homosexual writer coming of age well before the Age of Aquarius, its view of Williams's expanding experiences and shifting attitudes does represent a unique view of homoeroticism during his life.

Williams defended the finished product in an interview conducted with *New York Times* critic Mel Gussow when the book was first released by Doubleday. Gussow shares Williams's remarks: "The publisher 'was hoping I would write more about the plays,' he said. Instead, 'I even forgot one or two. I found it difficult to write about writing. Some people write about it. I just do it. I thought my plays exist for people to see. My life is more or less expressed in them.'"[25] In 2011, Marie Pecorari views Williams's strategy as a protective one that is, in her opinion, the writer "feigning not to be aware that the public/private difference is still a valid one"; she argues that instead of "separating his persona along a public/private dichotomy, Williams displaces the accepted line between outer and inner to arrive at a man/writer distinction. The more he puts his non-professional self on display, the better he can protect his writer self."[26] Jack Richardson, in his 1975 review, called the book a "raw display of a private life that has come to no pat conclusion about itself, a mixture of incongruous incidents and associations." In his description of the personal material in *Memoirs*, Richardson seems to suggest as much when he writes that the "happy one-night stands, the violent conclusions to a dalliance with rough trade, the long, deepening love for one person—all are remembered in a way that does not disguise or flaunt the problems of pederasty and treats the oddities of carnal appetite as both a comic and sublime fact of human feelings."[27] The "raw display" and the lack of "pat conclusion" created much consternation among readers and reviewers when the book was published, but from a distance those very elements made the book appropriate to its time.

In her more general remarks about the body of nonfiction that Williams produced over his lifetime, Pecorari argues that his nonfiction reflects "Williams's brand of understated, non-conformist experimentalism and its set of qualities" which, "however tenuous, could be used as guidelines to reread the works: its refusal to search for origins or foundations, to bring a sense of closure, its willingness to approach material already interpreted by others without trying to put new wine into old bottles."[28] Increased airing of the private lives of homosexuals seemed to many a display too "raw," and as these newly public narratives of diverse sexualities became part of the public sphere, they lacked the sense of "pat conclusion" that many Americans sought. The directives set forth in the Model Penal Code urged lawmakers to reconsider legal prescriptions and restrictions on sexuality, and the variance of revision from one state to the next revealed that no national consensus on sexual freedom existed. Debates about privacy and sexuality had grown more complicated and more visible, even as the transparency underscored the discrepancy between rights and morality. The back and forth of praise and condemnation, as well as the comments that hint at conclusions but do not make them, are representative of the initial reception of *Memoirs* and of its ongoing scholarly commentary. Pecorari's advice to adopt an approach of "understated, non-conformist experimentalism" for interpreting Williams's work reminds us that throughout his career, he interrogated the regulation of homosexuality, specifically, and the condemnation of diverse sexualities more generally, by utilizing indirect and sometimes contradictory narrative or thematic means.

Hooper suggests what he calls a general acknowledgment that with *Memoirs* "Williams did little either for himself or the cause of gay rights" and that he "chose the private/public genre of published memoirs to titillate his reader with both successful and unsuccessful sexual encounters" in order to "pander to what he thought would be his readership's prurience and enhance his image as a gay raconteur."[29] However, when *Memoirs* is viewed against the backdrop of sociological and legal upheaval about the place of the homosexual in American life and culture, the book's "private/public genre" would seem an appropriate form in which to present the life of a gay man born in 1911, a man who lived his private and his public lives in a century during which the right of privacy was developed and debated in the courts, a writer who created texts that challenged and excited audiences with accounts of "successful and unsuccessful sexual encounters," and one who complicated his fellow citizens' perceptions of the outcast writer in his fiction and in his non-fiction. It would seem appropriate for an American who waded into the murky waters of modern identity politics, revising his notion of self nearly as often as he revised one of his stories and plays.

Perhaps Hooper's description of *Memoirs* could be more aptly applied to what remains a notorious episode of Williams's public life, a personal revelation that preceded *Memoirs* by five years: his appearance on the David Frost show in January 1970. The television interview followed closely upon the playwright's release from the psychiatric ward at Barnes Hospital in St. Louis, where he had undergone treatment for alcohol and drug addiction, and less than a year since the police raided the Stonewall bar in Greenwich Village. When pressed by Frost about his homosexuality, Williams uttered a very public statement about his past: "I don't want to be involved in some sort of scandal, but I've covered the waterfront."[30] It is impossible to know if the most scandalous element of his remark was its allusion to homosexuality or its suggestion of promiscuity. Donald Spoto's commentary on this admission is particularly interesting, for he explains that although Williams would continue to speak very openly about his collapse and hospitalization, "he chose not to elaborate," here or in other interviews that followed, "on what had slipped out to Frost before a commercial interruption." Spoto suggests that in the late 1960s it had become fashionable for celebrities to "let it all hang out," and that the sharing of details with a "public famished for trash," at least in the case of Williams's confessions about his "stoned age," would produce public admiration for his honesty.

However, after reporter Tom Buckley published an interview he had conducted with Williams in Key West in the spring of 1970, Williams resented the appearance in print of the details of his home life and social intercourse, which he had offered to Buckley with casual abandon. Spoto theorizes on the apparent contradiction as follows: "Perhaps he wanted to be controversial—the hard-drinking, openly homosexual writer with nothing to hide—and at the same time, a man *of his own time*, a Southern gentleman from a politer era who would never abandon propriety and privacy [emphasis in the original]."[31] But the response Williams made to

Frost's question is also significant for what it reveals about his conception of his own sexuality. To some extent, an admission of covering the waterfront may not be as personally revealing as the details of his home life reported by Tom Buckley, for the first is, by its very nature, an example of conducted illegal sex. He had lived for decades with the reality that in those years that he picked up "trade" along the waterfront, whether the trade was sailors or queens, he would have been subject to prosecution by exposing himself to vice squads. But the intrusion of a reporter into one's home and a report on the very private "social intercourse" of a life gets at the heart of the issues of intimacy and legality that we have seen are complicated and fraught for Williams's characters, and, it seems, for him, both within the context of law and beyond its purview.

Williams's direct comments about law and society, pre- and post-Stonewall, provided some insights on his personal and public conceptions of self, although, as is often the case with him, his overt opinions tended toward the obscure. In an interview in 1966 with Walter Wagner, he spoke specifically about the civil rights movement and about his own position to what Wagner called the "main social stream" in America. Williams responded to the latter question by saying, "I am very much a part of it, I hope; I hope to be always," and he spoke of his admiration for young people going out to "face police bullies in the South, the Ku Klux Klan, the whole bit," and he suggests "some remarkable progress in that direction," that "finally American people have a sense of justice."[32] When Frost challenged him about his subject matter—"Why is it that your plays are so full of the less cheerful topics, like cancer and lobotomies and rape and adultery and incest and nymphomania and homosexuality?" Williams replied that "you're merely picking things out of the plays." Continuing to push, however, Frost concluded that it "just comes back again and again to the fact that all your plays do come out of your personal life, don't they?" But Williams resisted this pat conclusion by universalizing the portrait: these topics are part of "everybody's personal life," for we all live, he insists, with the rape of the individual by society, the cannibalism of one person of another, "in our fashion," and, when Frost asked specifically about homosexuality, Williams suggested that "everybody has some elements of homosexuality in him, even the most heterosexual of us." The "waterfront" remark followed immediately upon this part of the conversation; when what has been considered a shocking sexual admission on Williams's part is seen within the context of the conversation, the admission becomes part of a discussion about the heterogeneity of society and about the intricate connection between diverse sexual acts and a society whose identities and values are equally diverse.

In a 2011 panel discussion at the Tennessee Williams Scholars' Conference, four scholars discussed the topic of Williams's "coming out" on the David Frost show. In the published transcript of this discussion, Michael

Paller explained the shift to a communal identity that occurred in the gay community just months before Williams's television appearance: "After Stonewall, it's not unlike, I think, many minority communities, when there's a sudden moment where they're forging a communal identity. There's going to be dissent around it, but eventually there's going to be sort of one really significant, one mostly agreed-upon, identity. There's not a lot of room for dissent in terms of an emerging public identity."[33] This generalization does not allow for certain contingencies of both law and diversity. Given that many local and state jurisdictions continued to restrict and even threaten homosexuals who considered emerging from the closet to help forge a public identity, the early 1970s did not provide either the equal protection under the law or the cultural coherence that would have facilitated the communal identity that we speak of forty years hence through the lens of all that has changed since that period.

The panel discussion's consideration of legal restrictions was limited to those imposed upon dramatic representations. Savran suggested that in the earlier decades of his career Williams might have been "trying to safeguard his gay characters, which may seem peculiar—I mean, having them kill themselves may seem like a curious way of safeguarding them—but you have to remember that positive representations of lesbians and gay men were forbidden on the New York stage. So it's not as though Williams could simply invent all these wonderful gay characters. They were not allowed."[34] As Paller added, "Actually, technically, legally, no depiction of sex perversion was allowed," from around 1928 until 1968 because of the Wales Padlock Law. Savran asserted the difference between Williams's prose and his plays that has been noted elsewhere: "His prose—because it was not as public—was a place where he could write his sexuality and write his desires, which could not be represented on the stage."[35] Savran personalized the difference here, referring to the creative expressions of sexuality and desire as "his," emphasizing the connection between Williams's identity and the many versions of sexual identity that appeared in the plays and stories.

Williams spoke in interviews, before and after his Frost show appearance, about the homophobia that he experienced personally at his home in Key West because he had "come out." These interviews may have been an opportunity for testing the public's reaction to his personal sexual confessions, and Bak's 2011 essay documents the autobiographical musings that become part of, or provide a way of writing toward, the *Memoirs*. Don Lee Keith interviewed Williams in New Orleans a year after Stonewall, and in that interview he told Keith that he felt less comfortable in Key West after the appearance of an *Esquire* piece the prior year that reported an incident in which Williams was "beaten up by some sailors in a Key West bar" (which Williams denied). After the article came out, Williams said, "It hasn't been the same there [Key West]. They come by and throw rocks at my house and yell, 'Faggot.' Sometimes they throw eggs."[36] This story reveals a Williams vulnerable to what he claims were falsities about his sexual activities and attacks on him for his public acknowledgment of them. It also demonstrates that the public statements about his own sexuality, in interviews and in the *Memoirs*, could have endangered more than his reputation. Acts of violence against homosexuals who dared to be so visible and without shame occurred despite shifts in law, psychology, and public sentiment.

In 1972, reporter Jim Gaines describes the circumstances of his visit to Key West just after the New York premiere of *Small Craft Warnings*, with Gaines describing its positive reception as an occasion for "several theater critics" to declare that Williams's reputation "had been resurrected." Gaines tells this story about his evening with the playwright, recounting that a race riot had broken out the previous day, and that Williams wanted to visit the scene of civil disturbance. The night, Gaines writes, "was shot through by the flashing lights of police cars and the sound of sirens converging on the scene of more violence downtown. The restaurateur told us that someone had just been shot in the local pool hall. Williams was finally persuaded not to visit the riot area but to return to the safety of his home."[37] The playwright's interest in visiting the scene, as well as his insistence on talking with multiple interviewers during this period about acts of public violence against him, suggests his consciousness about current events and his interest in social upheaval and its legal implications. That this indication of interest occurred as his "stoned age" ended, in tandem with a renewed vigor for writing and for staging his plays, links his work with his social and political sensibilities. His desire to witness the scene of violence serves as a reminder that Williams's vision of difference is strongly driven by his interrogation of the physical enactment of cultural discord.

When he repeated the story about certain Key West citizens and their response to the details of his sexual life in a conversation with Rex Reed, Williams theorized the range of attitudes about unconventional behavior or lifestyles: "Society is becoming very permissive to one's inalienable rights to pursue whatever personal choices make one happy in life. But among the unsophisticated, there still exists a conspiracy to destroy the sensitive people of the earth."[38] The latter sentence echoes a message he had delivered many times over the years, most compellingly in his imaginative work, that sensitivity makes people vulnerable to attacks initiated by the brutal. It is the first sentence that suggests a revision to what he had always maintained about the destruction of the sensitive, and how the publication of diverse attitudes might now be received. For he acknowledged the increased freedom that comes with a changing social climate: the permissibility to pursue happiness, conveyed with the constitutional language of "one's inalienable rights." Although Williams had never consistently worked to hide his homosexuality, his own and others' interrogations of his sexual history reveal that he understood the dangers of conflicted desires.

Although Williams was not subjected to physical violence during this period, attacks on his post-1961 dramatic canon were frequent and virulent. Philip C. Kolin wrote in 2002 that while "the later plays remain largely undiscovered country, elusively difficult to edit, classify, and interpret," there was an overemphasis on "antagonistic biographical criticism" that meant "reading these later plays through his personal and often decadent life, venomously attacking the script as if it were nothing more (or less) than a performance of his *Memoirs*." Kolin acknowledges, however, that the "diversity and breadth of this part of the Williams canon defies easy, homogenized rubrics."[39] Savran puts it somewhat differently, while also connecting private and public, person and writer: most critical narratives of the last two decades "read like dirges, bemoaning the decline and fall of a great prodigy whose writings document his own disintegration." The publication of *Memoirs*, Savran asserts, "was read by many as an invitation to attack Williams on account of his sexual practices and to link his alleged sharp decline" to moral decadence, one that "intensified after the death of Williams's longtime lover and companion, Frank Merlo, in 1963." In a description apt to this study, Savran goes as far as to insist that the post-*Iguana* plays "must be read in relation to what is unmistakably a concerted attempt by critics to *police* the consolidation of the canon by scuttling Williams's most radical works [emphasis mine]."[40] Kolin and Savran imply that moral judgments on Williams's life had permeated critical assessments of his work; considering that both statements point to *Memoirs* as the source or even cause of this new brand of critical policing, the implication is that if he is being punished for sexual promiscuity, it is not for its exposure in the imaginative texts, it is for exposure in his autobiographical texts.

John Clum suggests that when "Williams decided, after Stonewall, to move his openly gay characters from exposition to the stage," he opened himself up to "charges that such open homosexuality is 'too personal'" as well as to attacks from gay men that his homosexual character in *Small Craft Warnings* (1972) was "anything but a positive representation."[41] In *The Politics of Reputation: The Critical Reception of Tennessee Williams' Later Plays*, Annette Saddik documents the range of complaints from other critics what they consider to be Williams's missteps in his confluence of personal and theatrical elements. She notes, for example, that in his review of *In the Bar of a Tokyo Hotel*, Clive Barnes suggests that the "'play seems too personal'" and that "'more pity and less self would be a distinct advantage.'"[42] Saddik's perspective on the initial reception of the late plays is that Williams "was perceived as having been reduced to a babbling, drugged-out, dirty old man—capable of expressing himself only through the lewd ramblings of his *Memoirs*." Challenging what she sees as the common critical opinion of the time, that Williams's later work failed because it was too personal, she argues that this perspective "masks the real reason why these plays were not well received: they were not entertaining enough in terms of the expectations that go along with the 'sensitive realism' typical of Williams's earlier Broadway successes."[43] Saddik's 1999 book and subsequent scholarship counter the personal criticism by focusing on form and on developments in contemporary theater; the approach here is to explore the implications of the personal criticism and Williams's first-person texts for their considerations of sexuality, identity, and law as the playwright and the nation transitioned from repression to expression.

The relative success of *Small Craft Warnings*, which opened off-Broadway and later moved uptown, was buoyed by Williams's appearance in the show as Doc. The published edition of the text contains a preface to the play that consists of a brief essay by Williams dated 26 March, 1972. A note accompanying the essay indicates that he had planned to submit it to the *New York Times* as a preopening piece for the New York premiere of the play, but the newspaper conducted an interview with him instead. The essay's title, "Too Personal?," makes explicit Williams's concern with the confluence of his life and his career, and he begins the piece by bemoaning the fact that the "greatest danger, professionally, of becoming the subject of so many 'write-ups' and personal appearances on TV and lecture platforms is that the materials of your life, which are, in the case of all organic writing, the materials of your work, are sort of telegraphed in to those who see you and to those who read about you." Assuming that his readers might well wonder why he was willing to expose himself, his first reason reflects his ongoing interrogation of the tension between private and public: "When one has passed through an extensive period of that excess of privacy which is imposed upon a person drifting almost willfully out of contact with the world" and then finds himself still alive, the latter recognition brings with it "an almost insatiable hunger for recognition of the fact that he is, indeed, still alive, both as man and artist."[44] Williams's television appearances, interviews, and his stage appearance all seemed designed to satisfy the "insatiable hunger" of recognition even as they suggested an excess of publicity in reaction to the "excess of privacy" that he believed was imposed upon him by the internal and external forces that shaped his previous decade.

An early one-act version of *Small Craft Warnings* is titled *Confessional*, and as is often the case with Williams, both titles are telling. Taken together they reveal something significant about the work's structure and character construction, while also revealing much about the individual's relationship to law. Crotty writes that law "can often look largely irrelevant to the self," that law consists of rules and "by obeying these rules, we get the space we need to live our own lives." Indeed, he concludes that this arrangement is "crucial to the legitimacy of the legal system" and that "law is not just *unless* it is largely irrelevant to the most vital concerns of the individual [emphasis in original]."[45] To some extent, the play title that Williams settled on reflects a similar conception of the individual: each of us a "small craft" whose safety depends upon rules that we all must follow to maintain autonomy and safety from harm. That there are "warnings" that nonetheless come makes plain the need for rules.

In Crotty's book chapter titled "Dilemmas of the Self: Law and Confession," he argues that because "rights are most readily thought of as inhering in the individual," they tend to "reflect a model of the person as an individual—reasonable, autonomous, deliberative." What might be particularly apt for this consideration of the titles of *Confessional/Small Craft Warnings* is what Crotty says next: "This individualistic conception of the person has become in many ways implausible, even for the legal purposes it was supposed to serve. The simplifications it entails have come to seem increasingly distorted and distorting."[46] In order to explore the relation between conceptions of the law and conceptions of the self, Crotty turns to Augustine's *Confessions*, from which derive, he says, "two powerful (but inconsistent) models of the self—a self that is free, autonomous, and responsible; and a darker, more fascinating self that is deeply conflicted and incapable or encompassing itself." Crotty's assertion that our legal selves are complex and contradictory to law and, one would presume, to our perceptions about identity, and his interrogation of legal confessions as a way to underscore his argument remind us that Williams's early title and one approach to the play is as a series of confessional statements. Thus might we look for the ways that he and his characters apply or occupy legal conceptions or insights about the power and the problems of confessions, with attention paid very specifically to the sexual and to the theatrical nature of confession. For various reasons, this text has deep legal implications for Williams, his identity, and his reputation as private and public citizen.

Small Craft Warnings is significant because of its timing in Williams's life and career: he drafted it as *Confessional* prior to his brief period of institutionalization, during what he and the critics agreed was the lowest period of his life, personally and professionally, but the full-length version was staged in 1972, and is considered evidence of an upswing in both areas of his life. Although the reviews were mixed, the play represents his post-crisis comeback, at least in the eyes of the public. The inscription in the first edition of the published script is to "Bill Barnes: You said to go on, and I went." But he had never really gone away. This play's parallels to *Battle/Orpheus* are significant to this study, for it recalls the earlier work specifically and a good part of his early work more generally. The set, a *"somewhat nonrealistic evocation of a bar on the beachfront in one of those coastal towns between Los Angeles and San Diego,"* recalls the similar description of the *Orpheus* set, which is described as representing *"in nonrealistic fashion a general dry-goods store and part of a connecting* '*confectionary' in a small Southern town.*"[47] Both sets represent public spaces, where citizens gather; both are run by a proprietor tied to the premises. In both cases, the owner lives upstairs, residences evident and yet cast in shadow, and the latter detail is made explicit in the scripts. The later play calls for the stairs to be "*masked above first few steps,*" while the *Orpheus* set features "*stairs that lead to a landing and disappear above it.*" Thus do both settings represent the public and the private space of American lives, with indications of the "*shadowy and poetic as some inner dimension of the play.*"[48] In *Battle* and *Orpheus* the sexual activity, or rather lack thereof, that took place above the confectionary was the subject of speculation among the townspeople, for what the local women found when they snooped suggested that Myra/Lady sought out only illicit and illegal sex rather than the licensed acts of marital relations.

The bar setting of *Small Craft Warnings*, with its motley cast of regulars, recalls Eugene O'Neill's *The Iceman Cometh*, and, more generally, what Brenda Murphy describes as the "tradition of the American saloon play, in which a collection of down-and-out characters with illusions about themselves are presided over by a benign figure who protects them from the importunities of the outside world."[49] Clive Barnes began his review of the original New York production of *Small Craft Warnings* by making this point into a larger claim about American theater and life: "Only Americans write plays set in the poised, never-never land of a bar. Saroyan, O'Neill, Charles Gordone, Tennessee Williams, all have used the bar as a symbol of the transience of American society, a resting period outside the punctuation of events and yet at the same time an indication of a world adrift." Both comparisons suggest that the bar setting offers refuge and exile at once, and as Barnes provides a sketch of the characters populating this particular "never-never land," the descriptive list underscores Williams's continued focus on illicit and illegal sexual activities. There's the hustler, who is "content that his sexual prowess is a sure meal ticket"; "the drunken, discredited doctor who apparently lives on illegal abortions"; and a "couple of homosexuals, the elder upset because the younger wants to show affection." Nothing much happens, Barnes explains, and no "genuine outside event, except for the doctor's drunken killing of a mother in childbirth, intrudes upon the evening's drinking."[50] But crime is piled on top of crime, even in the reviewer's matter-of-fact summary, all of them originating with sex acts, and even the disagreement between the gay lovers, a generational split, suggests that the older man's hesitation to go public is out of fear of arrest.

Paller argues that, beginning with this play, Williams works in the "land of the living," with characters who are "sad and rueful survivors, chastened and seeking understanding and forgiveness for a multitude of sins"; Paller hypothesizes that Williams himself "needed forgiveness, and the plays he wrote between 1971 and 1981 suggest that he was trying to believe that he was not beyond it."[51] Forgiveness, atonement, and reconciliation have spiritual and legal connotations, and in this context we might imagine that Williams's "confession" on the David Frost show is part atonement for his sexual sins, moral and criminal. Happening as it does in the immediate aftermath of his confinement in a psychiatric hospital advances such an interpretation of his actions, for throughout the Williams canon are conflations of mental and sexual instability and of incarcerations in institutions that house the insane, the criminal, or the criminally insane.

Williams's appearance in *Small Craft Warnings* shares more than temporal proximity with his Frost appearance and the publication of *Memoirs*. They are both revelatory of his late life reflections on the personal, the sexual, and the legal: the pair of homosexuals in *Small Craft Warnings*; Williams's return to a fictionalized younger self in the revision and staging of *Vieux Carré* (1977); and the co-existence of 1940 and 1980 versions of the playwright as the character of August in *Something Cloudy, Something Clear* (1981). Furthermore, these lightly veiled self-depictions reflect legal changes and public perceptions of homosexual relationships, for as homosexual acts were de-criminalized state by state, legal focus would gradually move from what homosexuals might do together to how they would be together. The issue of homosexual identity, which Williams explored throughout his work and throughout his own lifetime, came to include the nature of the same-sex relationship. *Small Craft Warnings* and *Something Cloudy, Something Clear* specifically take up this issue, and the genesis and production of both plays took place during a ten-year span when legal challenges to the prohibition of same-sex marriage began to appear in state courts.

The focus on law as institution, and on sexuality as the animalistic forces controlled by it, underscores the tensions between freedom and community. What might be explored, then, are the revisions to Williams's artistic vision when the world he had so often contested began to change, to shift toward more complex and ambiguous attitudes about individuals and institutions. The fracturing of a consistent framework of values, caused and effected by demographic changes, polarizing political events, and a gradual shift in beliefs meant that while the cultural imaginary that shaped him was still available, its power, both real and imagined, was now considerably less monolithic for viewers of multiple generations. To some extent, it was impossible for Williams to continue to sustain a singular battle against values in flux.

In *Long Road to Freedom: The Advocate History of the Gay and Lesbian Movement*, the 1971 timeline is introduced by Arnie Kantrowitz as "the year we began to make ourselves real. For decades, homophiles had spoken in polite whispers. In 1969 a gay battle cry had been sounded at Stonewall. In 1970 we got organized and began to argue over our goals. Nineteen seventy-one was the year we grew loud enough to be heard, and like us or not, America could no longer deny that we were there."[52]

Paller's contextualization of the possible reception by young audience members of Williams's depictions of homosexuality helps to explain why *Small Craft Warnings* might have been seen as negatively depicting gay life. The "abusive treatment of homosexuals in newspapers, magazines, and journals," Paller writes, "would have had its effect on Williams's reputation among young gay men and women." Just as this younger generation was "becoming fed up with their treatment by police and politicians," they might have wondered why Williams was not more defiant, for "what relevance to their lives was a gay playwright who wrote by indirection, was even-handed in his treatment of heterosexual and homosexual characters," and who did not "use his fame to speak out and be 'proud' in an era that would increasingly insist on pride and political correctness as artistic criteria?"[53] Paller concludes that if "gay audiences were going to demand plays that simply valorized their lives, or that made a conscious effort to stand up for gay people rather than suggest that as human beings their problems and loneliness were no more easily resolved than those of heterosexuals, they would be disappointed" by *Small Craft Warnings*.[54]

As the first openly homosexual work from Williams's *Small Craft Warnings* may also be understood on a continuum of Williams's representations of illegal sexuality and the complicated responses of both those who engage in it and those who witness it. Such a perspective broadens a discussion of how diverse sexuality is treated in the play, shifting the focus from homosexuality to the various ways that Williams continues to interrogate figures and situations that exist outside of the mainstream in order to evoke audience sympathy. As Paller himself says, it is not "being a homosexual that Quentin or Williams mourns here;" rather, for "all these characters, heterosexual and homosexual, mere sex, automatic, unsurprising, like the jabbing of a hypodermic needle, has become an inadequate substitute for spontaneous awareness."[55] Not a married one in the bunch, this particular collection of misfits have, as have many others in Williams's canon, attempted to forge relationships while pursuing activities that only increase their distance from the center.

Marc Robinson constructs a lineage of dramatists that includes a discussion of Williams, who in this study follows Gertrude Stein rather than the more common critical assertion that Williams succeeds Eugene O'Neill in the American dramatic canon. Analyzing the scene in *Orpheus Descending* in which Lady meets briefly with her old flame, David, Robinson notes the awkward and rushed qualities of the scene as written, but suggests that skilled performers might play the exchange with fine results. He suggests that "Williams writes the clumsiness into the text as a way of exposing on stage the reality of suffering—a reality that is never neat, never gracefully paced." This interpretation of the stylistic influence of the script on both performance and interpretation provides an excellent example of the formal experimentation that Williams engaged in throughout his career and, in this particular case, the scene was created in the revision of a very early text, *Battle of Angels*. Reminding us of Williams's suggestion that "'all good art is an indiscretion,'" Robinson argues that the statement is a reminder that "as his characters unsoul themselves they help bring into view the artist himself." Rejecting advice early in his career that he ought to be careful about baring all, emotionally, Williams "kept giving, forever indiscriminately, as though the mere act of revelation kept something alive in him." Robinson takes issue with the playwright's approach in one notable instance: Williams's appearance as Doc in a production of *Small Craft Warnings* was "a gallant move, surely, a testimony to his commitment to his art," but also "pathetic, one self-exposure too many. Couldn't he just stop? . . . Didn't he understand that with every attempt to create he was really destroying more of himself?"[56] The intersections of creation, revelation, and destruction that Robinson underscores are significant throughout Williams's career, for as we have seen, this thematic triangle is visible throughout his work, and is in keeping with his insistent interrogation of privacy and its many implications: personal, social, and legal.

Robinson's implication of self-destruction has been one component of a pervasive narrative of slippage in Williams's career, even in the face of his continued commitment, that has been echoed or challenged by a wide range of reviewers, critics, and theater practitioners. Although the narrative of failure has persisted, particularly in the context of his late period, it has been transformed over several decades into but one version of a very complex and as yet incomplete critical narrative. In the years since his death, Williams's reputation gradually but steadily experienced a renaissance that has not abated, marked by the regular production of a wide variety of his theatrical texts, from the never-before-staged to the familiar classics; a host of new or reprinted works in several genres published; new critical studies appearing regularly; festivals celebrating his life and work, popular and academic; the publication of two best-selling biographies, one in 1995 and one in 2014. If Williams was, as so many who knew him have suggested, concerned about his legacy, he need not have worried. Perhaps what would most please him is that the late plays are neglected no longer, for they have been the subject of much insightful scholarship, they have been produced in theaters large and small, and they have been adapted for the screen. Williams's penchant for writing veiled autobiography and for creating fictions about his real life was not new, but the particularities of the way that he shaped his past and his present during the twenty years before his death reveal the complexities of identity construction in a nation that had become increasingly focused on the "me," not just in personal contexts, but in legal and political ones.

Why is it that during the "me" decade of the 1970s, Williams's "me" was disdained? One possibility could be his representations of diverse sexuality during the period, perhaps particularly the explicit connections that his memoir and his essays make between his own transgressive past and present and the characters he created. As the rigid sexual mores that had been supported in public, in popular film, in advertising, not to mention in public policies, had become more ambiguous, Williams's own work, which for many viewers and readers had come down on the side of morality by dramatizing or narrating the punishment of sexual transgressors, began to shift as well. A diminished moral coherence is visible (and celebrated) in the narrative and performing arts of the decade, and while some such work was met in its moment with great acclaim, some was only belatedly appreciated for its boundary crossings. The majority of Williams's late career creative efforts fall into the latter category. What is now visible from some distance is that his creative production during the 1960s and the 1970s aptly reflected the fractured nature of a society that could no longer cling to the solid structure of the past, which had been built on illusion and repression, and did so in texts that were themselves incoherent and therefore difficult to understand and interpret.

He lifted the curtain of privacy from his own life just as issues of privacy were being examined throughout the public sphere, but his attempts to reflect contemporary tensions were not as well received as they had been during his two decades of great commercial and critical success. The law as a system in flux during the late 1960s and throughout the 1970s was represented in Williams's work as an insistence for openness that was nonetheless met by older and more established attitudes. The growing discrepancy between illegal acts and prosecuted acts made for what appeared to be an increasingly open culture that had forever banished some secrets while obscuring others. Paller points to the "technique that Williams would employ (although not necessarily consciously) for so long and well: he would confront his need to conceal with the equally strong need to reveal." Most of Williams's best work, Paller contends, was "created through and because of this tension," and when the "social conventions that required concealment began to ease in the 1970s and the outward necessities that created his conceal/reveal strategy began dissolving, so did the primary condition that produced his best work."[57] But a consideration of the legal history of the period indicates that the "primary condition" had not been quite so thoroughly revised.

It is tempting to wonder if the acts of punishment that Williams so often included in his early texts, acts that targeted his transgressive characters and represented the restrictive legal and political establishment seeking conformity, were later directed at him, metaphorically, by some critics. Certainly there is an attachment to sameness that influences critics, scholars, even audiences, when it comes to the evaluation of artistic works. We seek to understand and analyze through categorization; we claim interest in diversity while rewarding sameness. As the likelihood decreased that he and other real-life versions of what he called the "fugitive kind" would be criminally prosecuted for their sexual activity, it is possible that Williams (and, indirectly, his characters) were critically prosecuted in the press and in the scholarship. At the same time, Williams expressed an irrational paranoia about his worth, even as the changing times enabled him to represent, more transparently, his true sexual self. Perhaps his own fear, which he had for so long sublimated through the creation and punishment of vulnerable characters, was increasingly expressed both inside and outside his work, and the blurred line made it difficult for author and for critics to separate personal imaginings from creative inspiration.

Homosexuals have been targeted for who they are, but they have been criminally prosecuted for what they do, albeit often unfairly or falsely. Hence the privileging in this study is on what Williams's characters have done or are charged with doing, even though what you do is clearly related to who you are. In drama, the duality of the textual and performative interplay underscores this relationship, and in Williams's early work, characters suspected of sexually deviant acts are identified as deviants; act and identity merge. The confluence in creative texts does not emerge from the law, but from the literary or theatrical representation of character. When we analyze the acts of sexual transgression in Williams's plays, very few of them taking place on stage, then the personhood and the identity of the figures accused of or who confess to having committed the acts come into play. Transgressive sexuality becomes part of a character's construction and works from opposing sides to condemn those accused of it. If a character is said to belong to a group regularly associated with transgression, or to a group that has become a site of residency for the disgust or revulsion that is an inevitable part of a culture's construction, then that person will be associated with or suspected of acts that engender disgust. It is no accident that many or all of the various groups appealing for equal rights during the 1960s and the 1970s had been identified in Williams's works as legal criminals and transgressors. As the fight for civil rights of women, homosexuals, people of color, the mentally ill, and the disabled began to gain public attention and began to challenge laws that discriminated against them or oppressed them, fictional representations of such groups were increasingly examined for the ways that such renderings supported or challenged the status quo. For Williams, gender identity and sexual orientation became the most visible and the most contested of such examinations.

With Williams himself "out," and with an increased focus on the confessional Williams, the critical emphasis on homosexuality in all his work became a topic of intense attention; theories about how his representations of homosexuality, his own and his characters, could have affected audience and critics' responses as the culture diversified and conversations about such diversity became more frequent in the scholarship on his work. Paller's book, published in 2005, examines Williams's reputation in the Stonewall era and sets the playwright and his work into the context of these changing times, theorizing how many in the gay community might have received it when it first appeared. As part of a generation that did not necessarily identify themselves as gay, Williams "did not write gay plays," according to Paller, nor did he "feel the need to create positive images of gay men." Paller contrasts this depiction of Williams with a description of the next generation of theater artists: "Many lesbians and gay men who came of age in the 1960s experienced their sexuality differently than people of Williams's generation had;" many more "were able to embrace their homosexuality proudly and publicly," and "were likely to view theatre as a useful tool for community-building and for disseminating sexual and politically positive self-images." Concluding that members of two generations with such different approaches to sexual orientation would have surely misunderstood each other, Paller proposes that *Small Craft Warnings*, when it appeared in 1972, "was taken by some as Williams's first utterance of what it meant to be a gay man in the post-Stonewall era," while, he continues, "what Williams offered as a personal mediation on his own life would be taken by many, including gay critics writing years later, as a homophobic portrait of gay men."[58]

What this study of the writer's work and the law has helped to demonstrate, however, is that whatever the intentions of Williams's offerings, his ability to place the most personal stories (his or his characters') in contact with most or all of the major institutions of American life, chief among them the law, and his insistence on examining the power dynamic of such contacts, meant that both his pre- and his post-Stonewall texts had political urgency. Williams lived outside of the law throughout his life, and the shift that Paller notes is not, primarily, a legal one, given that many US jurisdictions continued to maintain restrictions against homosexual acts until the 1990s. Even those Americans who enjoyed legal rights in their home states would not have been immune to prosecution if they traveled, and in their home jurisdictions they might still be threatened by harassment or violence. It is not necessary that Williams acknowledge his focus on homosexual activity, and indeed he denied it as such: in his 1973 essay, titled "Let Me Hang It All Out," he wrote that "at the risk of alienating some of my friends in Gab Lib, I have never found the subject of homosexuality a satisfactory theme for a full-length play," and "despite the fact that it appears as frequently as it does in my short fiction," sexual activity of a person does not "provide the story with its true inner substance."[59] The example he uses to explain his position is "One Arm," and his claim is that this short story concerns an emotional cripple healed through human contact; however, transgressive sexual activity is the source of that human contact, and issues of criminality and disgust drive the plot and determine the story's resolution.

S. Alan Chesler's 1977 essay "Tennessee Williams: Reassessment and Assessment" provides an incomplete yet telling critical summary of the writer's reputation and reception. Noting Williams's popularity as the result of "his plays' direct appeal to basic human emotions," the appeal emerges from, according to Chesler, Williams's "concentrated treatment of man's purely emotional response to his environment and the original, often symbolistic, means he employs to dramatize this concern." He continues: "By combining impressionistic and expressionistic staging devices with the naturalist's keen observations and the realist's objectivity in handling his materials, Williams has created a new poetic drama in the United States." The contributions that Williams made to the American theater and to the next generation of playwrights include "dealing with subjects that had before his time been carefully avoided." Through his handling of sex and violence, according to Chesler, Williams paved the way for the next generation of playwrights; the "general favorable critical and popular reception of their bold treatment of sex and their hard-hitting dialogue is doubtlessly to some degree the result of Williams's having broken ground for them in these areas."[60] It is the nature of the poetic drama that Chesler says is likely to make permanent Williams's literary reputation, although he acknowledges that Williams was still alive and still writing when the volume was published. Near the end of the essay he includes a long list of plays, some early and some late, under a general category of work, which indicated that Williams was not in sufficient control of his craft; the list is useful in reminding readers that the deemed insufficiency was not limited to the post-*Iguana* dramas. In closing the essay, however, Chesler's assessment and reassessment remains focused on the early period, noting that works such as *Menagerie* and *Streetcar* have retained their stature while more recent texts, which he names as *Cat*, *Iguana*, and *Suddenly*, had, by the time of the essay's publication, gained in critical acceptance, even praise.[61]

If Chesler's approach was to speculate on continued influence, Judith Thompson suggests that his late plays "do not so much mark either a structural or thematic change from the kind of drama that established his 'early and popular reputation' as they represent an increasing emphasis on the comic strain that has informed his work from its beginning." Further commenting on the lack, in her opinion, of a radical departure in form or content in texts created or produced after 1960, she argues that the embrace of absurdist techniques visible in the late plays "represents an organic outgrowth of existential themes and concerns fundamental to his dramatic vision." These themes and concerns include the "difficulty of human communication"; the "conflict between subjective impressions and objective reality"; the absurdity of a universe marked by "the existential condition of the fragmented or divided self-condemned to 'solitary confinement inside our own skins.'"[62] In several of the plays Thompson examines from the period that she calls "After *Iguana*," she notes a "context and focus that encompasses representatives of the entire community in its gaze rather than concentrating on a single 'divided self;' one that is more concerned with the integration of a 'society' than with the resolution of conflict within a single individual."[63] This critical perspective suggests a Williams turned outward to the world rather than inward to a self in contest; what I have attempted to demonstrate, however, is that throughout his career his engagement with the world and its structures has been in evidence. As laws restricting sexual activity came under increased scrutiny in the public sphere, it is possible that his approach to character formation was influenced by the dialogues of community difference that were created or revised during the last two decades of Williams's life.

Saddik provides a useful demarcation of Williams's various modes of representation, by considering the extent to which the early dramatic works function as realistic drama; this focus on form is a perspective that serves her argument and that might well serve mine. Once she has surveyed various definitions and limits of the term "realism," she asserts that what she considers his realistic plays "exhibit an awareness of the ironic link between realism as a literary form," which reinforces an industrial capitalist view of the subject as "the origin of meaning, knowledge, and action," and industrial capitalism itself as a force that undermines any sovereignty his characters may experience in society. At the same time, his early work offers a "subtle but powerful challenge to realism's ideological goals by manipulating the mythology of industrial capitalism rather than completely reinforcing it"; beginning with *The Glass Menagerie*, she argues, "capitalism emerges as the new world order which ultimately devours rather than empowers his characters."[64] Imagine, if you will, that "industrial capitalism" is in every instance here replaced by the word "law," and "capitalist," by "legal."

Given the connections Williams makes between law and (economic) privilege or mobility, and his persistent interest in the ways law contributes to the devouring of rather than the empowering of his characters, his legal representations make multiple contributions to realistic literature in general and to his realistic plays in particular. Moreover, the law as depicted in the early plays helps to both situate the individual subject as the origin of meaning while manipulating law's mythologies of justice and rights. Quite apart from the ways that Williams's use of law problematizes his attitudes, and his society's attitudes, about sexual activity in the postwar years, particularly the effects that transgressive sexual acts have on a theoretically endangered body politic, his attention to law's tropes and law's language shows Williams's dramaturgy working at dual but not cross-purposes, infusing the public sphere with reflections of itself while challenging the long-term viability of what those reflections suggested about past, present, and future.

In her chapter "Critical Expectations and Assumptions," Saddik quotes extensively from a 1957 article written by composer Warren Lee and published in the *Chicago Review*. On the surface an explication of the poor reception that Samuel Beckett's *Waiting for Godot* received when it reached the United States in 1956, Lee and then Saddik underscore the larger purpose of Lee's essay: "a complaint about the commodification of theatrical and literary criticism in the United States," and the unwillingness of what Lee calls America's "Wealthy Man" to accept a "kind of literature—and specifically drama—which is not easily accessible and pleasantly entertaining, and which does not reinforce positive American cultural myths and values."[65] What has become clear in the range of critical perspectives that Williams faced (and attempted to face down) as he confronted a new age of theater production and a new age of personal and public sexual visibility, is that changing theories about the making of art and the makeup of society aligned with similar changes in law. Two years before Saddik's book, Ruby Cohn's essay that surveys the late plays ends with a prediction and a suggestion: "I am not so naïve as to think I will convert critics to the qualities of these late plays, but I do hope that actors or directors will reach for their wealth."[66] Why would Cohn think that the critics will not be persuaded but the theater practitioners would nonetheless embrace such "wealth"? The answer may lie in the contemporary development that this perceptive scholar and avid theater-goer was astute enough to recognize as potentially powerful and lasting: that drama and theater, while never one, had increasingly parted ways, the latter responding to wildly changing conditions of theater production while the former remained bound to more traditional modes of textual study.

In 1998, Mark W. Rocha wrote the entry on three late plays in Kolin's *Guide to Research,* cautioning readers "not to see these three plays of the 1970s," *Small Craft Warnings, Vieux Carré,* and *A Lovely Sunday for Creve Coeur,* as forming a 'period' in either the life or work of Williams," but arguing that they can be connected "to a time in Williams's career that can be termed 'post': post-Broadway (the end of serious drama on Broadway) and post-Stonewall (the beginning of the gay liberation movement marked by riots in Greenwich Village, June 1969)."[67] What we might consider about Williams's last two decades is that the world he often represented in his earlier works is one of social stability that had come with a dear price for many: a world of clear expectations for the individual, enforced by ever-present and powerful institutions. The making of laws, bound by tradition and by text, continued to forge and maintain preferences and precedents set by history, while ongoing changes in law's interpretations, theories, and practice might allow for improvisation and the infusion of new attitudes and strains of creativity. What we see in the theatrical production from this period, which parallels the development of critical legal studies, is that contradictions and conflicts might be more readily acknowledged and assimilated.

Having already considered, at least summarily, the actual changes or lack of change in sexual legislation, it remains to be noted how methods of law's theories might add to the analysis of Williams's late life and public identity. It should come as no surprise that as parallel structural forms, literary and legal, began to shift and to embrace new modes, they would do so in response to some of the same changing conditions in the external world. By looking for such similarities and comparing the fissures we can identify in Williams's mode of construction, with comparable fissures in legal decisions and revisions, we find, as we have when comparing the early works to the restrictively structured postwar laws about sexuality, that the loosening of laws, slowly, haltingly, and with multiple unanswerable ambiguities, corresponds with similar patterns in literary studies. Paller calls the creative results of this period "uneven and, for his career, disastrous." Critics saw in the plays produced during these years, according to Paller, "the steep, shocking demise of America's foremost playwright" and noted that "most calamitous for Williams, personally as well as professionally, was the critical response to *In the Bar of a Tokyo Hotel* in 1969." That play was not included in Kolin's 1998 *Guide to Research and Performance*, and as recently as 2002 Allean Hale writes that although many of the late plays "are being reassessed and are being found of unique value," *Tokyo Hotel* "remains almost unexamined, still condemned as Williams's greatest failure."[68] Savran provides a reading of the play in his book, foregrounding it in a way that suggests the representative nature of the work from the period while arguing for the "politics of masculinity" in Miller and Williams. Reminding his readers of the latter's claim for the revolutionary quality of his work, Savran concludes his study by "taking Williams at his word and examining the revolution 'implicit' in his work through an analysis of how textual pleasure is coupled with a process of *desubjectification*, an unbinding and deconstruction of the sovereign subject." It is such an approach, he claims, as will help to "identify and credit a radical—and deeply utopian—potential" that is so intrinsic to the Williams canon that it often goes unnoticed.

Tellingly, Savran notes the significance of bodies to what is otherwise a heavily theoretical undertaking, for what he argues has gone "previously undetected" is the "profligacy of words that disrupts traditional notions of narrative continuity and dramatic form, in company with its double: a profligacy of bodies that disrupts postwar moral and sexual norms."[69] I have elsewhere marked a sea change in Williams criticism with the publication of the three-volume critical analysis on twentieth-century American drama by Bigsby, noting the latter as the first critic who dared to call Williams political. On the other hand, Bigsby's perspective is typical of the critical assessments that emerged soon after Williams's death, as when the critic writes that "throughout the plays he wrote in the 1960s and early 1970s he presented a series of grotesques, figures reduced to a single dominating feature." Noting that such figures have, throughout the canon, shared "only a common desperation," where "they once had other resources, no matter how ironic, now they seem completely drained of any resistant spirit. The cry of the pure in heart seems to give way to the whine of the self-pitying."[70]

My emphasis on bodies is significantly more corporeal than Savran's, specifically as the extreme sexual grotesques of the later texts worked in companionship and contrast with the legal ideals and the legal realities that all Americans confronted during changing times. The assertion that Williams's text marks a larger cultural shift toward public recognition of homosexuality puts a recent essay on *Memoirs* into context: for when Tony Fong examines the "Queer Gaze" of the *Memoirs*, he argues that despite "repeatedly turning the reader's eyes away from himself and onto the bodies of his many lovers, Williams's gaze ironically places his own corporeality at centre stage."[71] Williams as narrator directs the "queer gaze" outward, as he did throughout his career, but this time he fails to divert the reader's eyes; the author's body becomes a central focus. In what might be called his confessional period, he himself became the illegal body in full focus. He had been hiding in plain sight behind his subversive characters, whose created lives seemed, to the public eye, considerably more notorious than his own. He had protected himself from scandal and moral judgment by deflecting attention onto his imaginative work, and indeed many of his texts directed readers toward condemnation by applying the legal language of disgust to the sexual scenarios he narrated or dramatized. As what seemed to be the universal denunciation of deviance began to diminish, Williams dared to reveal his own transgressive past, and, in doing so, participated in the critical revision reflected in the reception of his late work and its ongoing significance. Williams's late works provide ample evidence of late-life "corporeality at centre stage." Not surprising for a writer whose own body was in decline, of course, but in the case of Williams's characters, the transition to mature depictions of sexuality, illegal and otherwise, and their movement from off-stage, or the periphery, to the spotlight, is significant for considering the critical responses to this stage of his career. The connection between the physical and the sexual was not new, for he explored it throughout his career; however, there is a recognizable shift from deformity to disease, from uniqueness to aberration, as Williams and his characters age. Ollie from "One Arm" is missing an arm, but his attractiveness is intact, even enhanced by the loss. The stage directions from *Battle* describe Val Xavier as "fresh and primitive" with a "strong physical appeal."[72] Blanche needs to hide her aging face from harsh lighting, but the clothing of her youth still fit her slender figure. Brick has a limp, but it is temporary. There are exceptions, of course, but the physical marks of decline, especially as they are connected to carnality, are a fruitful way to frame this explication of Williams's late life representations of transgressive sexuality.

Titles predicative of doom become more frequent in the last two decades: *I Can't Imagine Tomorrow*, the double-bill that comprised *Slap-*

stick Tragedy, Demolition Downtown, Small Craft Warnings, and *A House Not Meant to Stand*. *Vieux Carré*, a play that Robert Bray rightly calls the playwright's "beloved French Quarter opus" and that in production, Bray argues, should convey the "ambience of the French Quarter," can be noted for a title that conveys not only place but time, set as it is in New Orleans's "old square."[73] These titles suggest Williams's increased focus on destruction and decay, and the plays themselves are rife with issues of illness and aging. They have often been, as has already been suggested here, considered as part of Williams's self-revelatory period. All of these elements bear on the later plays' depictions of sexuality, and specifically transgressive sexuality, for physical deterioration, elderly characters engaging in sexual acts, and the lengthening shadows of Williams's own homosexuality produce ever more complex reactions among critics and audiences.

As the plays become more open in their diverse representations of sexuality, they feature more variance in the age and physical condition of the illegal bodies. In a period when overt support for sexual variance was more necessary than ever, in order to change laws and to prevent public backlash occurring in light of such changes, Williams's plays made it more challenging for American theatregoers to react with sympathy to his ever more abstract scenarios. As Saddik argues, Williams's movement toward more minimalistic dialogue, for example, does not necessarily indicate a shift away from realism; "the fact that he was depending less and less on the ability of discursive language to communicate accurately and completely an idea or emotion" is a movement toward nonrealistic drama, with the focus on "expressing meaning that can only be articulated through incomplete, fragmented dialogue and the silences which surround it."[74] Adapting to postmodern literary trends and theatrical conditions was necessary for Williams, both in his evolution as a writer and in his efforts to convey accurately the realities of the contemporary world. But the revisions made to his dramaturgy during this period meant that the risk of rejection might occur because of both the content of his late plays and the form, especially given that the public grappled with increased sex exposé in fiction and in real life. Close consideration of the double-bill *Slapstick Tragedy* demonstrates Williams's attachment to issues of sexuality and law while indicating the more explicit and extreme depictions that mark the late plays. A pair of short plays originally produced together, they are nonetheless quite different from each other, and a comparative discussion will reveal a divided highway of Williams's career from the 1960s to his death.

Williams's moves away from realistic representation were, according to Saddik, due to his determination "to displace the emphasis on external reality in order to suggest a new perception of reality and experiment with alternative structures."[75] She calls the two plays that comprise *Slapstick Tragedy* "attempts at an absurdist dramatic style."[76] *The Mutilated* and *The Gnädiges Fräulein* share more than a premiere date of February 22, 1966, the stage at Broadway's Longacre Theatre in New York City, and sympathetic direction by Alan Schneider, a champion of absurd theater who directed American premieres of plays by Samuel Beckett, Edward Albee, and Harold Pinter. Despite what Allean Hale rightly calls the "efforts of a superb cast," the double bill closed after just seven shows and the two plays have been staged only rarely since then. In his production notes for *Fräulein*, Williams writes that he thinks the two plays should be performed together, and suggests that the Bird-Girl of *Mutilated* could appear as the cocaloony in the other play. *Mutilated* is set in the French Quarter, and *Fräulein* in imaginary Cocaloony Key, off the coast of Florida, but both specific settings share the sensibility and familiarity of Williams's many depictions of transient residences. Although only one of the plays indicates as much in the title, physical mutilation is present in both plays. The Fräulein has had her eyes plucked out by the birds with whom she competes for fish, and ex-stripper Trinket Dugan from *Mutilated* has had a mastectomy.

In 2010, Stefanie Quinlan summarized the criticism of *Fräulein* by noting that when commentators do not dismiss it "outright as a failed play, they often equate it with Williams's personal life."[77] Hale begins her essay on *Fräulein*, subtitled "Tennessee Williams's Clown Show," by ranking it as perhaps the "most unusual and most difficult" of the late plays, and after summarizing the first production and the existing criticism, she moves into an extended discussion of a production at the University of Illinois-Urbana in 2000, for which she served as dramaturge. By informing us that the theatre department took up Williams's definition of the play's style as "'akin to vaudeville, burlesque and slapstick, with a dash of pop art thrown in,'" she reminds us that Williams conceived of the play as what we would now call "postmodern," a pastiche of old and new, high and low.[78] In her essay on *Fräulein*, Una Chaudhuri approaches the animality of the play from the perspective of postmodernism, "which comes to the animal as it does to other margins of dominant discourse": as to a figure, she continues, "capable of inspiring and guiding a new journey" in which "postmodern travelers favor odd and ungainly beasts, 'unfamiliars' with strange—and strangely powerful—forms."[79]

Scholarly commentary on the plays, whether they are considered together or separately, is peppered with the language of the grotesque; the carolers in *Mutilated* (the play is set at Christmastime) rightly sing of a miracle, but one performed for the "strange, the crazed, the queer," a "sanctuary for the wild," and even the mutilated "will be touched by hands that nearly heal."[80] At the time of the Broadway production of the double bill, Richard Watts Jr. wrote that *Mutilated* was both the "more conventional" and, in his opinion, the "better play."[81] In Kolin's view, the two old women in *Mutilated*, Celeste and Trinket, are "two doyens" who are "vintage Williams denizens of desire," and, like other "forlorn women" in Williams's texts, "they are waiting for a lover" and "sexual desire is their (and Williams's) life force."[82] Kolin sees a "bifurcated Blanche DuBois" in the two women, but the differences between the ways that transgressive sexualities are staged in *Streetcar* and in *Mutilated* are substantial, and Williams's departure from or revision of earlier patterns is significant to his depictions of law.

June Bennett Larson described the doyens as the embodiment of the "duality of flesh and spirit," Celeste a "frumpish, alcoholic whore whose chief attraction is a more than ample bosom," while Trinket "poses as a ladylike ex-stripper turned wino recluse" because of her mutilation. They are, she continues, "inhabitants of a small and isolated world of outcasts who have been abandoned by, or have abandoned, society." Notably, what Larson calls their companions are the "whores, pimps, hotel clerks, sailors, bartenders, and 'drag queens.'" The list describes the social and economic environment in which sexual crimes often take place, and in which such crimes continue to be the focus of police investigation. The "Bird-Girl" is the freakiest of all the freaks in the play, a local attraction who Larson calls the "embodiment of human degradation."[83] The action of the play commences with Celeste's release from the "jug," where she was been serving time for shoplifting. Her residency at the House of Detention meant the loss of her room at the Silver Dollar Hotel, and the management has seen fit to lock up her belongings in the basement. The displaced criminal figure is a common one that dates back to Williams's apprentice Depression-era plays, and indeed the play is set in the French Quarter of 1939, one of the playwright's stock urban transient backdrops ever since he had first lived the boardinghouse life there himself. Although the combination of poverty, transience, and illegality might seem dated by its period setting, audiences in the 1960s would recognize these conditions from their own experiences of contemporary urban life.

Larson's analysis, from her perception of the two women as representing "the duality of flesh and spirit" to the catalog of outcasts, is also an indication of well-trodden Williams terrain. Watt's notion of *Mutilated*'s conventionality is apt, but perhaps his assessment of relative success is contestable. From a theatrical standpoint, the play takes fewer chances than does *Fräulein*, and if evaluated by volume of scholarly interest since *Slapstick Tragedy* first appeared on stage, *Fräulein* has attracted more attention and more significant analysis. It keeps pace with Williams's embrace of a postmodern sensibility, as Chaudhuri's essay makes clear. On the other hand, *Mutilated* offers a rather uncomplicated look back from the 1960s to 1939; however, it is not one of the late memory plays, akin to *Vieux Carré* and *Something Cloudy, Something Clear*, for the latter plays put past and present onstage together, and, in doing so, challenge cultural perceptions of homosexuality across time.

Mutilated focuses on the aged bodies of the women and their physical inability to attract men, for money or for pleasure. Kolin compares them to earlier Williams women, from *Streetcar*'s Blanche to Lucretia in *Portrait of a Madonna* and Bertha in *Hello from Bertha*, all plays written during the 1940s. Although the similarities of the aging woman cut across all these plays, the yearnings for reciprocated sexual desire in the early works are almost entirely focused on love affairs from the past and on lovers who do not appear on stage. Blanche's potential relationship and possible marriage to Mitch is staged in the play's present; what Blanche seeks, however, is safety and respectability, not passion or even love. The desire of her youth, represented by her marriage to poet Allan, and the imagined relationship with former beau Shep Huntleigh, are told of, not seen by audiences, and Lucretia Collins and Bertha offer similar narrative remembrances of absent lovers. In Blanche's seductive toying with the paper boy and her flirting with Stanley, she acts out her desire for sexual transgression, but she refrains from the first while the latter relationship proves more about power than about sex, and it is Stanley who ultimately crosses into criminal territory.

The women of *Mutilated*, on the other hand, actively seek sexual companionship despite their age, and in this regard their bodies can be linked to Williams's own late-life need for physical companionship, particularly that which is illegally obtained. In *Memoirs* he wrote of being alone in a hotel room in the present, having left his little black book in Venice. Not to be deterred from procuring services, he used the phone book to locate the number for a madam he knew "to send over a paid companion." The young man who attends to his needs "must have read and remembered 'Desire and the Black Masseur,'" Williams reports, for he gave his "tired old body the roughest pounding and squeezing," and he protests to the young man, "'Hey, now, I'm not a masochist.'"[84] In her 2015 book on the late plays, which uses as its subtitle the first line of *Mutilated*, the "strange, the crazed, the queer," Annette J. Saddik argues that this play and others "perform female identity, desire, and desir(ability) as an ongoing negotiation between lack and excess, swinging between the two poles, embracing the ambiguous, monstrous woman who often embodies these poles simultaneously." Such women are "unstable in the most celebratory sense, and they maintain their power through leading an unapologetic life" and by "defeating those who seek to exploit their instability in order to take advantage of them and living passionately in the face of death."[85] In scene two of *Mutilated*, which consists entirely of a monologue by Trinket, she convinces herself to seek out a companion, for "not daring to expose the mutilation has made me go without love for three years now," and tonight, she professes, "I'll give myself the Christmas gift of a lover, yes, I'll find him tonight and he will be—beautiful!" and perhaps "kind, even, so kind I can tell him about my mutilation."[86] Like Williams, Trinket is prepared to pay for affection, and so while the landscape is as it always was for Williams, with sexual indulgence coming at a legal and financial cost, the protagonist is no longer the payee but is now the payer.

In this version of pre–World War II New Orleans, stage center is occupied by the aged and the mutilated, and the supporting characters are the youthful opportunists who expect to be compensated for their favors. Saddik rightly argues that the play's "philosophy on the satisfaction of desire is rooted in an overt system of exchange: 'love' and 'friendship' are for sale."[87] The possibility of "love" for Trinket takes the form of two sailors, who are themselves transgressors, for they enter a bar off-limits to military personnel, and when Trinket attempts to lure them away with her, one of them suggests that they have sex in the alley. She is flattered rather than insulted by his assumption that she is a "whore," but she immediately shows him her "wad of greenbacks," insisting that "money isn't my problem, my problem is not economic." Her problem, she tells him after some hesitation, is a "human problem."[88] Celeste appears with the other sailor, the one that Trinket had already decided she "wanted for Christmas," and accusations of prostitution and shoplifting commence, along with a threat from Trinket that, with the help of the "biggest lawyer in town," she will have Cricket "committed to the hospital for the CRIMINAL INSANE."[89] In order for each of them to pursue "the satisfaction of desire," they must negotiate not only with the objects of interest, but with each other. Access to money, previous criminal history, and the limited access to "trade" are all part of the "overt system of exchange" that the text dramatizes. The physical deterioration of the two women heightens the competition, and this "symbiotic pair of friends" offer a view to Williams's perspective on the illegal body as his own declines: an aging, fragmented but still longing self.

Once Trinket gets the sailor of interest into her apartment, she alludes to her criminally suspect activities, and thereby to what she proposes to him: she tells him that she prefers the Silver Dollar Hotel to others she could afford, for she has a private entrance for "when you—have a guest with you at night." Slim rightly surmises that a big hotel would have "house dicks in it." Although she does not admit that specific reason for seeking privacy, Slim responds *"suspiciously"* with "Hmmmm."[90] But Trinket seems to hold herself above Celeste as law-abiding, and she tries to explain her former position in public relations to Slim by *"snatching a photograph from the dresser"* to show him, a framed newspaper photo in which she is standing "between the Mayor and the president of the International Trade Mart."[91] Unfortunately, her narrative reveals that her plan to hold a funeral for "Mr. Depression" as a morale boost to the city was a public relations disaster, and her career ended; she conflates the failed efforts with her mastectomy's hit to her sense of self, and Slim conflates them too.

Saddik explores the significance of the pseudonym "Agnes Jones," first used by Trinket when she underwent her mastectomy, then by Celeste when she was arrested for shoplifting and again, upon her release, for possible employment at the Rainbow Bakery. With Trinket's use of an "alias" for her surgery, Saddik suggests, the name "becomes a shameful and clandestine identity attached to social seclusion and shame." Celeste uses it to shield her true identity from the police who arrest her, and, in both cases, the name protects the woman using it from institutional identification, medical and legal. Illness and crime are conflated, and the scene with Slim and Trinket in the latter's room continues its focus on accusation and defense, on physical and mental depravity and their ties to illegality. Celeste climbs the stairs to Trinket's room and yells out the name they have both used as cover for their true identities; each accuses the other of crimes, with Celeste calling Trinket's "worse mutilation" the "crime of the Christian commandments, STINGINESS, CHEAPNESS, PURSE PRIDE," and she calls Trinket a "FINK, MUTILATED FINK!"[92] Acts or accusations of criminal activity, sexual or otherwise, often culminate in violence or annihilation. In *Mutilated*, the death figure Jack in Black appears, even as a reconciliation instigated by Trinket brings the two women together to celebrate Christmas Eve, when they are joined in renewed faith by what Celeste claims is an appearance by Mary the Virgin Mother, and Trinket proclaims that the *"pain in my breast is gone!"*[93] The rejuvenation of the "miracle" holds off death, for Jack in Black declines to descend for now: "Expect me, but not yet, not yet!"[94] Forgiveness, a vision of Our Lady, and a deferred death sentence resolve this slapstick tragedy.

Saddik aligns Williams's late plays with Aleks Sierz's identification and theory of what he calls the "in-yer-face" theatre of 1990s Britain to describe plays that rely and thrive on shock value in order to "elicit a visceral reaction and jar audiences out of their complacency."[95] She does not claim that playwrights who embraced the "in-yer face" style were familiar with Williams's late work; rather, she draws the comparison in order to underscore the shift in his work and its anticipation of contemporary trends toward the extreme. She argues that the playwright's tendency to shock audiences with physical and emotional violence was always present, but as his career progressed, and as theater and culture underwent contemporary shifts, "he depicted this cruelty more graphically and literally." A new social permissiveness made it possible for Williams "to dismiss the subtlety of symbolism and metaphor that marked the early plays and instead turn to the outrageous and the extreme in dealing with intersections of the personal and political."[96] *Slapstick Tragedy* in its totality represents both the early and the late depictions of physical and emotional violence with its roots in transgression. In locale and time period, *Mutilated* recalls Williams's explicit focus on transience, with criminal activity both a cause and effect of liminal living.

Although the specific offenses recall those that Williams wrote about as early as the 1930s, from petty theft to prostitution, in *Mutilated* these crimes are ascribed to aging women rather than to youthful vagrants.

In another rooming house setting, *Fräulein*'s action takes place on fictional Cocaloony Key, what Polly calls a "little bit of heaven dropped from the sky one day, the southernmost tip of terra firma of the—"; a version of Key West, that is, set in the present time but abstracted from reality with Williams's renaming and with his fanciful descriptions of the human and nonhuman creatures that populate the place.[97] Molly, the proprietor of the rooming house, tells reporter Polly that there is "always a 'vacancy' sign" in the big window of the cottage, ever since Molly "knocked out the walls of the private bedrooms to make the big dormitory" and "they's always room for one more."[98] Although Molly brags that she has "REAL PERSONAGES" residing with her, ones that would provide society editor Polly with a "gold mine of material in the class category," she goes on to concede that on weekends her place fills up, and the meaning of the SRO sign becomes "standing room only."[99] Chaudhuri argues that the play "encapsulates paradigmatic elements" of Williams's late plays and extends them to their signifying limits," and the set and setting "are a case in point." She argues that the setting "performs Williams's drift away from classical dramatic modernism by eschewing the normative domestic interior of dramatic realism"; the "big dormitory" is "surely the extreme version of the transient spaces in which Williams increasingly located his attempts to stage the kinds of 'limit experiences' which increasingly interested him."[100] Although Chaudhuri seems to suggest that this development is unique to the late plays, the rooming house with a big window and dormitory beds for rent by the night was depicted by Williams in his 1937 play, *Fugitive Kind*. But her larger point about the extremity of his move away from a domestic interior is useful for, as she notes, the "civic values and kinship relationships once articulated by the stage living room are nowhere to be found in the nightmarish boardinghouse" of *Fräulein*.

Fräulein deals less explicitly with legal issues, but it is more extreme in its depiction of the grotesque body, and the Fräulein's physical deterioration is staged; the play thus takes *Mutilated*'s dialogue about assaults to the body and weaves it into the action. The Fräulein is increasingly disfigured in the play: when she first appears, her eye is covered by a "large blood-stained bandage"; later in the scene, the bloody bandage covers the whole upper half of her face and her costume is "spangled with fresh drops of blood"; at the end of the play, her costume has been torn away and her flesh-colored tights are "*streaked and dabbled with blood*. Patches of her fuzzy orange hair have been torn away."[101] Linda Dorff argues that the transformation allows the character "to cross over temporarily from her disfiguration from a 'social derelict' into an ironic caricature of a saint, purified for a moment by her blinded vision."[102] In an essay that compares *Fräulein* to Alfred Hitchcock's film *The Birds*, which was released three years before the first production of *Slapstick Tragedy*, Kolin argues that this final appearance of the Fräulein reveals a condition of utter destruction, her body conveying a state in which "her identity, her art, and her humanity" have been stripped away, and the body, "as in the film, is the site of the outrageous, the discontinuity between reason and representation."[103] He notes that Cocaloony Key, analogous to the southernmost key where Williams owned a home for thirty years, Key West, resonates as a community "on the border, on the edge, between sea and land, continent and the vast deep." It is located "at the very end of a respectable, putatively rational, America," a site where difference looms large and the location is "purposely borderline to accommodate the transformations enacted on stage."[104]

William Prossner suggests that the play "moves the audience into its own demented world" and the drama is thus "experienced from the inside, not merely observed in troubled characters" but a "wild journey that becomes more adventurous and bizarre as the evening progresses."[105] As Williams continues to craft texts that challenge his audiences to consider boundary sites and boundary lives as not so different from their own, he may be asking for more than observance and compassion. The pairing of the two plays that make up *Slapstick Tragedy* is significant for what they share in theme and situation, but also for their considerable formal complementarity. *Mutilated* is the more realistic of the two, reminiscent of earlier works that explicitly dramatize legal transgressions, including sexual transgressions. *Fräulein* narrates the dangers of the "permanent transient" who risks arrest if caught "on the street at that desperate hour" in a "state of the Union where they's eighteen different kinds of vagrancy charges that a lone man on the streets at night can be charged with," but unlike *Mutilated* it does not focus on such figures and their plights. The two plays, together, however, suggest that transgressive bodies, especially when exposed to the elements, urban or natural, are subject to grotesque deterioration, physical attack, the uselessness that comes with age. *Slapstick Tragedy* demonstrates an attempt to transform the relationship of characters and audience members; in the first play we are observing a New Orleans street life that is familiar Williams territory, with a chorus to remind us that we witness the "strange, the crazed, the queer." In the second play, the frame of the unrealistic set, as if "Picasso designed it," indicates a dislocation "characteristic or Picasso's cubist paintings," according to Allean Hale. She then extends the visual art reading of the play, suggesting that as "Warhol's endless rows of tomato soup cans were comments on American culture, so was Williams's satire on the Wasp inhabitants of Cocaloony Key and their attitudes toward the gays who frequented Key West."[106] If *Fräulein* has, as Prossner suggests, moved the audience into "its own demented world," then it may be that Williams has finally succeeded in moving us into the boarding house, into the madhouse, into the holding cell of the county jail, all of them located "at the very end of a respectable, putatively rational, America."

Williams continued to write for almost two decades after *Slapstick Tragedy* and to experiment with style, subject matter, and setting. To suggest that this work points ahead in several ways is not to suggest it as a summation or even fully representative pair of texts. But it does indicate some significant features of much of the work that follows it. For one thing, it was a commercial failure. Following *The Milk Train Doesn't Stop Here Anymore* to Broadway, the production of *Slapstick Tragedy* lasted but a week before closing and predicted the ongoing downward turn in ticket sales to which there were few exceptions. In a preface to *Slapstick Tragedy* first published in *Esquire* with the play texts, Williams suggests that in production, the two plays "may seem to be a pair of fantastic allegories on the tragicomic subject of human experience on this risky planet."[107] As Brenda Murphy notes, Williams's work from the 1970s continues "the same interest in new forms of theatre that had developed in the 1960s, and for the most part is far less referential, more imagistic, more what he called 'plastic,' more immediately symbolic than his earlier work, with less concern for plot or craft."[108] Murphy notes that *Mutilated* is important among Williams's later efforts because it "takes the existential condition of the misfit as the subject of the play, using its dramatic form to bring some resolution to the human situation of being marginalized."[109] With its nonrealistic setting that is nontheless specified as the Silver Dollar Hotel on South Rampart Street in New Orleans, it mines Williams's memories of the French Quarter in the late 1930s. He returned more personally to this time and place in the later memory play, *Vieux Carré*, but both plays concerned themselves with illegal and physically deteriorating bodies, combining the experiences that Williams had as a young man with the attitudes and insights of an older one.

Saddik argues that Williams's later plays "use exaggeration and distortion of reality, humor, and satire as social commentary," and that they "face life's tragic elements and laugh at them, a liberating laughter that destabilizes boundaries and breaks through imposed limitations."[110] There are examples, in his *Memoirs* and in some of the plays of the same period, of his continued interest in liminal bodies and borderland lives, and depictions of law-breaking can still be found. But experimentation and abstraction in many of these works often shift depictions away from the specificity of warrants, arrest records, and law enforcement, and when these do exist, they have lost some of their restrictive impact and specificity of jurisdiction. His representations demonstrate a continued commitment to portray the "strange, the crazed, the queer," and to shine the light on a ranges of cultural marginality, but as the legal environment moves slowly away from the regular prosecution of difference, and diverse sexualities move toward center stage, in theater and in the news, the frequency of law-breaking scenarios written into his texts declines.

On the other hand, representations of transgressive bodies are, in some cases, connected to Williams's own body. His confessions about his sexual history, in the David Frost interview and in the pages of *Memoirs*, render his life, to borrow a phrase from Ruckel, a "text of scandal." His performance as Doc in *Small Craft Warnings* may have been motivated by a desire for ticket sales, but the decision to appear in the show placed his body on stage (a rare thing in itself) as a criminal who flees the jurisdiction after the death of mother and child during the childbirth he botches while drunk. The original production also featured transsexual Candy Darling as Violet; Darling was a member of Andy Warhol's core group of actors and a friend of Williams, and in *Memoirs* he included several accounts of their outings together post-performance, such as this one: "I left the theatre in costume, going to Candy's dressing room before leaving and asking her to go with me to Joe Allen's restaurant, a night spot for theatre people." Darling "dressed up in a glamorous fifties style," with a "very becoming blond wig" and a black velvet cloche hat. He went on to suggest that the two "must have made quite an entrance" at the restaurant, and noted that he was wearing the Stetson hat he bought to wear in the play.[111] The increased visibility of transgressive bodies in his life and in his work, in performance and in society, demonstrates that his relationship to the culture continued to be focused on portrayals of diverse sexuality that challenged norms even if illegality was not the explicit focus. The "politics of recognition" that developed in the 1960s manifested itself in a variety of ways in Williams's texts, and he created new kinds of literary and theatrical art to align himself with, or to complicate, the development of a more radical public sphere.

NOTES

1. Robert Spitzer, "A Proposal About Homosexuality and the APA Nomenclature: Homosexuality as One Form of Sexual Behavior and Sexual Orientation Disturbance as a Psychiatric Disorder," Diagnostic and Statistical Manual of Psychiatric Disorders (DSM-II), December 1973, accessed October 19, 2015, http://www.torahdec.org/downloads/dsm-ii_homosexuality_revision.pdf
2. Richards, *The Sodomy Cases*, 72–73.
3. *Lawrence v. Texas* 539 U.S. 558 (2003).
4. Eskridge, *Dishonorable Passions*, 138.
5. Eskridge, *Dishonorable Passions*, 158.
6. Quoted in Eskridge, *Dishonorable Passions*, 164.
7. Eskridge, *Dishonorable Passions*, 170–172.
8. Williams, *New Selected Essays*, xiii–xiv.
9. Lahr, *Tennessee Williams*, xv.
10. Victor A. Kramer, "Memoirs of Self-Indictment: The Solitude of Tennessee Williams," *Tennessee Williams: A Tribute*, ed. Jac Tharpe (Jackson: University of Mississippi Press, 1977), 664.
11. Kramer, "Memoirs of Self-Indictment ," 667–668.
12. Kramer, "Memoirs of Self-Indictment ," 671.

13. John S. Bak, "'White Paper' and 'Cahiers Noirs': Williams's Many Ur-*Memoirs*," *Études Anglaises* 64.1 (2011): 9.

14. Williams, *Memoirs*, xvii.

15. Terri Smith Ruckel, "A 'Giggling, Silly, Bitchy, Voluptuary': Tennessee Williams's *Memoirs* as Apologia Pro Vita Sua," *The Southern Quarterly* 38.1 (Fall 1999), 94.

16. Ruckel, "A 'Giggling, Silly, Bitchy, Voluptuary,'" 95.

17. Ruckel, "A 'Giggling, Silly, Bitchy, Voluptuary,'" 100.

18. "Homsexuality and Sexual Orientation Disturbance: Proposed Change in DSM-II," *Torah Declaration*, accessed 10 August 2015, http://www.torahdec.org/Downloads.aspx.

19. Roy Cain, "Disclosure and Secrecy among Gay Men in the United States and Canada: A Shift in Views," *Journal of the History of Sexuality* 2.1 (1991), 25.

20. Cain, "Disclosure and Secrecy," 26.

21. Ruckel, "A 'Giggling, Silly, Bitchy, Voluptuary,'" 100.

22. Ruckel, "A 'Giggling, Silly, Bitchy, Voluptuary,'" 102.

23. Bak, *Tennessee Williams*, 227.

24. Bak, *Tennessee Williams*, 227.

25. Mel Gussow, "Tennessee Williams on Art and Sex," *New York Times* 3 November 1975, 49.

26. Marie Pecorari, "'Scratches upon the Caves of Our Solitude': Weighing in on the Essays," *Études Anglaises* 64.1 (2011), 24.

27. Jack Richardson, "Unaffected Recollections: Memoirs," *New York Times* 2 November 1975, 293.

28. Pecorari, "'Scratches upon the Caves of Our Solitude,'" 32.

29. Hooper, *Sexual Politics*, 71.

30. Tennessee Williams, "Will God Talk Back to a Playwright? Interview with David Frost/1970," *Conversations with Tennessee Williams*, ed. Albert J. Devlin (Jackson: University Press of Mississippi, 1986), 145–146.

31. Donald Spoto, *The Kindness of Strangers: The Life of Tennessee Williams* (New York: Ballantine Books, 1985), 324–325.

32. Interview with Walter Wagner, "Tennessee Williams," in *Conversations with Tennessee Williams*, 132.

33. Annette Saddik et al., "Out of the Closet, Onto the Page: A Discussion of Williams's Public Coming Out on the David Frost Show in 1970 and His Confessional Writing of the '70s," *Tennessee Williams Annual Review* 12 (2011), 15.

34. Savran, in Saddik, "Out of the Closet," 15.

35. Savran and Paller, in Saddik, "Out of the Closet, 16.

36. "New Tennessee Williams Rises from 'Stoned Age,'" Interview with Don Lee Keith, in *Conversations with Tennessee Williams*, 158.

37. "A Talk about Life and Style with Tennessee Williams," Interview with Jim Gaines, in *Conversations with Tennessee Williams*, 213–214.

38. "Tennessee Williams Turns Sixty," Interview with Rex Reed, in *Conversations with Tennessee Williams*, 184–207; 189.

39. Philip C. Kolin, *The Undiscovered Country: The Later Plays of Tennessee Williams* (New York: Peter Lang, 2002), 1–2.

40. Savran, *Communists, Cowboys, and Queers*, 131–132.

41. Clum, *Still Acting Gay*, 132.

42. Annette J. Saddik, *The Politics of Reputation: The Critical Reception of Tennessee Williams' Later Plays* (Madison, NJ: Fairleigh Dickinson University Press, 1999), 27.

43. Saddik, *The Politics of Reputation*, 150.

44. Williams, *The Theatre of Tennessee Williams*, Vol. V, 217.

45. Crotty, *Law's Interior*, 90.

46. Crotty, *Law's Interior*, 90–91.

47. Williams, *The Theatre of Tennessee Williams*, Vol. V, 225.

48. Williams, *The Theatre of Tennessee Williams*, Vol. III, 227.

49. Brenda Murphy, *The Theatre of Tennessee Williams* (London: Bloomsbury: 2014), 168.
50. Clive Barnes, "Stage: Williams Accepting Life As Is," *New York Times* 3 April 1972, 50.
51. Michael Paller, *Gentleman Callers: Tennessee Williams, Homosexuality, and Mid-Twentieth-Century Drama* (New York: Palgrave Macmillan, 2005), 173.
52. Arnie Kantrowitz, Introduction to "Speeding Up," *Long Road to Freedom: The Advocate History of the Gay and Lesbian Movement*, ed. Mark Thompson (New York: St. Martin's Press, 1994), 49
53. Paller, *Gentleman Callers*, 189.
54. Paller, *Gentleman Callers*, 192–193.
55. Paller, *Gentleman Callers*, 198.
56. Robinson, *The Other American Drama*, 57.
57. Paller, *Gentleman Callers*, 20.
58. Paller, *Gentleman Callers*, 158.
59. Williams, "Let Me Hang It All Out," *New Selected Essays*, 172.
60. Chesler, "Tennessee Williams," 878, 880.
61. Chesler, "Tennessee Williams," 880.
62. Thompson, *Tennessee Williams' Plays*, 184–185.
63. Thompson, *Tennessee Williams' Plays*, 197.
64. Saddik, *The Politics of Reputation*, 63–64.
65. Saddik, *The Politics of Reputation*, 139–140.
66. Ruby Cohn, "Tennessee Williams: The Last Two Decades," in *The Cambridge Companion to Tennessee Williams*, ed. Matthew C. Roudané (Cambridge, UK: Cambridge University Press, 1997), 242.
67. Mark W. Rocha, "*Small Craft Warnings, Vieux Carré*, and *A Lovely Sunday for Creve Coeur*," in *Tennessee Williams: Guide to Research and Performance*, ed. Philip C. Kolin, 183–184.
68. Allean Hale, "In the Bar of a Tokyo Hotel: Breaking the Code," in *Magical Muse: Millennial Essays on Tennessee Williams*, ed. Ralph F. Voss (Tuscaloosa: University of Alabama Press, 2002), 148.
69. Savran, *Communists, Cowboys, and Queers*, 145.
70. Bigsby, *A Critical Introduction*, 110.
71. Tony Fong, "'I Look into Their —Myriad Eyes:' The Queer Gaze of Tennessee Williams's *Memoirs*," *University of Toronto Quarterly* 84.1 (2015): 34.
72. Williams, *The Theatre of Tennessee Williams*, Vol. I, 16
73. Robert Bray, "*Vieux Carré*: Transferring 'A Story of Mood,'" *The Undiscovered Country: The Later Plays of Tennessee Williams*, ed. Philip C. Kolin (New York: New Directions, 2002), 144, 153.
74. Saddik, *The Politics of Reputation*, 40.
75. Saddik, *The Politics of Reputation*, 78.
76. Saddik, *The Politics of Reputation*, 78.
77. Stefanie Quinlan, "*The Gnädiges Fräulein*: Tennessee Williams's Southernmost Belle," *Tennessee Williams Annual Review* 11 (2010), 53.
78. Allean Hale, "*The Gnädiges Fräulein*: Tennessee Williams's Clown Show," in *The Undiscovered Country: The Later Plays of Tennessee Williams*, ed. Philip C. Kolin (New York: New Directions, 2002), 40, 48.
79. Una Chaudhuri, "'AWK!' Extremity, Animality, and the Aesthetic of Awkwardness in Tennessee Williams's *The Gnädiges Fräulein*," in *The Undiscovered Country: The Later Plays of Tennessee Williams*, ed. Philip C. Kolin (New York: New Directions, 2002), 55.
80. Tennessee Williams, *The Theatre of Tennessee Williams*, Vol. VII, 81.
81. Quoted in Philip C. Kolin, "*The Mutilated*: Tennessee Williams's Apocalyptic Christmas Carol," *American Drama* 13.2 (2004), 83.
82. Kolin, "*The Mutilated*," 83–84.

83. June Bennett Larsen, "Tennessee Williams: Optimistic Symbolist," in *Tennessee Williams: A Tribute,* ed. Jac Tharpe (Jackson: University of Mississippi Press, 1977), 419.
84. Williams, *Memoirs*, 231.
85. Saddik, *Tennessee Williams and the Theatre of Excess: The Strange, the Crazed, the Queer* (Cambridge: Cambridge University Press, 2015), 87.
86. Williams, *The Theatre of Tennessee Williams*, Vol. VII, 101.
87. Saddik, *Tennessee Williams and the Theatre of Excess*, 105.
88. Williams, *The Theatre of Tennessee Williams*, Vol. VII, 107.
89. Williams, *The Theatre of Tennessee Williams*, Vol. VII, 109–110.
90. Williams, *The Theatre of Tennessee Williams*, Vol. VII, 112.
91. Williams, *The Theatre of Tennessee Williams*, Vol. VII, 114.
92. Williams, *The Theatre of Tennessee Williams*, Vol. VII, 117–118.
93. Williams, *The Theatre of Tennessee Williams*, Vol. VII, 128.
94. Tennessee Williams, *The Theatre of Tennessee Williams*, Vol. VII, 129.
95. Saddik, *Tennessee Williams and the Theatre of Excess*, 139.
96. Saddik, *Tennessee Williams and the Theatre of Excess*, 139.
97. Williams, *The Theatre of Tennessee Williams*, Vol. VII, 219.
98. Williams, *The Theatre of Tennessee Williams*, Vol. VII, 223.
99. Williams, *The Theatre of Tennessee Williams*, Vol. VII, 226.
100. Chaudhuri, "'AWK,'" 55–56.
101. Williams, *The Theatre of Tennessee Williams*, Vol. VII, 230, 245, 260.
102. Linda Dorff, "Theatricalist Cartoons: Tennessee Williams's Late 'Outrageous' Plays," *Tennessee Williams Annual Review* 2 (1999), 19.
103. Philip C. Kolin, "'A Play about Terrible Birds': Tennessee Williams's *The Gnädiges Fräulein* and Alfred Hitchcock's *The Birds*," South Atlantic Review, 66.1 (2001), 14.
104. Kolin, "'A Play About Terrible Birds,'" 16.
105. William Prossner, *The Late Plays of Tennessee Williams*, Foreword by Ed Sherin (Lanham, MD: Scarecrow Press, 2009), 33.
106. Hale, "In the Bar of a Tokyo Hotel," 45.
107. Williams, "*Slapstick Tragedy*: A Preface," *New Selected Essays*, 148.
108. Murphy, *The Theatre of Tennessee Williams,* 152.
109. Murphy, The Theatre of Tennessee Williams, 165.
110. Saddik, *Tennessee Williams and the Theatre of Excess*, 5.
111. Williams, *Memoirs*, 35.

Conclusion

With Dignity for All

In August 1981, Judge Stephen M. Lachs of the Los Angeles Superior Court wrote to Tennessee Williams on behalf of the Los Angeles Gay and Lesbian Community Center (LAGLC). At the time, Lachs was serving as a member of the organization's board of directors, and he wrote to invite Williams to attend the group's annual fundraising event as the recipient of the center's Humanitarian Award. As Judge Lachs noted in his letter, the LAGLC, then in its twelfth year, "was the first, and continues to be the most comprehensive provider of social services to gay men and women in the world," and Lachs called it "an exceptional organization existing in exceptional times." He goes on: "And what times they are! Who would have thought that a book such as your *Memoirs* could have been published to such wide acclaim or that I could have been appointed a judge while being openly gay? Who would have imagined that GLCSC would be providing services with full community and governmental support, to tens of thousands of clients a year?" No person, he claimed, "could be more deserving of such an award and few would be able to command the universal respect that you would. Your work has enriched our lives for so long; we would be deeply honored for you to allow us to share our appreciation with you.... If I was with you in person, I could perhaps better express the depth of feeling we all have about making this request."[1] Several strands of history come together in this letter: a recently established and growing legacy of community support and spirit in gay and lesbian urban communities, made possible through government funding; the pride of a citizen serving his city and embracing his identity in a way that would not have been possible just two decades prior; the emotion accompanying the request that a well-known artistic figure accept the gratitude of the many who had been personally affected by his creative texts and his public life.

Not unique in its expression of gratitude for Williams's life and work, the letter represents one of many such requests that Williams received every year: to make an appearance, to accept an award, to donate money or a personal item to be auctioned off, to give advice about the writing life, to read and endorse another writer's first novel. When Williams was awarded an Honorary Doctorate of Literature from the University of Hartford in 1972, the text of the award praised the writer's artistic mission and its outcome: "'It is not,' you have said, 'the essential dignity but the essential ambiguity of man that needs to be stated.' Your poetic statements of our essential ambiguity make us more fully alive; they dignify us all."[2] Among the many requests were those that asked him for a personal item, a belt or a pair of shoes. Sacred Heart College in Belmont, North Carolina, did so, for instance, along with the plea: "Please don't throw this appeal in your trash can! We know you must get many requests, but you must also realize that your name carries a great deal of weight with many people; and a number of persons would be honored to have something which was yours."[3] Arriving as they did from a great diversity of individuals and organizations, such tributes attest to Williams's reputation as a sensitive and skilled author who captured for many life's isolation and pain while conveying the human capacity for compassion.

What these statements have in common is their depiction of Williams as a writer who greatly affected the masses exposed to his work, whether on stage, on screen, or in print. His creative work did so through its elicitation of emotion and its depictions of dignity in the face of complexity and suffering. To read through Williams's papers from his Key West cottage, now housed in Columbia University's Rare Book and Manuscript Collections, is to realize that reports of his diminishing influence on culture and letters in the latter years of his life are but one version of a complex life narrative; the awards and honors he continued to receive until his death attest to the significant influence he had on audiences, even during the years when he struggled to have his late plays produced.[4] This recognition makes explicit that one of Williams's enduring contributions was his public exploration of the individual emotional life, its varieties and vagaries; by exploring the risks and rewards of intimacy, his work engaged in an ongoing dialogue about the need for compassion in human relationships.

In her book *Upheavals of Thought: The Intelligence of Emotions*, Martha Nussbaum argues that the "relationship between compassion and social institutions is and should be a two-way street: compassionate individuals construct institutions that embody what they imagine; and institutions, in turn, influence the development of compassion in individuals." In many of Williams's representations of the law and its legislation of sexual identity and behavior, the compassion is one-sided, springing primarily from individuals, usually only those who have themselves experienced social marginalization. It may be that sympathy and conciliation are not indicative of institutions or their representatives in his work; indeed, what is forthcoming for the most part is indifference or, more often, condemnation. Williams presents this lack as an absence, and indeed, Nussbaum argues that institutional compassion is quite powerful and influential, for it can "either promote or discourage, and can shape in various ways, the emotions that impede appropriate compassion: shame, envy, and disgust."[5] In forging a concrete plan to promote empathy across social barriers erected to impede compassion, Nussbaum turns to works of art, naming and calling for works that "present these barriers and their meaning in a highly concrete way," in order that citizens are required to grapple with them; the goal being reception that results in emotional growth prompted by exercising the "muscles of the imagination" and "making people capable of inhabiting, for a time, the world of a different person."[6] The worlds that Williams created were marked by violence, and the violent acts often emerged from sexual desire and energy. But passion and sympathy are often aligned in his texts to engender understanding and intimacy, and he portrayed the need for connection between characters and between characters and their environments.

Nicholas de Jongh includes a report on the first London premiere of *Streetcar* in his survey of dramatic representations of homosexuality in London and New York theaters from the 1920s to the 1980s. He argues that the fourteen curtain calls for *Streetcar* served as "indices of a rare excitement that was only exacerbated by the critics' vituperative reviews." *Sunday Times* critic Harold Hobson, de Jongh reports, wrote of the "'spirit of daring'" Williams introduced into the London drama that "'was in many quarters received with a venomous opposition'"; *Streetcar* was spoken of as "nasty" and "vulgar," and "'many theatre goers walked out of the performance in noisy disgust.'" The adjectives used by other London critics to condemn the work: "sordid," "sexual," "lewd," and "repugnant," not to mention "immoral," are, of course, echoes of the words used to condemn deviant behavior under the law, and synonyms for words that Williams used in the play: "degenerate" and "disgusting." The impact of the "spirit of daring" that Hobson refers to, de Jongh reminds us, "must be remembered when assessing the way in which Williams managed to depict sexuality, particularly female sexuality, on stage, and also how he portrayed young men as clear objects of desire." He "dealt with the wild cards of sexuality, when such desiring was not to be mentioned on the stage." He devoted his plays "to those for whom the good news does not arrive, the sexual and social outsiders, the misfits, the fugitives, the downcast and down-at-heel." It was "in these ways that Williams's developed homosexual sensibility brought him into alliance with the nonconformists. For he believed that his occupation as a writer, and involuntary vocation as homosexual, allied him with those seeking freedom to be themselves."[7] Williams's ways of expressing love and desire were certainly considered throughout his career uncongenial to conventional American society, but the complex tension between the repulsiveness of many of his representations and their compelling evocation of compassion challenged audiences to replace the condemnation of difference with understanding and acceptance.

In a review of Robert Caro's fourth installment of his serial biography of Lyndon B. Johnson, reviewer and former president Bill Clinton writes the following about Johnson's era and its success in effecting change: "L. B. J., Shriver and other giants of the civil rights and antipoverty movements seemed to rise all around me as I was beginning my political involvement. They believed government had an essential part to play in expanding civil rights and reducing poverty and inequality. It soon became clear that *hearts* needed to be changed, along with laws. Not just Congress, but the American people themselves needed to be *got to*" [emphasis in the original].[8] In Jonathan Haidt's 2012 book, *The Righteous Mind: Why Good People Are Divided by Politics and Religion*, Haidt summarizes what has been long recognized as a dominant attitude toward the emotions and decision-making: "Western philosophy has been worshipping reason and distrusting the passions for thousands of years. There's a direct line running from Plato through Immanuel Kant to Lawrence Kohlberg." Calling this attitude the rationalist delusion, Haidt explains that "when a group of people make something sacred, the members of the cult lose the ability to think clearly about it. Morality binds and blinds."[9] And in an interview published in 2001 in *Women Who Write Plays: Interviews with American Dramatists*, Emily Mann talks about the dangerous and volatile nature of theater and the necessary contributions it makes to "public conversations that matter." She also suggests that the particular quest of late-twentieth-century theater is to "start looking at those values that are not market-driven," values such as "tenderness, love, intimacy."[10] The long-standing view in the West that law and politics must be guided by reason, and that emotion and reason are sentinels of opposing ways of decision-making, has had a tremendous effect on aesthetics and its place in political argument.

Consider emotion's impact on literature and theater, for example: in both realms of creative production, it has been common to condemn, artistically if not politically, imaginative works that used the conventions of emotion in order to sway citizens in their civic opinions. Tennessee Williams's postwar drama was acclaimed for its quality of expression and for its poetic heights, but the path to acceptance that Williams's theater might have had some political effect on his age, intended or no, has been an uphill one, no doubt because the author's statements about his politics over the years were fraught with contradiction and, often, with a vagueness that suggested a desire to be seen as politically involved rather than a conviction. But just as the acceptance that feeling is often integral to good decision-making has spread from psychology to neuroscience and has shifted from the margins to mainstream thinking, the insistence that the revision of public attitudes can depend on both overt and covert methods, even to the extent that the latter might not be visible to he or she who is propagating for change, has begun to win over many who had previously equated authorial intention with authorial success when it came to the effects that letters might have on politics or on law.

Even those unfamiliar with the bulk of Williams's canon are probably aware of his focus on individual rights and freedom and, more specifically, his reputation for the humanity if not the primacy of midcentury Americans living outside the mainstream, for those he called, aptly employing the language of law, the "fugitive kind." Nussbaum's argument for a "politics of humanity" promotes the transformation of current laws in the area of sexual orientation, from the existing "piece-meal and local" nondiscrimination laws to the adoption of "a federal nondiscrimination statute that will do for sexual orientation what Title VII did for gender."[11] In her conclusion she argues that the law has been relatively slow-moving in this area, and that to date, the impetus toward a politics of humanity has come "perhaps above all, from the arts, which have given us models of dignity, equality, and joy that can hardly fail to work upon people's insides in ways that prompt change."[12] Williams's many texts, featuring characters not easily dismissed or rejected as "other," challenged the public discourse of disgust that supported the criminalization of diverse sexual activity. His work confirmed that compassion and acceptance are not easy, and that fear and loss all too often close us off from human communion. But it also demonstrated to readers and audience members that the pathway to mutual respect, when carved out by sympathy and imagination, can lead to a change of heart and mind, shifting the balance of opinion toward a change in law.

In *Lawrence v. Texas* in 2003, Justice Anthony Kennedy wrote the six–three decision to overturn a ban on sodomy, claiming that the case should be resolved by "determining whether the petitioners were free as adults to engage in the private conduct in the exercise of their liberty under the Due Process Clause of the Fourteenth Amendment to the Constitution." While Kennedy notes that there existed "broad statements of the substantive reach of liberty under the Due Process Clause" in earlier cases, the "most pertinent beginning point" for the deliberation was the court's decision in *Griswold* v. *Connecticut* (1965).[13] The decision in *Lawrence v. Texas* served to remind the American public that privacy rights had, for at least fifty years, an explicit connection to sexual freedom, and Kennedy's opinion, according to Richards, rested on the "recognition of comparable normative connections between the irrational prejudice of homophobia and the abridgement of the right to intimate life of homosexuals."[14] Richards's study of the sodomy cases ends with a consideration of the significance that *Lawrence* could have in regards to other sexual offenses and to same-sex marriage, but as for the latter, it would be six years after Richards's book was published before the high court would write its decision in *Obergefell v. Hodges* (2015), which overturned state-instituted bans on same-sex marriage.

One month before the *Obergefell* decision, Harvard history professor Jill Lepore argued in *The New Yorker* that it was Sandra Day O'Connor's concurring opinion in *Lawrence* that "marked the way forward for L.G.B.T. litigation that turned, increasingly, to marriage equality."

Both Kennedy's and O'Connor's opinions were based on rights described in the Fourteenth Amendment, but O'Connor had "based her decision on the equal-protection argument rather than on the privacy," and her reasoning, not Kennedy's, "marked the way forward for L.G.B.T. litigation that turned, increasingly, to marriage equality."[15] Lepore argued that while both good and bad constitutional arguments "fill every last nook of a very cramped space, and then they harden" over time, "arguments based on a right to privacy have tended to weaken and crack; arguments based on equality have grown only stronger."[16] What the *Obergefell* decision, based on the equal-protection argument, demonstrated, moreover, was that while constitutional arguments may harden, they may also result in the opening of hearts.

The majority opinion for *Obergefell* seems at times to be a summary of Tennessee Williams's dialogue with America and its laws. The decision narrates the changing times that Williams lived through and wrote through, for it notes that well into the twentieth century, "many States condemned same-sex intimacy as immoral, and homosexuality was treated as an illness. Later in the century, cultural and political developments allowed same-sex couples to lead more open and public lives. Extensive public and private dialogue followed, along with shifts in public attitudes." Ultimately, the Court argued, "fundamental liberties protected by the Fourteenth Amendment's Due Process Clause extend to certain personal choices central to individual dignity and autonomy, including intimate choices defining personal identity and beliefs."[17] This landmark decision, its argument defining parameters for identity and autonomy, its repeated use of the word "dignity," justify legally a vision of human life that Tennessee Williams advanced in his creative work throughout his career. The honorary doctorate from the University of Hartford commended him for his poetic statements of humanity's "essential ambiguity" that "make us more fully alive" and "dignify us all." We need only look to any of the texts discussed in this study to find ambiguity and dignity sharing the stage and page in Williams's many representations.

In the *Obergefell* decision, Judge Kennedy reminds the people that until the mid-twentieth century, "same-sex intimacy long had been condemned as immoral by the state itself in most Western nations, a belief often embodied in the criminal law."[18] Williams's depictions of midcentury life featured many examples of the state's condemnation of same-sex intimacy, and his work made visible to audiences and readers that criminal laws were often interpreted or expanded to punish perceived immorality more broadly. What society considered to be sexual transgressions, whether committed by anyone among the "strange, the crazed, the queer," the unmarried, the mutilated, the impoverished, were contained by a legal system that seemed to have lost sight of ambiguity's value in the construction of human dignity. But his many sympathetic representations of illegal bodies moved American audiences to compassionate response, and closer to the embrace of what Hannah in *The Night of the Iguana* suggested as a philosophical credo, that nothing human except the unkind or the violent ought to elicit disgust or judgment.

NOTES

1. Letter from Stephen M. Lachs, Judge, August 26, 1981, Tennessee Williams Papers, Rare Book and Manuscript Library, Columbia University Library.

2. Honorary Doctorate of Literature Award from the University of Hartford, 3 December 1972, Tennessee Williams Papers, Rare Book and Manuscript Library, Columbia University Library.

3. Letter from Sacred Heart College, Tennessee Williams Papers, Rare Book and Manuscript Library, Columbia University Library.

4. Williams's stories continued to be published in the later period, appearing in the magazines *Playboy*, *Esquire*, *Playgirl*, and *Vogue*, in literary journals, and in collected volumes. The "Preface to *Slapstick Tragedy*" and the two play scripts that constitute the double-bill were published in *Esquire* in August 1965.

5. Martha C. Nussbaum, *Upheavals of Thought: The Intelligence of Emotions* (Cambridge, UK: Cambridge University Press, 2001), 405.

6. Nussbaum, *Upheavals*, 431.

7. de Jongh, *Not in Front of the Audience*, 66-68.

8. Bill Clinton, "Seat of Power," *New York Times* 6 May 2012: BR1.

9. Jonathan Haidt, *The Righteous Mind: Why Good People Are Divided by Politics and Religion* (New York: Pantheon Books, 2012), 28.

10. Alexis Greene, ed., "Interview with Emily Mann," *Women Who Write Plays* (Hanover, NH: 2001), 287.

11. Nussbaum, *From Disgust to Humanity*, 208.

12. Nussbaum, *From Disgust to Humanity*, 205.

13. *Lawrence v. Texas* 539 U.S. 558 (2003) (opinion).

14. Richards, *The Sodomy Cases*, 158.

15. Jill Lepore, "To Have and to Hold: Reproduction, Marriage, and the Constitution," *The New Yorker*, May 25, 2015: 38.

16. Lepore, "To Have and to Hold," 35.

17. Obergefell v. Hodges, 575 U.S. ___ (2015).

18. Obergefell v. Hodges, 575 U.S. ___ (2015).

Bibliography

Angyal, Andras. "Disgust and Related Aversions." *The Journal of Abnormal and Social Psychology* 36.3 (1941): 393–412.
Bak, John S. *Homo americanus: Ernest Hemingway, Tennessee Williams, and Queer Masculinities*. Madison, NJ: Fairleigh Dickinson University Press, 2010.
———. *Tennessee Williams: A Literary Life*. New York: Palgrave, 2013.
———. "Tennessee v. John T. Scopes: 'Blanche' Jennings Bryan and Antievolution." *Tennessee Williams Annual Review* 8 (2006).
———. "'White Paper' and 'Cahiers Noirs': Williams's many Ur-*Memoirs*," *Études Anglaises* 64.1 (2011): 7–20.
Bandes, Susan A., ed. *The Passions of Law*. New York: New York University Press, 1999.
Baraka, Amiri. "Tennessee Williams Is Never Apolitical." In *Tenn at One Hundred: The Reputation of Tennessee Williams*, ed. David Kaplan. East Brunswick, NJ: Hansen Publishing Group, 2011.
Barnes, Clive. "Stage: Williams Accepting Life as Is." *New York Times* 3 April 1972: 50.
Bérubé, Allan. *Coming Out Under Fire: The History of Gay Men and Women in World War Two*. New York: The Free Press, 1990.
Bibler, Michael P. *Cotton's Queer Relations: Same-Sex Intimacy and the Literature of the Southern Plantation, 1936–1968*. Charlottesville: University of Virginia, 2009.
Bigsby, C. W. E. *A Critical Introduction to Twentieth-Century American Drama*. Vol. 2. Cambridge, UK: Cambridge University Press, 1984.
"Bill of Rights." *The Charters of Freedom*. June 10, 2014. http://www.archives.gov/exhibits/charters/bill_of_rights.html.
Bloustein, Edward J. "Privacy as an Aspect of Human Dignity." 39 *New York University Law Review* 971 (1964).
Bowers v. Hardwick, 478 U.S. 176 (1986).
Brandeis, Louis D., and Samuel D. Warren. *The Right to Privacy*. New Orleans: Quid Pro Law Books, 2010. Kindle edition.
Bray, Robert. "*Battle of Angels* and *Orpheus Descending*." In *Tennessee Williams: A Guide to Research and Performance*, ed. Philip C. Kolin. Westport, CT: Greenwood Press, 1998.
———. "Vieux Carré: Transferring 'A Story of Mood.'" *The Undiscovered Country: The Later Plays of Tennessee Williams*. Ed. Philip C. Kolin. New York: New Directions, 2002. 142-154.
Brownmiller, Susan. *Against Our Will: Men, Women, and Rape*. New York: Simon and Schuster, 1975.
Burks, Deborah G. "'Treatment Is Everything': The Creation and Casting of Blanche and Stanley in Tennessee Williams' 'Streetcar.'" *Library Chronicle of the University of Texas at Austin* 41 (1987): 16–39.
Cain, Roy. "Disclosure and Secrecy among Gay Men in the United States and Canada: A Shift in Views." *Journal of the History of Sexuality* 2.1 (1991): 25–45.
Case, Claudia Wilsch. "Inventing Tennessee Williams: The Theatre Guild and His First Professional Production." *Tennessee Williams Annual Review* 8 (2006): 51–71.
Caserio, Robert L. "Queer Passions, Queer Citizenship: Some Novels about the State of the American Nation 1946–1954." *Modern Fiction Studies* 43.1 (1997): 170–205.
Chaudhuri. Una. "'AWK!' Extremity, Animality, and the Aesthetic of Awkwardness in Tennessee Williams's *The Gnädiges Fräulein*." In *The Undiscovered Country: The*

Later Plays of Tennessee Williams, ed. Philip C. Kolin. New York: New Directions, 2002. 54–67.

Chauncey, George. *Gay New York: Gender, Urban Culture, and the Making of the Gay Male World, 1890–1940.* New York: Basic Books, 1994.

Chesler, S. Alan. "Tennessee Williams: Reassessment and Assessment." In *Tennessee Williams: A Tribute,* ed. Jac Tharpe. Jackson: University Press of Mississippi, 1977.

Childress, Steven Alan. "Foreword." In *The Right to Privacy,* Samuel D. Warren and Louis D. Brandeis. New Orleans: Quid Pro Law Books, 2010. Kindle edition.

Clum, John. "The Sacrificial Stud and the Fugitive Female in *Suddenly Last Summer, Orpheus Descending,* and *Sweet Bird of Youth.*" In *The Cambridge Companion to Tennessee Williams,* ed. Matthew C. Roudané. Cambridge, UK: Cambridge University Press, 1997. 128–146.

———. "'Something Cloudy, Something Clear': Homophobic Discourse in Tennessee Williams." In *Displacing Homophobia: Gay Male Perspectives in Literature and Culture,* eds. Ronald R. Butters, John M. Clum, and Michael Moon. Durham, NC: Duke University Press, 1989. 149–167.

———. *Still Acting Gay: Male Homosexuality in Modern Drama.* Updated edition. New York: St. Martin's Press, 2000.

Cohn, Ruby. "Tennessee Williams: The Last Two Decades." In *The Cambridge Companion to Tennessee Williams,* ed. Matthew C. Roudané. Cambridge, UK: Cambridge University Press, 1997.

Corber, Robert J. *Homosexuality in Cold War America: Resistance and the Crisis of Masculinity.* Durham, NC: Duke University Press, 1997.

Crandell, George W., ed. *The Critical Response to Tennessee Williams.* Westport, CT: Greenwood Press, 1996.

———. "Tennessee Williams Scholarship at the Turn of the Century." In *Magical Muse: Millennial Essays on Tennessee Williams,* ed. Ralph F. Voss. Tuscaloosa: University of Alabama Press, 2002.

Crotty, Kevin M. *Law's Interior: Legal and Literary Constructions of the Self.* Ithaca, NY: Cornell University Press, 2001.

de Jongh, Nicholas. *Not in Front of the Audience: Homosexuality on Stage.* London: Routledge, 1992.

D'Emilio, John. "The Homosexual Menace: The Politics of Sexuality in Cold War America." In *Passion and Power: Sexuality in History,* eds. Kathy Peiss and Christina Simmons. Philadelphia: Temple University Press, 1989.

——— and Estelle B. Freedman. *Intimate Matters: A History of Sexuality in America.* New York: Harper & Row, 1988.

Devlin, Albert J. "Audrey Wood and Tennessee Williams: A Revealing Correspondence." In *Tenn at One Hundred: The Reputation of Tennessee,* ed. David Kaplan. East Brunswick, NJ: Hansen Publishing Group, 2011.

Devlin, Albert J., ed. *Conversations with Tennessee Williams.* Jackson: University Press of Mississippi, 1986. 38–39.

Dickson, Vivienne. "*A Streetcar Named Desire*: Its Development through the Manuscripts." In *Tennessee Williams: A Tribute,* ed. Jac Tharpe. Jackson: University Press of Mississippi, 1977.

Dorff, Linda. "Theatricalist Cartoons: Tennessee Williams's Late 'Outrageous' Plays." *Tennessee Williams Annual Review* 2 (1999). 13–34.

Draya, Ren. "The Fiction of Tennessee Williams." In *Tennessee Williams: A Tribute,* ed. Jac Tharpe. Jackson: University Press of Mississippi, 1977.

Eskridge, Jr., William N. *Dishonorable Passions: Sodomy Laws in America, 1861–2003.* New York: Viking Penguin, 2008.

———. *Gaylaw: Challenging the Apartheid of the Closet.* Cambridge, MA: Harvard University Press, 1999.

Fong, Tony. "'I look into their myriad eyes:' The Queer Gaze of Tennessee Williams's *Memoirs.*" *University of Toronto Quarterly* 84.1 (2015): 34-54.

Fout, John C., and Maura Shaw Tantillo, eds. *American Sexual Politics: Sex, Gender, and Race since the Civil War*. Chicago: University of Chicago Press, 1993.

Freedman, Estelle B. "'Uncontrolled Desires': The Response to the Sexual Psychopath, 1920–1960." *Journal of American History* 74 (June 1987): 86–87.

Frontain, Raymond-Jean. "Tennessee Williams and the 'Arkansas Ozark Way.'" *Tennessee Williams Annual Review* 9 (2007): 77–94.

"Glass Menagerie' Is Best Play of Year, Drama Critics Decide." *New York Times*, 11 April 1945, 18.

Goldstein, Ann B. "History, Homosexuality, and Political Values: Searching for the Hidden Determinants of *Bowers v. Hardwick*." In *Homosexuality and the Constitution, Volume 1: Homosexual Conduct and State Regulation*, ed. and with introductions by Arthur S. Leonard. New York: Garland, 1997. 43–73.

Gussow, Mel. "Tennessee Williams on Art and Sex." *New York Times* November 3, 1975: 49.

Haidt, Jonathan. *The Righteous Mind: Why Good People Are Divided by Politics and Religion*. New York: Pantheon Books, 2012.

Hale, Allean. "In the Bar of a Tokyo Hotel: Breaking the Code." In *Magical Muse: Millennial Essays on Tennessee Williams*, ed. Ralph F. Voss. Tuscaloosa: University of Alabama Press, 2002.

———. "*The Gnädiges Fräulein*: Tennessee Williams's Clown Show." In *The Undiscovered Country: The Later Plays of Tennessee Williams*, ed. Philip C. Kolin. New York: New Directions, 2002. 40–53.

Hart, Harold H. *Sexual Latitude: For and Against*. New York: Hart Publishing, 1971.

———. Letter to Tennessee Williams. April, 1970. Tennessee Williams Papers. Rare Book and Manuscript Library. Columbia University Library.

Herron, Ima Honaker. *The Small Town in American Drama*. Dallas: Southern Methodist University Press, 1969.

"Homosexuality and Sexual Orientation Disturbance: Proposed Change in DSM-II." *Torah Declaration*. Accessed 10 August 2015. http://www.torahdec.org/Downloads.aspx.

Hooper, Michael S. D. *Sexual Politics in the Work of Tennessee Williams: Desire over Protest*. Cambridge, UK: Cambridge University Press, 2012.

Kahan, Dan M. "The Anatomy of Disgust in Criminal Law." *Michigan Law Review* Vol. 96
1621: 1622.

Kantrowitz, Arnie. Introduction to "Speeding Up." In *Long Road to Freedom: The Advocate History of the Gay and Lesbian Movement*, ed. Mark Thompson. New York: St. Martin's Press, 1994.

Kaplan, David, ed. *Tenn at One Hundred: The Reputation of Tennessee*. East Brunswick, NJ: Hansen Publishing Group, 2011.

Klassen, Albert D., Colin J. Williams, and Eugene E. Levitt. *Sex and Morality in the U.S.: An Empirical Enquiry under the Auspices of The Kinsey Institute*, ed. and with an introduction by Hubert J. O'Gorman. Middleton, CT: Wesleyan University Press, 1989.

Kleb, William. "Marginalia: *Streetcar*, Williams, and Foucault." In *Confronting Tennessee Williams's* A Streetcar Named Desire: *Essays in Critical Pluralism*, ed. Philip C. Kolin. Westport, CT: Greenwood Press, 1993. 27–41.

Kolin, Philip C. "'A Play about Terrible Birds': Tennessee Williams's *The Gnädiges Fräulein* and Alfred Hitchcock's *The Birds*." *South Atlantic Review*, 66.1 (2001). 1–22.

———. ed. *Tennessee Williams: A Guide to Research and Performance*. Westport, CT: Greenwood Press, 1998.

———."*The Mutilated*: Tennessee Williams's Apocalyptic Christmas Carol." *American Drama* 13.2 (2004). 82–97.

———. *The Undiscovered Country: The Later Plays of Tennessee Williams*. New York: Peter Lang, 2002.

Kramer, Victor A. "Memoirs of Self-Indictment: The Solitude of Tennessee Williams." In *Tennessee Williams: A Tribute*, ed. Jac Tharpe. Jackson: University Press of Mississippi, 1977.

Lahr, John. *Tennessee Williams: Mad Pilgrimage of the Flesh*. New York: W. W. Norton & Co., 2014.

Lawrence v. Texas, 539 U.S. 558 (2003).

Leonard, Arthur S, ed. *Homosexuality and the Constitution*. New York: Garland Press, 1997.

Leverich, Lyle. *Tom: The Unknown Tennessee Williams*. New York: New Directions, 1995.

Lithwick, Dahlia. "Extreme Makeover." Books, *New Yorker*, 12 March 2012: 76.

Malamud Smith, Jana. *Private Matters: In Defense of the Personal Life*. Emeryville, CA: Seal Press, 2003.

Maroney, Terry A. "A Proposed Taxonomy of an Emerging Field." *Law and Human Behavior* 30 (2006): 119–142.

Matthew, David C. C. "'Towards Bethlehem': *Battle of Angels* and *Orpheus Descending*." *Tennessee Williams: A Tribute*. Ed. Jac Tharpe. Jackson: University Press of Mississippi, 1977. 172-191.

Miller, William Ian. *The Anatomy of Disgust*. Cambridge, MA: Harvard University Press, 1997.

Murphy, Brenda. *Tennessee Williams and Elia Kazan*. Cambridge, UK: Cambridge University Press, 1992.

Murphy, Brenda. *The Theatre of Tennessee Williams*. London: Bloomsbury: 2014.

Nelson, Deborah. *Pursuing Privacy in Cold War America*. New York: Columbia University Press, 2002.

Nelson, Richard. "Introduction." In *Stopped Rocking and Other Screenplays*, Tennessee Williams. New York: New Directions, 1984.

Nicolay, Claire. "Hobos, Sissies, and Breeders: Generations of Discontent in Cat on a Hot Tin Roof." *The Tennessee Williams Annual Review* 12 (2011): 1–46.

Nussbaum, Martha C. *From Disgust to Humanity: Sexual Orientation and Constitutional Law*. New York: Oxford University Press, 2010.

———. *Hiding from Humanity: Disgust, Shame, and the Law*. Princeton, NJ: Princeton University Press, 2004.

———. *Upheavals of Thought: The Intelligence of Emotions*. Cambridge, UK: Cambridge University Press, 2001.

Obergefell v. Hodges, 575 U.S. ___ (2015).

Olmstead v. United States. 277 U.S. 438 (1928).

Paller, Michael. *Gentleman Callers: Tennessee Williams, Homosexuality, and Mid-Twentieth-Century Drama*. New York: Palgrave Macmillan, 2005.

Palmer, R. Barton, and William Robert Bray. *Hollywood's Tennessee: The Williams Films and Postwar America*. Austin: University of Texas Press, 2009.

Pecorari, Marie. "'Scratches upon the Caves of Our Solitude': Weighing in on the Essays." *Études Anglaises* 64.1 (2011): 21–32.

Peden, William H. "Mad Pilgrimage: The Short Stories of Tennessee Williams." *Studies in Short Fiction* 1 (Summer 1964): 243–250.

Penn, Donna. "The Sexualized Woman: The Lesbian, the Prostitute, and the Containment of Female Sexuality in Postwar America." In *Not June Cleaver: Women and Gender in Postwar America, 1945–1960*, ed. Joanne Meyerowitz. Philadelphia: Temple University Press, 1994. 358–381.**[au: edit ok?]**

Peters, Brian M. "Queer Semiotics of Expression: Gothic Language and Homosexual Destruction in Tennessee Williams's 'One Arm' and 'Desire and the Black Masseur.'" *Tennessee Williams Annual Review* 8 (2006): 109–121.

Posner, Richard A., and Katharine B. Silbaugh. *A Guide to America's Sex Laws*. Chicago: University of Chicago Press, 1996.

Prossner, William. *The Late Plays of Tennessee Williams*. Lanham, MD: Scarecrow Press, 2009.

Quinlan, Stefanie. "*The Gnädiges Fräulein*: Tennessee Williams's Southernmost Belle." *Tennessee Williams Annual Review* 11 (2010), 53–64.
Richards, David A. J. *The Sodomy Cases*: Bowers v. Hardwick *and* Lawrence v. Texas. Lawrence: University Press of Kansas, 2009.
Richardson, Jack. "Unaffected Recollections: Memoirs." *New York Times* 2 November 1975: 293.
Robinson, Marc. *The Other American Drama*. Cambridge, UK: Cambridge University Press, 1994.
Roudané, Matthew C., ed. *The Cambridge Companion to Tennessee Williams*. Cambridge, UK: Cambridge University Press, 1997.
Ruckel, Terri Smith. "A 'Giggling, Silly, Bitchy, Voluptuary': Tennessee Williams's *Memoirs* as Apologia Pro Vita Sua." *The Southern Quarterly* 38.1 (Fall 1999): 94–103.
Saddik, Annette J. *The Politics of Reputation: The Critical Reception of Tennessee Williams' Later Plays*. Madison, NJ: Fairleigh Dickinson University Press, 1999.
———. *Tennessee Williams and the Theatre of Excess: The Strange, the Crazed, the Queer*. Cambridge, UK: Cambridge University Press, 2015.
Saddik, Annette, et al. "Out of the Closet, Onto the Page: A Discussion of Williams's Public Coming Out on the David Frost Show in 1970 and His Confessional Writing of the '70s." *Tennessee Williams Annual Review* 12 (2011), 15.
Savran, David. *Communists, Cowboys, and Queers: The Politics of Masculinity in the Work of Arthur Miller and Tennessee Williams*. Minneapolis: University of Minnesota Press, 1992.
Sklepowich, Edward A., "In Pursuit of the Lyric Quarry: The Image of the Homosexual in Tennessee Williams' Prose Fiction." In *Tennessee Williams: A Tribute*, ed. Jac Tharpe. Jackson: University Press of Mississippi, 1977.
Solove, Daniel J. *Understanding Privacy*. Cambridge, MA: Harvard University Press, 2008.
Spitzer, Robert. "A Proposal About Homosexuality and the APA Nomenclature: Homosexuality as One Form of Sexual Behavior and Sexual Orientation Disturbance as a Psychiatric Disorder." Diagnostic and Statistical Manual of Psychiatric Disorders (DSM-II). December 1973. Accessed October 19, 2015. http://www.torahdec.org/downloads/dsm-ii_homosexuality_revision.pdf apa.
Spoto, Donald. *The Kindness of Strangers: The Life of Tennessee Williams*. New York: Ballantine Books, 1985.
Summers, Claude J. *Gay Fictions Wilde to Stonewall: Studies in a Male Homosexual Literary Tradition*. New York: Continuum, 1990.
Tharpe, Jac, ed. *Tennessee Williams: A Tribute*. Jackson: University Press of Mississippi, 1977.
"Tennessee Williams." New Directions Books. Accessed October 16, 2012. http://ndbooks.com/author/tennessee-williams.
"The Universal Declaration of Human Rights." *United Nations Website*. Accessed May 3, 2013. http://www.un.org/en/documents/udhr/.
Thompson, Judith J. *Tennessee Williams' Plays: Memory, Myth, and Symbol*. Revised edition. New York: Peter Lang, 2002.
Tischler, Nancy. *Tennessee Williams: Rebellious Puritan*. New York: The Citadel Press, 1961.
Turley, Jonathan. "The Scarlet Letter Lives On." *USA Today* 26 April 2010: A9.
Vannatta, Dennis. *Tennessee Williams: A Study of the Short Fiction*. Boston: Twayne Publishers, 1988.
Vidal, Gore. "Introduction" to *Collected Stories* by Tennessee Williams. New York: New Directions, 1985, xx.
Vogel, Ursula. "Whose Property? The Double Standard of Adultery in Nineteenth-Century Law." In *Regulating Womanhood: Historical Essays on Marriage, Motherhood and Sexuality*, ed. Carol Smart. London: Routledge, 1992. 147–165.
Voss, Ralph F. ed. *Magical Muse: Millennial Essays on Tennessee Williams*. Tuscaloosa: University of Alabama Press, 2002.

Whitmore, George. "George Whitmore Interviews Tennessee Williams." In *Gay Sunshine Interviews*, vol. 1, ed. Winston Leyland. San Francisco: Gay Sunshine, 1984, 316.
Wiegman, Robyn. "The Anatomy of Lynching." In *American Sexual Politics: Sex, Gender, and Race since the Civil War,* eds. John C. Fout and Maura Shaw Tantillo. Chicago: University of Chicago Press, 1993.
Williams (Brownlaw), Isabel. Letter to Tennessee Williams. 24 March 1937. Tennessee Williams Collection. Harry Ransom Center, Austin, TX.
Williams, Tennessee. *Collected Stories*. Introduction by Gore Vidal. New York: New Directions, 1985.
———. *Conversations with Tennessee Williams*. Ed. Albert J. Devlin. Jackson: University Press of Mississippi, 1986.
———. *Hard Candy: Collected Stories*. New York: New Directions, 1985.
———. Letter to Lucy Freeman. September 8, 1962. Tennessee Williams Collection. Harry Ransom Center, Austin, TX.
———. Letter to Andreas Brown. 1963, n.d. Tennessee Williams Collection. Harry Ransom Center, Austin, TX.
———. *Letters to Donald Windham 1940–1965*. Ed. and with comments by Donald Windham. New York: Penguin, 1980.
———. *Memoirs*. New York: Doubleday and Company, 1975.
———. *New Selected Essays: Where I Live*. Ed. John S. Bak. New York: New Directions, 2009.
———. *Notebooks*. Ed. Margaret Bradham Thornton. New Haven, CT: Yale University Press, 2006.
———. "One Arm." Screenplay draft. Tennessee Williams Collection, Rare Book and Manuscript Library. Columbia University Library.
———. "One Arm" [story]. May 1942. Tennessee Williams Collection. Harry Ransom Research Center, University of Texas at Austin.
———. "One Arm." In *Stopped Rocking and Other Screenplays*. New York: New Directions, 1984.
"Tennessee Williams Turns Sixty.'" Interview with Rex Reed. Conversations with Tennessee Williams. Ed. Albert J. Devlin. Jackson: University Press of Mississippi, 1985. 184-207.
Williams, Tennessee. "A Talk about Life and Style with Tennessee Williams" Interview with Jim Gaines. *Conversations with Tennessee Williams*. Ed. Albert J. Devlin. Jackson: University Press of Mississippi, 1985. 213-223.
"New Tennessee Williams Rises from 'Stoned Age.'" Interview with Don Lee Keith. *Conversations with Tennessee Williams*. Ed. Albert J. Devlin. Jackson: University Press of Mississippi, 1985. 147-160.
———. "One Arm." *Collected Stories*. Introduction by Gore Vidal. New York: New Directions, 1985. 175-188.
"Tennessee Williams." Interview with Walter Wagner. Conversations with Tennessee Williams. Ed. Albert J. Devlin. Jackson: University Press of Mississippi, 1985. 124-133.
"Will God Talk Back to a Playwright? Interview with David Frost/1970." Conversations with Tennessee Williams. Ed. Albert J. Devlin. Jackson: University Press of Mississippi, 1985. 140-146.
———. *Selected Letters, vol. 1, 1920–1945*, eds. Albert J. Devlin and Nancy M. Tischler. New York: New Directions, 2000.
———. *Selected Letters, vol. II, 1945–1957*, eds. Albert J. Devlin and Nancy M. Tischler. New York: New Directions, 2004.
———. *Small Craft Warnings*. New York: New Directions, 1972.
———. *Stairs to the Roof*. New York: New Directions, 2000.
———. *Stopped Rocking and Other Screenplays*. New York: New Directions, 1984.
"A Streetcar Named Desire." [draft fragments]. n.d., Tennessee Williams Collection, Harry Ransom Research Center, University of Texas at Austin.

———"The Battle of Angels" [notes and fragments]. n.d., Tennessee Williams Collection, Harry Ransom Research Center, University of Texas at Austin.

———. "The Battle of Angels" [play]. n.d., Tennessee Williams Collection. Harry Ransom Research Center University of Texas at Austin.

———. *The Theatre of Tennessee Williams*. Volumes I–VIII. New York: New Directions, 1971–1992.

Wilson, Edmund. "Playwright's Diary," *New York Times Book Review* 4 March 2007, 20.

Wolter, Jürgen C. "Tennessee Williams's Fiction." In *Tennessee Williams: A Guide to Research and Performance*, ed. Philip C. Kolin. Westport, CT: Greenwood Press, 1998.

Index

adultery, double standard for, 78–79
Albee, Edward, 178
Alioto, Joseph, gay suppression and, 152
Allen, Joe, 187
American South, policing behavior in, 117–118
Anatomy of Disgust, The (Miller), 68
Andrus, Cecil, 98n112
Angyal, Andras, 84–85
anti-Communist era
homophobia and, 38
homosexuals and, 11. *See also* Cold War era
Arendt, Hannah, 144–145
Augustine's *Confessions*, 165

Bak, John S., 9, 31–32, 108, 115, 154–155, 157
Balcony, The (Genet), 16–17
Baraka, Amiri, 17
Barnes, Bill, 165
Barnes, Clive, 166
Battle of Angels (Williams), 12, 13, 169, 177
epilogue of, 141–142
failure of, 121–124
language of disgust and, 123
published version of, 136–138
racial-sexual politics in, 133–135
themes of, 115–116
transgressive sexuality in, 126–131
voice of conventional morality in, 125–126. *See also* Battle/*Orpheus* (Williams); *Orpheus Descending* (Williams)
Battle/Orpheus (Williams), 22, 115–116
moral/criminal representations in, 120–121
revisions of, 121
sex-law connection in, 134–138, 140–141
Small Craft Warnings and, 165–166
themes of, 115–116
violence in, 116–117. *See also Battle of Angels* (Williams); *Orpheus Descending* (Williams)
Beckett, Samuel, 174, 178
Berlin, Irving, 1
Bérubé, Allan, 7
Bibler, Michael P., 111
Bigelow, Paul, 1, 10, 12
Bigsby, C. W. E., 49, 105–106, 176–177
Bill of Rights, amendments addressing privacy, 32, 47, 53n18
Birds, The (Hitchcock), 185
Bishop, Elizabeth, 13
Black, Clara Atwood, 13
Blackstone, William, 48
Bloustein, Edward, 34
Bowers v. Hardwick, 46–48, 144
dissenting opinions in, 48–50
Goldstein's analysis of, 50
overruling of, 50
Williams's texts and, 50. *See also* sodomy laws
Brandeis, Louis D., 32–33
Brando, Marlon, 44
Bray, William Robert, 108, 116, 177
"Broken Tower, The" (Crane), 49, 145
Brown, Andreas, 14
Brownlow, Isabel Williams, 101
Brownmiller, Susan, 43
Buckley, Tom, 159–160
Burger, Warren, 48

Caro, Robert, 193–194
Carpenter, Dale, 46
Case, Claudia Wilsch, 102, 125

Cat on a Hot Tin Roof (Williams), 22, 107–111, 172
   seen as homophobic text, 107
   subversive agenda in, 108–109
Chaudhuri, Una, 179, 180, 184
Chauncey, George, 6, 7, 10, 75–77
Chesler, S. Alan, 103, 116, 172–173
Childress, Steven Alan, 32, 35
Christianity, Williams and, 102, 124
civil rights movement, Williams and, 116, 160
Clinton, Bill, 193–194
Clum, John, 58, 62–63, 64–66, 106, 107, 126, 133, 142, 163
Cohn, Ruby, 174
Cold War era
   and attitudes toward homosexuality, 59, 85
   cultural changes during, 109
   impacts of, 21
   privacy and, 145. *See also* anti-Communist era
Collected Stories (Williams), 57
Communists, Cowboys, and Queers: The Politics of Masculinity in the World of Arthur Miller and Tennessee Williams (Savran), 17
compassion, Williams's work and, 192–193
Comstock Act of 1873, 75
Confessional (Williams), 164–165
Confessions (Augustine), 165
confinement
   in *Battle/Orpheus*, 137
   Williams's interest in, 131–132
Corber, Robert J., 17, 59
   on "Hard Candy", 66
   on language of disgust, 67
Council of the American Law Institute, Model Penal Code of, 49–50, 98n112, 151, 158
Crandell, George W., 20
Crane, Hart, 49, 63, 145
"crimes against nature"
   state/local regulation of, 28, 30, 76, 110. *See also* homosexuality; legal prohibitions; same-sex activity; sodomy laws; transgressive sexuality

Crotty, Kevin M., 15, 164–165

Dakin, Walter, 1
Darling, Candy, 187
de Jongh, Nicholas, 63–64, 193
D'Emilio, John, 11
Demolition Downtown (Williams), 177
"Desire and the Black Masseur" (Williams) 72, 181
detainments, 1
Devlin, Albert, 3
Devlin, Patrick, 81–82
Dewey, John, 13
Diagnostic and Statistical Manual of Psychiatric Disorders (DSM-II), homosexuality.classification in, 149
Dickson, Ruth, 25–26, 27
Dickson, Vivienne, 40
difference, Williams's portrayals of, 27
disgust. *See* language/power of disgust
Doe v. Commonwealth's Attorney, 149
Dorff, Linda, 184–185
Douglas, William O., 36, 47
Draya, Ren, 65, 94
Due Process Clause
   Lawrence v. Texas and, 149, 195
   privacy of sexual freedom and, 46
   and protection of liberty, 50

Eighteenth Amendment, repeal of, 6
emotion, and administration and structure of law, 51–52
emotional life, Williams's explorations of, 192
Eskridge, William N., Jr., 7, 28, 30, 38, 76, 150, 151
   on prosecution of same-sex activity, 110
   on sex panics and World War II, 6
Evans, Oliver, 1, 4
   TW's commitment to, 12

Farrell, James, 13
Faulkner, William, 60
Federal Bureau of Investigation (FBI), Williams's file and, 104
films. *See* specific films
Flagrant Conduct (Carpenter), 46
Florida, vagrancy laws in, 1

Index

Fong, Tony, 177
Fourteenth Amendment, Due Process Clause and. *See* Due Process Clause
Freedman, Estelle B., 11, 42, 118–119, 121
Freeman, Lucy, 14
friendships, Williams's commitment to, 12
Frontain, Raymond-Jean, 76–77
Frost, David, Williams's interview with, 159, 160, 167, 187
Fugitive Kind (Williams) (play), 184
Fugitive Kind, The (Williams) (film), 115

Gaines, Jim, 162
Gassel, Sylvia, 143–144
"gay," evolution of term, 6
gay activism, impacts on sodomy laws, 152
gay culture, in New York's Prohibition years, 6
Gay Fictions (Summers), 58
"gay fictions", 58–59, 73
gay men
  responses to Williams's work, 17, 163–164
  YMCAs and, 11
gender/sexual identity, politics of, 17
Gilman, Richard, 81
Glass Menagerie, The (Williams), 101, 172, 174
Gnädiges Fräulein, The (Williams), 178, 184–186
  commentaries on, 179, 180–181
Goldberg, Arthur, 36
Goldstein, Anne B., 50
Griswold v. Connecticut, 36, 47, 121, 144, 149, 195
Gussow, Mel, 157

Haidt, Jonathan, 194
Hale, Allean, 175, 178, 185–186
"Hard Candy" (Williams), 21, 64–71
  power of disgust in, 67–71
  risk theme in, 69–70
Hart, Harold H., 25, 27
Hart Crane and the Homosexual Text (Yingling), 63
Hello from Bertha (Williams), 181

Herron, Ima, 142
heterosexuality, moving beyond norm of, 115
Hitchcock, Alfred, 185
Hobson, Harold, 193
Hollywood's Tennessee: The Williams Films and Postwar America (Palmer & Bray), 108
Holt v. Florida, 121
homophobia
  anti-Communist era and, 38
  Cold War politics and, 108
  internalized, 67–68
  Kinsey report and, 108
homosexual activity
  laws prohibiting, 2, 3. *See also* legal prohibitions
  Homosexual Conduct law (Texas), 45–46
homosexuality
  Cat on a Hot Tin Roof and, 107, 108–111
  during Cold War era, 59; in DSM-II, 149; in prose works, 64; in prose works *versus* plays, 59–60; public-private split in, 65–67, 68; sex panic surges and, 6; as social suicide, 73; transition in attitudes toward, 58–59, 167; Williams's attitude toward, 90–91; in Williams's prose works, 58, 61–63
homosexual life, World War II period and, 11
homosexuals, and surrender of rights, 6
homosociality, *Cat* and, 109
Hooper, Michael S. D., 62, 75, 122, 133–134, 158–159
Hoover, J. Edgar, 117
Hopkins, Miriam, 122
House Not Meant to Stand, A (Williams), 177
Hunter, Kim, 44

I Can't Imagine Tomorrow (Williams), 177
identity: individual right to control, 33–34; integrity of, "One Arm" and, 73–74; legal restrictions on, 41; privacy and, 34; shame and, 91

identity politics, Williams and, 17
illegal bodies, 20; female, 122, 139; in later plays, 178; vulnerability of, 2; Williams and, 19, 39, 182, 187. *See also* homosexuality; legal prohibitions
Illinois, sodomy laws in, 151
internalized homophobia, charges of, against Williams, 67–68
In the Bar of a Tokyo Hotel (Williams), 175

Jackson, Esther M., 103
Johnson, Lyndon B., 193–194
jurisprudence, law-and-emotion, 51–52

Kameny, Franklin Edward, 150, 151
Kantrowitz, Arnie, 167–168
Kass, Leon, 82
Kaufman, Moisés, 71
Kazan, Elia, 44, 45
Keith, Don Lee, 161–162
Kelly, James, 60
Kennedy, Anthony, 46, 149–150, 195, 196
Kiernan, Kip, 90–91, 99n119
Kindness of Strangers: The Life of Tennessee Williams (Spoto), 105
Kinsey, Alfred C., 13, 59, 77, 83, 108
Kinsey Report, impacts of, 108
Kleb, William, 31
Koch, Ed, 152
Kolin, Philip C., 163, 175, 180, 181
Kramer, Victor A., 154
Krapp's Last Tape (Beckett), 16–17

Lachs, Stephen M., 191
Lahr, John, 8, 91, 153–154
Langner, Lawrence,Williams's correspondence with, 13
language/power of disgust, 20, 177; apparent *versus* overarching use of, 38–39; *Battle of Angels* (Williams) and, 123; desire and, 87–88; in "Hard Candy", 65, 67–69, 67–71; *Iguana* and, 30; in "One Arm", 71–89; representations of homosexuality and, 21; restrictive sex laws and, 68–69; usage in law, 28; Williams's rejection of, 26–27; Williams's use of, 28–29. *See also* "Hard Candy" (Williams); "One Arm" (Williams)
Larson, June Bennett, 180
Laughlin, James, 74–75, 83–84
Lawrence v. Texas, 45–46, 50, 149, 195
Leavitt, Richard, 104
legal prohibitions, 20–21; on homosexuality, 2, 3, 6; neglect in Williams scholarship, 18–19; post-World War II, 67; and power over life and death, 74; revisions of, 18–19; on sexual behavior, 12; Williams's awareness of, 19
legal significance of Williams's work, neglect of, 16, 58
legal statutes, and language of disgust, 28
legal system: impacts of, 174; 1960s-1970s changes in, 170
Lepore, Jill, 195–196
lesbians: exclusion of, 6; 1960s and, 172; Tennessee Williams Scholars Conference and, 161; in urban communities, 191; World War II era and, 7, 11
Leverich, Lyle, 8, 10, 12, 75, 104, 122
liberty, Williams's work and, 30
Lithwick, Dahlia, 46
Long Road to Freedom: The Advocate History of the Gay and Lesbian Movement (Kantrowitz), 167–168
Los Angeles Gay and Lesbian Community Center (LAGLC), 191
love, physical dimension of, in Williams canon, 46–47
Lovely Sunday for Creve Coeur, A (Williams), 175
lynching, Wiegman's essay on, 132–133

Magnani, Anna, 4
Malamud Smith, Janna, 12, 15, 91
Mann, Emily, 194
Maroney, Terry A., 51
marriage equality. *See* same-sex marriage
married couples, zone of privacy and, 36
masculinity, politics of, 106

Massee, Jordan, 12
masturbation, prohibitions against, 28
Mattachine Society, 150
Matthew, David C. C., 116
McCarthyism: *Cat* and, 108–109. *See also* anti-Communist era; Cold War era
McGovern, George, 104
Mead, Shepherd, 104–105
Melton, Fred, 12
Memoirs (Williams), 3, 4–5, 8, 22, 153–157, 167, 181; critical attacks against, 162–163; political context of publication, 103–104; political past in, 104; "queer gaze" of, 177; sexuality and law in, 153–157; and social-legal transitions, 159
Merlo, Frank, 1, 163
Milk Train Doesn't Stop Here Anymore, The (Williams), 186
Mill, John Stuart, 82
Miller, Arthur, 105
Miller, William Ian, 68, 80
mob violence, in *Battle/Orpheus*, 117–118, 131, 139
Model Penal Code, 49–50, 98n112; penal code revisions and, 151, 158
Moore v. East Cleveland, 47
morality, connection with disgust, 68
moral values: in *Iguana*, 26–27; national, Williams's challenges to, 153
Murphy, Brenda, 45, 186
Mutilated, The (Williams), 178, 179–180, 184, 186
mutilation: in *Fräulein*, 184–185; in "One Arm", 80–81, 85–87; in *Slapstick Tragedy* plays, 178

National Gay Task Force, 149
Nelson, Deborah, 47, 144–145
New Orleans: "Bohemian" life of, 12; Williams's move to, 9
New Selected Essays: Where I Live (Williams), 104, 153–154
Nicolay, Claire, 108–109
Night of the Iguana, The (Williams), 27–29, 172; and connection between sexuality and legal regulation, 27–28; and politics of humanity, 29–30; premiere of, 26; privacy rights in, 46; Supreme Court debates and, 21; and Williams's statement of moral compass, 26–27
Nixon, Richard M., 104
nondiscrimination laws, 195
Notebooks (Williams), 3, 9, 10
Nussbaum, Martha C., 87–88, 192–193, 195; on disgust and law, 81–82; on politics of humanity, 29–30, 95

Obergefell v. Hodges, 195–196
obscenity, legal interpretations of, 75
O'Connor, Flannery, 60
O'Connor, Sandra Day, 195–196
Olmstead v. United States, 33
"One Arm" (Williams), 21, 61, 138, 172, 177; connection and redemption in, 91–94, 102–103; and documentation of composition process, 72; and integrity of identity, 73–74; mutilation and disgust in, 80–81, 85–87; power of disgust in, 71–89; public-private tensions in, 77; screenplay for, 72, 81, 82, 85–86; stage version of, 72
One Arm and Other Stories (Williams), 59, 60
O'Neill, Eugene, 168
Origins of Totalitarianism, The (Arendt), 144–145
Orpheus Descending (Williams), 101, 168; comparison with *Battle*, 138–143; women in, 143. *See also Battle of Angels* (Williams); *Battle/Orpheus* (Williams)

Palko v. Connecticut, 47
Paller, Michael, 160–161, 166–167, 168, 170, 172, 175
Palmer, R. Barton, 108
"pansy craze", 6
Passions of Law, The (Maroney), 52
patriarchal gender hierarchy, homosexual love and, 6
Pecorari, Marie, 157–158
Peden, William H., 60–61
Penn, Donna, 11

212   Index

Peters, Brian M., 72, 76
Pines, Burt, 152
Pinter, Harold, 178
plantation, transgressive sexuality and, 111–113
plays: critical response to, 163; early, 174; later, 163, 174, 177, 186–187; post-1961, 173–174, 177–187. See also specific plays
politics of humanity: arts and, 195; *Iguana* and, 29–30; *Streetcar* and, 30–32; and transformation of laws on sexual orientation, 95
politics of masculinity, 106
politics of recognition,: impacts of, 150–151; Kameny's petition and, 150
Politics of Reputation: The Critical Reception of Tennessee Williams' Later Plays (Saddik), 163–164
Portrait of a Madonna (Williams), 181
postmodernism, in later plays, 179, 180–181
power of disgust. See language/power of disgust
privacy: Cold War era and, 145; legal definition of, 65; in *Orpheus*, 138; and protection of wealth, 110–111; shame and, 91. See also right to privacy
privacy anxiety, spheres of, 144
Prohibition, gay community and, 6
prose works, 161; early assessments of, 59–60; homosexuality and public-private split in, 65–67, 68; homosexuality in, 59–60, 61–63, 64; popular reception of, 60; re-assessments of, 58
Prossner, William, 185–186
prostitutes, male *versus* female, 6
prostitution, economic necessity of, 76–77
protagonists, Williams's choice of, 20
psychiatric confinement, sex and, 42–44
public-private split, 3, 65–67, 154
public restrooms, homosexual sex and, 7
Pursuing Privacy in Cold War America (Nelson), 47

Quinlan, Stefanie, 179

rape, Brownmiller's study of, 43
Reed, Rex, 162
Remember Me to Tom (E. D. Williams), 14
Richards, David A. J., 6, 39, 59, 195
Righteous Mind: Why Good People Are Divided by Politics and Religion (Haidt), 194
right to privacy: balance with connection, 35; Bill of Rights and, 32, 47, 53n18; *Bowers v. Hardwick* and, 47; Brandeis and, 32–33; court cases on, 45–46; development of, 39; *versus* equal-protection argument, 196; *Griswold v. Connecticut* and, 121; identity and, 34; Kameny's petition and, 150; in late twentieth century, 52; *versus* need for self-revelation, 13; sexual freedom and, 195; Solove on, 33–34, 61–62; in *Streetcar*, 31–32; totalitarianism and, 144–145; UN Universal Declaration of Human Rights and, 33; zone of, for married couples, 36. See also privacy
risk theme, in "Hard Candy", 69–70
Roberts v. United States Jaycees, 48–49
Robinson, Marc, 17, 168–169
Rocha, Mark W., 174
Rodriguez y Gonzalez, Pancho, Williams's correspondence with, 15
Roe v. Wade, 144, 149
Ross, Don, 101
Roth v. United States, 39
Ruckel, Terri Smith, 155, 187

Saddik, Annette J., 163–164, 174, 178, 181–182, 183, 186
same-sex activity: *Cat* and, 109–111; prosecution of, 110; in Southern plantation literature, 111
same-sex marriage: *Obergefell v. Hodges* and, 195–196; privacy *versus* equal-protection arguments for, 196
same-sex relationships, inclusion in plays, 167
Savran, David, 17, 22, 58, 62, 63, 106, 122, 163, 175–176; on "Hard Candy",

66; on language of disgust, 67–68; on legal persecution of gays, 67
Schneider, Alan, 178
self, models of, 165
self-revelation, dangers of, 13
sex legislation: 1960s revisions of, 151–153; uneven progress in, 153
sex panics, 6, 117–118, 121; postwar, 38; in 1930s, 42–43
Sexual Behavior in the Human Male (Kinsey), 13, 59, 108
sexual freedom, Due Process Clause and, 45–46
sexuality: American, Kinsey study and, 77; in fiction *versus* theater, 63–64; right to privacy and, 33
Sexual Latitude: For and Against (Hart), 25–26
sexual orientation discrimination, Koch and, 152
sexual politics, *Streetcar* and, 30–32
sexual psychopath laws, 118–119
shame, and privacy and identity, 91
Shriver, Sargent, 194
Sierz, Aleks, 183
Sklepowitch, Edward A., 61, 64
Slapstick Tragedy (Williams), 177, 178–186. *See also Gnädiges Fräulein* (Williams), *The Mutilated, The* (Williams)
Small Craft Warnings (Williams), 157, 164–165, 175, 177; *Battle/Orpheus and*, 165–166; negative responses to, 163, 168; setting and production, 166–167; significance of, 165–166; Williams's appearance in, 164, 167, 168, 169
sodomy: arrests and, 22, 74; criminalization of, 28
Sodomy Cases, The (Richards), 6, 39
sodomy laws, 48; in Arizona, 89; arrests and, 110; in Idaho, 98n112; in Illinois, 151; *Lawrence* and, 195; legal challenges to, 46; scope of, 122–123; sexual acts included in, 50–51; *Streetcar* and, 39–40; in Texas, 149; violators of, 76; in Virginia, 149. *See also Bowers v. Hardwick; Lawrence v. Texas*

Solove, Daniel J., 13; on privacy, 33–34, 61–62, 65
Something Cloudy, Something Clear (Williams), 167, 181
Sontag, Susan, 17
Spoto, Donald, 105, 159
state laws, changes in, 22
Stein, Gertrude, 168
Stevens, John Paul, *Bowers v. Hardwick* and, 50
Stonewall era, 159, 161, 163–164, 167–168, 172
Stopped Rocking and Other Screenplays (Williams), 71
stories. *See* prose works
Streetcar Named Desire, A (Williams), 4.47 4.63: gay issues in, 39–40; influence on shift of public opinion, 39; legal issues in, 43–45; London premiere of, 193; politics of humanity and, 30–32; postwar sex panic and, 38; premiere of, 26; privacy rights in, 46; rape scene in, 41–42; revisions of, 40–42; right to privacy and, 34–37; staged *versus* film versions, 54n40; Supreme Court debates and, 21; transgressive sexuality in, 37; women in, 143
Suddenly Last Summer (Williams), 172
Summer and Smoke (Williams), women in, 143
Summers, Claude J., 58
Supreme Court decisions: *Bowers v. Hardwick* and, 46–48; decisions on sexual freedoms, 19; *Iguana* and, 21; on right to privacy, 45–46, 121, 144; *Streetcar* and, 21. *See also* specific cases
Sweet Bird of Youth (Williams), 143; women in, 143

Tennessee v. John Scopes, 31
Tennessee Williams: An Intimate Biography (D. Williams & Mead), 104–105
Tennessee Williams: A Tribute (Sklepowitch), 61, 103
Tennessee Williams: Rebellious Puritan (Tischler), 16–17

Tennessee Williams Scholars' Conference, 160–161
Texas, sodomy laws in, 149
Texas Bar Association, Model Penal Code and, 151
Thatcher, Molly Day, 123–124
Thompson, Judith, 173
Thornton, Margaret Bradham, 9
Tischler, Nancy, 16–17, 102
totalitarianism, privacy rights and, 144–145
transgressive sexuality: in *Battle of Angels*, 126–131; in *Battle/Orpheus*, 142; character construction and, 171; defining "transgress", 53n35; in early *versus* late plays, 180; focus on, 20; in heterosexual individuals, 40; in *Iguana*, 28–29, 30; legal regulation and @2 2.40; legal system and, 196–197; mixed messages about, 37–38; in "One Arm", 78–79; plantation and, 111–113; power structures and, 43–45; in prose works, 63; in *Streetcar*, 37; Williams and, 187; Williams's broadened understanding of, 122–123; Williams's late life representations of, 177–178; Williams's political engagement with, 105; in Williams's works, 16, 51
Truman, Harry, 1
Truman administration, focus on homosexual activity, 74–75

Understanding Privacy (Solove), 13
U.S. Constitution: Ninth Amendment and right of privacy, 36. *See also* Due Process Clause
United Nations Universal Declaration of Human Rights, privacy and 33
University of Hartford, Williams's honorary doctorate from 191–192, 196
University of Iowa, Williams's graduation from 8
Upheavals of Thought: The Intelligence of Emotions (Nussbaum) 192–193

vagrancy laws, in Florida 1

Vannatta, Dennis 59–60, 60–61
"Vengeance of Nitrocris, The" (Williams) 2.0
Vidal, Gore 57, 60
Vieux Carré (Williams) 167, 175, 177, 181, 186
violence: acts of, 161–162; proximity of, 2; threat of, 7, 17
Virginia, sodomy laws in, 149
Virginia Code, 149
Voeller, Bruce, 149
Vogel, Ursula, 78–79

Wagner, Walter, 160
Waiting for Godot (Beckett), 174
Wales Padlock Law, 161
Ward, Michael J., 122
Warhol, Andy, 187
"War on the Sex Criminal," Hoover and, 117
Warren, Samuel D., 32
Watts, Richard, Jr., 180
Where I Live: Selected Essays (Williams), 104
White, Edmund, 3
Whitmore, George, 104
Wiegman, Robyn, 132–133
Williams, Dakin, 104–105
Williams, Tennessee: attitude toward homosexuality, 90–91; biographical writings on, 17; coming out and, 159, 160–162; context of legal/sexual mores and, 22; contributions of, 172; critics of, 17; cultural impact of, 22; detainments of, 1; developing sexual identity of, 8; diaries and letters of, 3; family relationships and, 8, 10; and fears of revealing homosexuality, 15; hospitalization of, 159; influence on contemporary life 19; Laughlin correspondence and, 1; letters as confessions 15–16; Merlo and, 1; moral vision of, 101–103, 106–107; New Orleans and, 9; physical attacks on, 1; political perspectives of, 116–117; private and public identities of, 3; publications about, following death of, 104–105; recognition of

contributions, 192; relationship with family, 15; renaissance of, 169; on sensitivity and humanity of homosexuals, 4; social influences on, 5–6; sources of subject matter, 19; as Southern Puritan 143; statement of moral compass, 26; upbringing of, 22

Williams scholarship, neglected areas of, 3, 16, 19

Windham, Donald, 12, 72, 84; correspondence with Williams, 1, 74, 90, 104

Wolter, Jürgen C., 61–62, 94

women: adultery and, 78, 122; *Holt v. Florida* and, 121; as illegal bodies, 122, 139; legislation affecting, 19; in *Mutilated*, 180–183; in New South, 112; role in plays, 17; sex crimes against, 109; sexual stereotypes of, 39; sodomy laws and, 75; and state of fear, 43; in Williams's plays, 143

Women Who Write Plays: Interviews with American Dramatists (Mann), 194

Wood, Audrey, 3, 14, 75; Williams's correspondence with, 1, 41

World of Tennessee Williams, The (Leavitt), 104

World War II era: and boundaries of sexual behavior, 119–120; homosexual life and, 11; and wartime vice control powers, 7

Yingling, Thomas E., 63
YMCAs, gay men and, 11

Zoo Story (Albee), 16–17